CONTENT	PRESENTATION	PRESENTATION

Attention and Interest
Attention-getting techniques
Converting attention to interest

Humor
Devices of humor
(1) Exaggeration
(2) Understatement
(3) Irony
(4) Anticlimax
(5) Word play
Analyzing your own humor
Avoiding humor pitfalls
(1) Offensive humor
(2) Irrelevant humor
(3) Inept joke telling
(4) Overintroducing humor
(5) Overused material
Sources of humorous material

7 Credibility
Assessing your speaking image
(1) Competence
(2) Concern
(3) Trustworthiness
(4) Dynamism
Building prespeech credibility
Credibility and speech content
Credibility and delivery

8 Style
Oral vs. written style
Clarity
Appropriate language
Vivid, varied language

9 Persuasive Strategies
Content and audience attitudes
(1) Favorable audience
(2) Neutral audience
(3) Hostile audience
Audience-centered speech format
Climax or anticlimax format
Dealing with opposing arguments

20 Modes of Delivery
a Extemporaneous mode
b Coping with impromptu speaking
c Speaking from manuscript
d Memorizing speeches

21 Practice Sessions
a Timetable for practice sessions
b Early practice sessions
c Middle practice sessions
d Last few practice sessions
e Preparing speech notes
f Practicing to meet time limits

22 Overcoming Fear of Speaking
a Understanding fear of speaking
b Building your confidence
c Relaxation and tension release
d Positive self-suggestion
e Seeking outside help

23 Vocal Delivery
a Distracting characteristics
  (1) Voice quality
  (2) Articulation
  (3) Irrelevant pauses, sounds, and phrases
  (4) Repetitious inflection
  (5) Eliminating distracting habits
b Being heard and understood
c Vocal variety
d Acceptable pronunciation

24 Physical Delivery
a Your appearance
b Distracting mannerisms
c Your posture
d Your movements
e Your gestures
f Maintaining eye contact
g Your facial expression

25 Adapting to the Speech Situation
a Making evocative references
b Audience reactions
c Preventing distractions
d Coping with hecklers

26 Answering Questions
a Preparing for questions
b Responding straightforwardly
c Self-indulgent questioners

27 Guidelines for Special Occasions
a Ceremonial occasions
b Group presentations
c Chairing programs and meetings
d Group interviews
e Demands of the broadcast media

W9-DBA-907

THE
SPEAKER'S
HANDBOOK

THE
SPEAKER'S
HANDBOOK

Jo Sprague
San Jose State University

Douglas Stuart

HARCOURT BRACE JOVANOVICH, PUBLISHERS

*San Diego   New York   Chicago   Washington, D.C.   Atlanta
London   Sydney   Toronto*

Acknowledgments and Copyrights

Figures: 4–2, 3, 4 ABI/INFORM—A management and business information
database produced by Data Courier Inc., 620 South Fifth Street, Louisville, KY
40202, 502/582-4111, 800/626-2823 and DIALOG. 4–10 From *The Suburban
Environment and Women* by Donald N. Rothblatt, Daniel J. Garr and Jo Sprague.
Copyright © 1979 Praeger Publishers. Reproduced by permission of Praeger
Publishers. 13–2 (left) Pilot Press Copyright Drawing and (right) Aviation
Publications. 27–1 National Forensic League.

Text: Quoted passages from a classroom speech, in Section 9, Ellen G. Watrous.
Speeches adapted for use in Appendix, Glenn Huxtable, Florida Association of
Realtors (for Sprague speech), *Vital Speeches of the Day*—published by City News
Publishing Co. (for Cunningham and Postman speeches).

Cover: Alice Harmon

ISBN: 0–15–583175–5
Library of Congress Catalog Card Number: 83–82520
Printed in the United States of America

PREFACE

The Speaker's Handbook is at once a reference guide for the individual speaker and a textbook for use in the public speaking classroom. It is a compendium of principles, examples, and exercises that covers all the topics one commonly confronts in preparing and delivering a speech. What distinguishes *The Speaker's Handbook* from other books on public speaking, though, is its flexibility: each of the twenty-seven sections stands by itself, so that speakers need consult only those parts of the book covering the aspects of speechmaking with which they need further help.

A glance at the front endpapers and the table of contents shows that topics are logically arranged to aid study and permit ready reference. *The Speaker's Handbook* is organized to encourage instructors to refer speakers — by means of the **Evaluation Checklist**, a sample of which appears on the endpapers at the back of the book — directly to those portions of the book dealing specifically with what is needed to improve a given speech. Thus, instead of devoting many hours to *reading about* how to prepare and deliver a speech, speakers can from the very start of the course draw upon their own innate and acquired skills to begin making speeches. When instructors identify steps in the speechmaking process where students need improvement, each speaker can be directed to specific sections of the *Handbook*. Of course, should an instructor prefer to spend more time on lectures and discussion, sections of the book — in any order the instructor wishes — may be assigned to the whole class.

Speech preparation, organization, content, and presentation are given appropriately detailed coverage, in clear, straightforward language. The thorough system of cross-referencing — endpapers, the index, a detailed table of contents, and tabbed and numbered running heads — provides rapid, accurate access to all topics discussed in the *Handbook*. A **Speaker's Preparation Checklist** and a **Sample Outline Checklist** (on the back endpapers) enable speakers to assure themselves that they have given adequate attention to every element of their work on a speech. These checklists employ numerous cross-references to guide speakers to the sections or subsections containing the information and explanations they require.

While the emphases in this book are practical, no textbook can be entirely free of theoretical assumptions. In general, *The Speaker's Handbook* draws most heavily on the classical rhetorical tradition — supplemented by contemporary findings of the social sciences — with stress on analysis, reasoning, support for assertions, and clear organization. Finally, we support the ethical position that a speaker earns the right to speak through research, thoughtful inquiry, and adherence to the ground rules of public deliberation; and we believe that although a speaker's effect on the audience is his or her central concern, this concern should not be equated with attempting to manipulate one's listeners.

Acknowledgments

Our greatest debt is to Peter Dougherty, who conceived of adapting the *Handbook* format to public speaking and who generated and nurtured enthusiasm for the project, both in us and in his associates at Harcourt Brace Jovanovich. His guidance and expertise made it possible for us to transform an idea into a manuscript. Matthew Milan, Jr., has guided the manuscript through its later stages, and Michael Werthman has greatly enhanced its clarity through his respect for the nuances of language. His scrupulous attention to detail and consistency has been essential to the refinement of a *Handbook* of this sort.

A special thanks to the students in Jo's most recent classes in Public Speaking and Argument and Advocacy for their feedback on drafts of this manuscript. The faculty and staff of the Department of Communication Studies at San Jose State University have been helpful and supportive in a number of ways.

Jo Sprague

Douglas Stuart

CONTENTS

27   Guidelines for Special Occasions   318

APPENDIX

Glenn Huxtable

PREPARATION

1	Speech Topics and Purposes
2	Topic Analysis
3	Audience Analysis
4	Research

INTRODUCTION

When we watch world-class figure skaters, we are fascinated by the apparent ease with which they perform what we know are extremely difficult moves. However easy they make it look, we do not think that on *our* first time out on the ice we can immediately perform triple axels. We can understand that years of training, dedication, and discipline have gone into making it seem so effortless. Not everyone figure skates. Everyone communicates. We all have our share of good ideas and transmit them more or less successfully in our everyday encounters. This success may lead us to underestimate the difficulty in making the transition to more formal and public modes of expression. As Lord Peter Wimsey said to novelist Harriet Vane, "I say — I've thought of a good plot for a detective story . . . you know, the sort people bring out and say, 'I've often thought of doing it myself, if I could only find time to sit down and write it.' I gather that sitting down is all that is necessary for producing masterpieces." Good composition, in speech as in writing, requires more than having a good idea and sitting down to write it.

1

When you are asked (or told) to give a speech, your immediate impulse may be to grab the first topic that enters your mind and start to practice expressing your ideas on the subject. After "sitting down" in this fashion, you may discover gaps in your knowledge that require a trip to the library. Once at the library, it can be hard to decide in which direction to press your research, especially if you are not sure of the audience you will be addressing. Later, back "sitting down," you may find that much of the information you have collected is not relevant to the purpose of your speech as it has evolved during this time. At this point you may stop to wonder if the experienced speakers you have heard ever go through such wheel spinning. After all, they make speaking in public seem so effortless that surely their preparation also must be free of perspiration. Let us assure you that their performance, like that of world-class figure skaters, is built on mastery of skills and techniques and reflects careful planning and hard work. They save time and avoid duplicated and wasted effort by organizing their preparation in a way that is consistent with the phases of the creative process.

It has been proposed that there are four steps to this process: preparation, incubation, illumination, and refinement.[1] For speakers the preparation stage includes the gathering of materials, the analysis of the topic and audience, and the first stabs at putting the parts together. Incubation is a period marked by frustration, even despair, when the problems seem insoluble and the speech is set aside. During this period, your unconscious mind and your peripheral awareness work on the problems. Suddenly, in a moment of illumination, the pieces fit together — or, there may be a dawning awareness that grows in intensity. Illumination may occur while you are working on the project, but it is just as likely to occur when you are driving down the freeway, taking a shower, or even sleeping. Exhilaration and relief accompany this phase. You work eagerly and fluidly. In a few hours it is possible to accomplish more than you have in several days. Then the time comes for refinement. After the creative spurt, there follows a comparatively long period of checking details, fine tuning, and polishing. Like the preparation phase, this stage is largely cognitive and requires concentration and discipline. Many creative products have never been shared with the world because the creator gave up during the refinement stage. Other fine ideas have failed to be appreciated because the speaker

---

[1]Based on Catherine Patrick, *What is Creative Thinking?* (New York: Philosophical Library, 1955), 1–48.

presented them directly after the illumination phase, without spending the needed time on refinement. This delineation of the four-step creative process is provided to stress the importance of allocating time for *each* step.

Sections **1 – 4** address the preliminaries that should precede the actual composition of your speech. The first discusses *ways to select a topic* and *clarify your purpose*. It is obvious that you cannot start to prepare a speech before you know *what* you are going to be talking about. It is less obvious that you also need to know *why* you are going to speak. The more focused your topic and the more concrete your goals, the easier your later steps of preparation will be. Framing a thesis sentence and selecting a title will follow readily from a clear understanding of the purpose of your speech. Implicit in every topic are several issues to be confronted or questions to be answered. Through *analysis of your topic* you can identify its relevant issues. This process is helpful in directing your research and provides cues for organizing your information. When you envision the preparatory research for your speech, the tendency is to dwell on the amassing of data, examples, and arguments that deal with the topic itself. An important but frequently overlooked type of research is *audience analysis*. Through direct and indirect methods you can obtain information about their characteristics and attitudes, which will help you plan your speech. Knowing *research* techniques and sources can give you access to a wide information base.

1

Speech Topics and Purposes

Select an interesting and manageable topic, and determine what response you hope to evoke with that topic.

Do not settle on the first topic that occurs to you. Consider a number of different topics and examine their various facets. When you have chosen a promising one, narrow it down and crystallize your reasons for speaking about that subject.

1a. Select a speech topic.

As a speaker you will find that you have varying degrees of freedom in topic choice, according to the situation. At one pole there is the office manager who is told to give an oral report on the effectiveness of the current secretarial assignment system. At the other pole there is the respected speaker who is given carte blanche to speak on a topic "you feel is important," or the speech student who is told "Friday morning you will speak third and persuade us to do something, anything."

Most speaking situations fall between these extremes. You may be asked to welcome delegates to a conference or to speak to the Rotary Club about the economy. In these cases it is still up to you to select a theme for your talk. Even when the general topic is set, you will need to home in on an approach that will fit you, the audience, and the situation.

(1) Draw the topic from your own experience, expertise, and interests.

You come to a speech situation with a body of knowledge already. Perhaps it is because of this that you have been asked to speak: "Could you speak to us about your experiences in the Peace Corps [Stock Market, Blue Angels]?" Other times your background is the springboard for discovering a topic or a slant on a topic that can be developed into a compelling and substantial speech. There are a number of questions you should ask yourself to help you do this.

In answering the questions that follow, do not stop to evaluate every answer as you write it down. You want to generate a list of possible topics by brainstorming. In this technique you do not let your internal censor dismiss any idea as not being good enough for a speech topic. The principle behind brainstorming is that any unworkable idea may trigger a good one, and a group of mediocre ideas may combine to make a great one; so you should not judge any one idea until you have amassed a list of many. Answer these questions in as many different ways as you can think of, even if some seem silly. Later, you will select your best topic in terms of audience and occasion.

What unusual experiences have you had?

Consider places you have traveled, jobs you have held, events in which you have become enmeshed. Perhaps you have ridden in a hot air balloon or held a subcabinet post or were a hostage in a bank robbery. Obviously, these are stories worth telling in the right context. However, do not overlook aspects of your experience that you take for granted but might be interesting to others. If you are one of seven children or have always been self-employed or grew up speaking one language at home and another at school, you can increase your audience's understanding of events unfamiliar to them by sharing your experiences with them.

What special knowledge or expertise do you have?

Each of us has developed mastery in certain areas. How do you make your living? If your knowledge of the real estate field has provided you with a good income, you can be certain that there will be an audience eager to hear about your techniques. Yet, a job need not be high-paying or prestigious to generate speech topics. People like to know how things work. People are often quite interested in hearing about procedures, even ones that are considered mundane by the persons performing them. Jokes aside, how *is* your baggage routed from one airport to another? What goes on backstage at a concert?

Or, instead of talking about the mechanics of your work, you can build a speech around the people you meet in that context. If you enjoy observing people and have a flair for describing their behavior, you could become an informal anthropologist and social psychologist. You can give special insights into human nature or some aspect of our culture through topics like: dog owners as seen through the eyes of a letter carrier, the curious tribal customs of the used car lot, and patterns of interactions observed in a dentist's waiting room.

Your course of study in school has increased your knowledge in areas that perhaps are obscure to your potential audience. Think too about the talents, hobbies, and skills you have developed. Could you build a speech around rewiring your house, playing a musical instrument as relaxation therapy, preparing gourmet meals for backpacking, or describing the British class structure as conveyed through mystery novels? You may have researched in depth topics that appeal to you: Peter Bogdanovich movies, holographic technology, varieties of beer, Sudanese history, cults, home computers.

> You have probably found that the more you learn about a topic, the more there is left for you to learn. Do not let this blind you to the fact that you still know more in this area of special interest than your potential audience.

What strong opinions and beliefs do you hold?

Say you are at a party and suddenly find yourself arguing fervently about gun control. The conversation up to this point had dealt with a number of equally controversial subjects, but your contributions had not been so impassioned. Which are the topics that stir you up in this way? These issues, which probably touch on your core values (See **14c**), frequently make good speech topics. You will be less self-conscious if you are speaking from a deep conviction. The audience will be more generous in spirit, even when they are in opposition, if they see you are speaking from the heart.

However, avoid those subjects where your emotional involvement is so intense that you cannot be effective. Sometimes discussions of family dynamics, religious conversions, or recent personal tragedies may be more cathartic that communicative. Do not risk losing objectivity, losing emotional control, or embarrassing your audience through an inappropriate level of self-disclosure.

Besides those issues that can provoke you into heated debate, there are others that fascinate you intellectually. Do you have a pet theory about the decline of the nuclear family, why relationships fail, what makes a good manager, or whether there is other sentient life in the universe? Explaining the basis of your beliefs can make an excellent speech.

What would you like to know more about?

You may, ever since signing the note for your most recent business loan, have been curious about the workings of the Federal Reserve System. After reading *The Gulag Archipelago* you might have become interested in the roots of the Russian Revolution. Coming out of the movie theater after seeing *Star Wars* for the forty-seventh time, you might have made a resolution to go to the library and look up information on the Space Shuttle. Use the occasion of giving a speech as an opportunity to research some topics that have piqued your curiosity.

(2) Select a topic appropriate to the audience and occasion. *See also* **3**.

By brainstorming through the questions in **1(1)**, you have created a possible subject list of great variety. To choose the one topic on which you will speak, you next need to think about the audience and the occasion. Two more questions you can ask yourself at this point are:
  Audience: What are *these* people's expectations?
  Occasion: What are these people's expectations *now*?
Knowing who the audience is and why its members are gathered together can help you rule out a number of topics. A speech on the fluctuating silver market could be interesting, but not to a seventh-grade

class. Japanese architecture would probably not be the best subject for a speech given to the American Medical Association. Selling a product, promoting a candidate, or proselytizing for a faith would be out of place in a eulogy.

When you have removed the inappropriate subjects from your list, you then need to find the *most* appropriate of the remainder. Empathy is your best tool. Imagine sitting on those hard chairs in the boardroom or classroom. What would you sit still to hear?

(3) Select a topic that is both timely and timeless.

You may still have more than one possible topic on your list, even after going through the processes in **1(1)** and **1(2)**. Other things being equal, the best topics are those that are both timely and timeless. There are certain issues that have always been and always will be part of human discourse. The rights of the individual versus the right of the group and the need for security versus the need for adventure were being discussed 1,000 years ago, 100 years ago, and this past year; they will continue to be discussed by our descendants. When you tie a contemporary event to one of these enduring human dialogues, you link the timely and the timeless. Neither one of these conditions by itself is an indication that the topic would be a good one. Consider the criterion of timeliness. If an event has been taking up three front-page newspaper columns a day for two weeks, a speech on that topic may be timely. But unless you can tell your audience what it all means in more universal terms, there probably is little for you to give them that they do not already know. You have wasted their time. The reverse is true also: your audience can miss or fail to be interested in the profundity of your topic if you do not tie it in to the fabric of their current existence. A profound, timeless topic should have a timely application. A timely speech should point out the timeless implication of the subject.

Table 1-1 shows how topics that are too narrowly contemporary or too broadly universal may be altered to meet these criteria. Notice the different kinds of speeches to which the timely/timeless standard can apply.

☐ **Exercise 1.** Suppose that each of the following five topics is of great interest to you and that you are qualified to speak about them:

1. The martial arts
2. Real estate as a tax shelter
3. Problems of our Social Security System

4. How television commercials are made
5. Why I am a Christian

Which would be best for each of the following audiences? Select more than one if you wish, but justify your answers.

a. A speech class where the assignment is to support a thesis with factual and statistical evidence from several different sources
b. A Kiwanis Club luncheon
c. A junior high Scout troop
d. A current event study group
e. A keynote address at a business conference

☐ **Exercise 2.**   Explain how each of the five topics above could be developed to reflect both timely and timeless concerns.

1b. Narrow your topic.

One of the old public speaking jokes goes as follows:

   A: I'm giving a speech at the Rotary Club tonight.

Table 1-1

Timely (but potentially trivial)	Timeless (but potentially diffuse)	Timely and Timeless
There was a major confrontation last week when the American Nazi Party held a rally downtown.	Freedom of Assembly must be protected for everyone.	Last week's confrontation over the America Nazi Party rally raised important questions about what restrictions, if any, should be placed on Freedom of Assembly.
My trip to Quebec.	Travel helps people understand the diversity of human cultures.	My trip to Quebec helped me understand my own culture by contrasting it with another.
Our soccer team won the conference!!	Sports programs contributed to the physical, social, and emotional development of youths.	By reflecting on this year's soccer season, we can see how these kids have developed physically, socially, and emotionally.
Our company has adopted a new profit-sharing plan.	The best management philosophy is one that treats the employees like partners.	Our new profit-sharing plan will benefit the employees directly and reflect an enlightened philosophy of management.

B: What are you going to talk about?

A: Oh, about fifteen minutes.

Speaker A's answer is not wholly facetious. It acknowledges the important principle that the selection of a topic is not complete until that topic has been narrowed to accommodate the constraints of time.

The main advantage of limiting a topic is that this ensures depth of analysis. To avoid superficiality, you have to keep one eye on the clock while preparing your speech. To get into a topic, to get under the surface, you have to limit yourself to the number of points that can be adequately developed in the time available. You can expedite your research and preparation by narrowing your topic from the beginning. Instead of looking up all the books and articles about higher education, you can focus on those related to the financing of community colleges, or pass/fail grading, or coed dormitories.

(1) Determine the number of ideas you can cover in the time allotted.

The average speaker speaks between 100 and 150 words per minute. If you speak very rapidly or very slowly, you may fall outside this range. Chances are, though, that your rate of speaking is somewhere near 125 words per minute. If you want to check your rate, see **23b(2)**.

A typical journalistic paragraph of simple sentences runs about 125 words. Thus, a very general rule of thumb is that an average speaker speaks about one short paragraph per minute. If your material is highly technical or interspersed with statistics, dialogue, and dramatic pauses, or if you speak slowly, you had better allot two minutes per paragraph. This system is very rough, but it allows you to do some realistic narrowing of your topic.

For instance, if you are planning to give an eight- to ten-minute informative speech on the criminal justice system in the United States, you will need to set aside at least one to two minutes for the introduction and one minute for the conclusion. This leaves six or seven minutes for the body of your speech. If you choose to talk about the history of the criminal justice system, the causes of crime, the way crime statistics are calculated, the workings of the probation department, and the difficulties of recruiting police officers, you could spend about one to one and one-half minutes on each subject. But could you do the subjects justice? By narrowing the topic to one of these areas you could develop two subpoints for three minutes each or three subpoints for two minutes each — a more realistic plan.

The same principle can be applied to longer speeches, business presentations, and lectures. A twenty-minute speech can be thought of as twenty short, simple paragraphs or ten longer, more-developed paragraphs.

Look at how something like that could be broken down:

	Minutes
Introduction	
Welcome audience	1
Tell anecdote about Uncle Bob	1
State topic and preview main points	1
First main point	
Explain and define	1
Subpoint	2
Subpoint	2
Second main point, etc.	
	—
	—
	—
Conclusion	2
	20

☐ **Exercise 3.** The Postman speech in the **Appendix** has 5,720 words. How long would it take to deliver?

☐ **Exercise 4.** Select a speech from the **Appendix**. Suppose that you were allotted one-third the time needed to give *that* speech. How would you limit the topic?

☐ **Exercise 5.** Look at the outline on comic books in **7b**. If you were to present that speech to avid comic collectors, how would you limit the topic? Look at the outline on women in the labor force in **5b**. How would you limit that topic if you were given fifteen minutes to speak to a high school social studies class?

(2) Select a few main ideas based on thorough analysis of the audience, the occasion, and your own strengths as a speaker.

In the preceding section, knowing that the criminal justice speech should be cut to one or two main points does not tell you *which* one or two to select. Consider the following questions; they can help you develop your ability to effectively narrow a topic.

Which aspects of your topic are best covered in the oral mode?

Is it wise to spend five minutes reading a list of numbers? Probably that data should be handed out for further study and the *meaning* of the key figures discussed.

A speech should not be used to transmit routine information, to discuss specialized problems of a small portion of the audience, or, of course, to indulge the speaker's ego.

When you look for points to cut, cut those that are best handled by memo, phone call, over coffee — or not at all.

Keep asking yourself: Is this an important topic to discuss in a public speech?

Which aspects of your topic are best suited to this audience and occasion?

Once again, consider this important criterion: Select those points that relate most directly to the needs, attitudes, knowledge, and expectations of your listeners.

Which aspects of your topic can you present most effectively?

Select those points on which you have the most knowledge and in which you have the most interest. Do you excel at explaining complex material, or making abstract ideas personal? Are you better with human-interest stories than statistics, or vice versa? Select those points that best fit your speaking personality.

1c. Clarify the purpose of your speech.

(1) Identify the general purpose of your speech.

What is your intention?

Are you trying to change people's minds?

Are you trying to teach them something?

Are you trying to entertain them?

For instance, if you have decided on "Jazz" as your topic and have narrowed that topic further to "Jazz Saxophone Players," there are several possible speeches you might give. Do you want to explain the harmonic theories of Ornette Coleman to your audience? Or do you want to convince them that Sonny Criss has not been given the attention he should? Or perhaps you will choose to inspire your audience by telling of the comebacks of Stan Getz and Art Pepper after these two musicians overcame drug problems.

The general purpose of a speech can be classified in one of these three ways:

INFORM   A speech designed to explain, instruct, define, clarify, demonstrate, teach.

PERSUADE   A speech designed to influence, convince, motivate, sell, preach, stimulate action.

EVOKE   A speech designed to entertain, inspire, help listeners relive, celebrate, commemorate, bond.

The *speech to evoke* is often called the *speech to entertain*, but we feel that that word unfortunately has come to connote snappy patter and one-liners, which is much too narrow a definition. An evocative speech elicits a certain feeling or emotional response. The emotion or feeling can be one of fun, escape, and diversion — entertainment, if you will — but it can also be solemn and serious as in a eulogy, where a sense of community and an appreciation of individual worth may be evoked.

You will quickly discover that no speech has only one purpose. Most have a combination, but with one purpose usually dominant. For instance, a classroom lecture is used primarily to teach, but can at the same time be used to shape attitudes. The purpose of a campaign speech is to get the folks to vote for the candidate, but the speech can also entertain. An excellent sermon might do all three: inform, persuade, and evoke.

A clear grasp of purpose is especially important in persuasive speaking. When you try to change people, not just educate or inspire them, you are more likely to run into resistance. It helps to know exactly what your goals are — and what they are not. You want to aim for a realistic target.

Some writers distinguish between persuasive speeches that seek to change actual behavior and those that simply try to influence beliefs and attitudes. Although an attitude is a predisposition to respond in a particular way, holding a certain attitude does not guarantee certain behaviors associated with the attitude. People may say they believe in recycling, but never get up the energy to separate their garbage. Generally, if you want action, you should set your goals in terms of action and tell the audience what to *do*, not what to think. An exception is a case where you will be speaking to a hostile audience (see **19**). Here it is better to set a realistic goal of obtaining agreement with your views; you risk losing the audience if you ask for too much too soon. In any persuasive speech then, ask yourself if you are *primarily* trying to change people's minds or *primarily* trying to change their actions.

It is also important in setting goals to think carefully about the nature and direction of the change you seek. There is a tendency to characterize persuasion as "getting people to start doing something": buy a product, vote for a candidate. This persuasive goal, known as *adoption*, is only one of four. You might also persuade a person to stop doing something (*discontinuance*); to keep doing something (*continuance*); or not to start doing something (*deterrence*).[1]

On the general topic of physical fitness you could choose one of a number of persuasive tacks for your speech, such as persuading your audience to

adopt an exercise program

OR

continue eating good foods

OR

stop eating junk foods

OR

avoid taking up cigarette smoking.

Continuance and deterrence only make sense as persuasive goals if there is some jeopardy or pressure in the opposite direction. Exhorting an audience to *continue* breathing would not require much in the way of persuasion. The football coach asking the booster club to *continue* supporting the team knows that his audience has other demands on their time and money. If a speech admonished the audience to "avoid the instant gratification syndrome of credit cards," it would only be relevant in a western culture, where there is great pressure in the opposite direction.

☐ **Exercise 6.**   Show how the topic of each of the speeches in the **Appendix** could be adapted to one other speech purpose.

---

[1]Wallace C. Fotheringham, *Perspectives on Persuasion* (Boston: Allyn & Bacon, 1966), 32.

☐ **Exercise 7.** Describe how each of the topics below could be made into a:

    1. Speech to Inform
    2. Speech to Persuade
    3. Speech to Evoke

Topics:

    Trains
    Natural Childbirth
    Investing in Gold
    Men's Fashions

(2) Determine the primary speech objective.

Knowing which of the three purposes — to inform, persuade, or evoke — is predominant in your speech will help you in the next step: deciding what you really want to accomplish with your topic. It is good to be as specific as you can in visualizing just what you want to happen. The key to an effective statement of objective is to phrase it in terms of audience behavior. Think not about what you want to do, but rather ask yourself: If my speech is a success, what will my audience do?

NOT: My objective is to sell this product.

BUT: My objective is to have you buy this product.

NOT: My objective is to explain photosynthesis.

BUT: My objective is to have you understand the workings of photosynthesis.

    In phrasing your primary speech objective, isolate the central reason for speaking. You will have many incidental goals, but you cannot select and organize your materials without a very clear set of priorities. Do not go any further until you can complete this sentence:
    If there were one *action I'd want my listeners to take after my speech it would be . . .*

(3) Determine the specific secondary speech objectives.

Your speech goals can be clarified even further. Implicit in every general purpose statement are many contributing subgoals. If your overall goal is to persuade the members of the audience to take up the guitar, you want them first to *decide* that it is a good idea, second to *purchase* a guitar, third to *sign up* for lessons, and last to *continue* to practice.

Notice the significance of the verbs in each case. The emphasis is on the behavior you want the audience to adopt. This sort of goal analysis has proved effective in recent years in both education and business. Teachers have learned to phrase their previously fuzzy goals as concrete behavioral objectives. Both teaching and learning have improved. In the business world, the Management by Objectives movement has helped employers and employees analyze tasks and set definite goals and deadlines.

The same procedures will help you plan your speech. Break your primary speech objective into components, paying particular attention to using phrasing with verbs that describe overt behavior rather than general states of mind.

"I want my audience to *appreciate* art" is fine for a primary speech objective, but you must go further and ask yourself how you will know if you have succeeded. What, exactly, are people *doing* when they are appreciating art? If you think about the specific behaviors or operations that go into appreciating art, you will come up with a list of goals like this:

I want my audience to:

- *go* to a gallery.
- *read* books on art.
- *create* a piece of art themselves.

Observe how specific objectives can be crystallized from the three general types of speech:

General Purpose: To Inform
Primary Objective: I want my audience to know what goes into a successful job interview.
Specific Objectives: I want my audience to:

- *distinguish* between the job interview and other types of interviews.
- *understand* what the interviewer expects.
- be able to *list* the four phases of the typical employment interview.
- *recognize* the importance of appearance and body language.

General Purpose: To Persuade
Primary Objective: I want my audience to commit themselves actively to environmental concerns.
Specific Objectives: I want my audience to:

- *use* public transportation, when possible.
- *minimize* the *use* of nonbiodegradable materials.
- *recycle* paper, glass, aluminum, and steel.
- *make* their dwellings energy *efficient*.
- *support* environmentally oriented political candidates and contribute money and time to environmental causes.

General Purpose: To Evoke
Primary Objective: I want my audience to experience a sense of community with all those who participated in or supported the Central High School tennis program.
Specific Objectives: I want my audience to:

- *recognize* the contribution and achievement of each group: players, coaches, staff, parents, booster club, and fans.
- *feel* pride in their individual contribution.
- *relive* some of the high points of the past season.
- *identify* with each other by laughing at "in jokes" that only someone involved in this program would understand.
- *share* in the warmth felt for Coach Pierce.

The specific secondary objectives are not necessarily of the same type as the primary objective they support. Sometimes, for instance, it is essential to inform the audience about specific points before they can be persuaded, or to lighten a primarily informative speech with some entertainment. As a rule, though, the majority of the specific objectives should be compatible with the general purpose of the speech.

☐ **Exercise 8.**   Look at all of the four speeches in the **Appendix**. Identify them by their type—informative, persuasive, or evocative. State the one-sentence primary objective you think each speaker had.

☐ **Exercise 9.**   List at least four secondary objectives that might be developed for each of the following primary objectives. Use specific, concrete verbs to describe the behaviors.

I want to teach my audience about gardening.
I want to have my audience experience the thrills of a trip to Australia.
I want to persuade my audience to drive more safely.

1d. Frame a thesis statement as a single declarative sentence that states the essence of your speech content.

In contrast to your "purpose" and objectives, which state your speech topic in terms of what response you want from your audience, your thesis sentence states your topic as a proposition to be proved or a theme to be developed. This sentence, sometimes referred to as the central idea, gives your speech a focus. Later, when you begin to organize your speech, it will give you a standard against which to test ideas.

(1) In informative or evocative speeches the thesis sentence is a concise distillation of the speech content.

A thesis sentence should not merely announce your topic. It should capsulize what you plan to say about the topic. Be sure that this statement includes enough information to differentiate your approach from other possibilities.

INFORMATIVE SPEECH

NOT: My speech is on the office of the future.

OR EVEN: The office of the future will be very different.

BUT: The office of the future will be virtually paperless, with a computer terminal at each desk providing text and voice messaging and data base access.

EVOCATIVE SPEECH

NOT: We are here to dedicate the new hospital wing.

OR EVEN: The opening of this wing is a great day for O'Connor Hospital and the community.

BUT: This new surgical wing reflects the efforts of many dedicated fund-raisers and increases the quality and quantity of medical care available in our community.

(2) In persuasive speeches the thesis sentence takes the form of a proposition that requires proof. There are three kinds of propositions.

1. PROPOSITION OF FACT. It may seem that if something is a *fact* there is no need to use persuasion to establish it, but there are issues in the factual domain that cannot be verified directly. There either is or is not life on other planets. The question is one of fact, but, because we lack the means to find out, we must argue from the data we have, drawing the most logical inferences therefrom. For example:

Lee Harvey Oswald did not act alone.
The Russian brigade in Cuba were assault troops.
More than two cups of coffee a day increases the chance of cancer of the pancreas.
Reduction of Japanese car imports will help the U.S. auto industry.

2. PROPOSITION OF VALUE. Persuasive speakers are often attempting to prove evaluative positions. Their goal is to judge the worth of something, to establish that it is good or bad, wise or foolish, just or unjust, ethical or unethical, beautiful or ugly, competent or incompetent. For example:

Reagan is a good president.
It is wrong to try to avoid jury duty.
The free enterprise system is the best economic model for the working class.
Charlie Parker was the greatest jazzman ever.

3. PROPOSITION OF POLICY. Most common and most complex among persuasive theses is the proposition of policy, which advocates a specific course of action. Here are some propositions of policy:

The federal government should legalize marijuana for private use.
You should vote for Dan Huboi for union president.
The state of Indiana should ratify the Equal Rights Amendment.
You should send your children to private schools.

When you undertake to prove a thesis sentence that is a proposition of policy, you must be very specific about what plan or program should be adopted by what specifically empowered group or agency. Otherwise, although your thesis includes the word *should/should not*, it is really a disguised proposition of value. Tax loopholes should be closed, for example, is only another way of saying: The present tax system is bad. To be a proposition of policy it must read: Congress should change the present tax structure to reduce oil depletion allowances, vacation home deductions, and home office deductions.

Notice that the types of propositions are cumulative: The proposition of value assumes certain propositions of fact, and the proposition of policy takes its direction from a proposition of value. Or, proving that something *should/should not* be done depends on proving that something is *good/bad*, which in turn requires establishing that something else *is/is not* the case. For instance, to establish the proposition of policy:

> Our local government should/should not commence the aerial spraying of Malathion to eradicate the Mediterranean Fruitfly,

one has to prove at least this proposition of value:

> It is appropriate/inappropriate to risk some danger to human health in order to protect an important agricultural product.

To accept this proposition of value, three propositions of fact need to be established:

> The effect of Malathion on human health is/is not minimal or nonexistent.
> Malathion is/is not effective in controlling the Mediterranean Fruitfly.
> The fruit attacked by the fly is/is not important to the agricultural economy of the area.

Propositions of fact:	IS/IS NOT
Propositions of value:	GOOD/BAD
Propositions of policy:	SHOULD/SHOULD NOT

☐ **Exercise 10.** Read one or more of the speeches in the **Appendix** and formulate a single declarative sentence that best sums up the content. You may find the actual sentence in the speech itself, or you may, in the case of an implicit thesis, have to draft a sentence of your own.

☐ **Exercise 11.** Identify which of the following are propositions of fact, value, or policy.

Converting to solar energy can save the average homeowner money.
New Wave music is simplistic and tasteless.
Cats make better pets than dogs.
Children should learn a foreign language before fifth grade.

☐ **Exercise 12.** Write a proposition of fact, value, and policy on each of these general topics:

Atheism
Nutrition
Women in the military

1e. If necessary, select a speech title.

While every speech needs a thesis and a purpose, not every speech needs a title. Those instances in which a title is necessary are: when there is to be advance publicity; when there is a printed program; and usually, when the speaker is going to be formally introduced. Unless there is a definite deadline to announce your title, you can defer selecting one until after the speech is composed.

A title can take any grammatical form. It can be a declarative sentence, a question, phrase, or fragment.

"Freedom of Speech is in Jeopardy"
"Is Free Speech Really Free?"
"Threats to Free Speech"
"Free Speech: An Endangered Species"

NOTE: Do not confuse the thesis statement with the speech title. The thesis statement is a declarative sentence essential for the organizing and composing of the speech. The title is not.

An effective title should pique interest in your subject and make the audience eager to listen. Sometimes a metaphor, quotation, or allusion that is central to the speech can be part of the title:

"Who Will Be David to This Modern Goliath?"
"Social Security: A House of Cards"
"With Malice toward All"
"Who Is Wise?"[2]
"A Flavor for Our Daily Bread"[3]
"Vulnerability and Vigilance"[4]
"Is God Over Thirty? Religion and the Youth Revolt"[5]
"Warm Flesh Beats Cold Plastic"[6]
"Being Heard As a Woman"

In an effort to be clever or profound, do not devise a title that will totally mystify your audience, like:

"You, a Sponge?"

OR

"The Heraclitus of Sycamore High"

Nor should you select a title that promises more than you deliver. That is false advertising. Do not announce

[2]Ronald W. Roskens, *Vital Speeches of the Day* 47, no. 17 (June 15, 1981): 529.
[3]Samuel B. Gould, *Representative American Speeches* 35, no. 4 (1962–63): 122–28.
[4]Elliot L. Richardson, *Representative American Speeches* 46, no. 3 (1973–74): 13–23.
[5]David C. H. Read, *Representative American Speeches* 39, no. 5 (1966–67): 129–37.
[6]Gerald M. Goldhaber, *Vital Speeches of the Day* 45, no. 22 (Sept. 1, 1979): 683–88.

"How to Double Your Income While Working Two Days a Week."

and then give a speech on how to make one's first investment in income property.

LIKEWISE: "Digging up Dirt at the White House"

might lead your audience to think that your speech has more titillating content than your recollections of work as a gardener in the White House Rose Garden. This may sell tabloids at the supermarket, but it is not considered good speaking technique.

Keep the title concise. Avoid the sort of title initiated by eighteenth-century novelists:

> *The Fortunes and Misfortunes of the Famous Moll Flanders &c. Who was Born in Newgate, and during a Life of continu'd Variety for Threescore Years, besides her Childhood, was Twelve Year a Whore, five times a Wife (whereof once to her own Brother), Twelve Year a Thief, Eight Year a Transported Felon in Virginia, at last grew Rich, liv'd Honest, and died a Penitent, Written from her own Memorandums . . . by Daniel Defoe.*

and perpetuated by academics:

> "A Quasi-experimental Investigation of Latency of Response, Self-disclosure and Turn Taking in Same Sex Dyads: Etiology, Manifestations and Implications."

Do not give your speech in your title.

☐ **Exercise 13.** Evaluate the titles of the speeches in the **Appendix**. Are they effective?
　　　Select titles for the speeches outlined in **5b** and **7b**.

2

Topic Analysis

Analyze your speech topic and generate a comprehensive list of the questions your speech must answer.

When chemists analyze a substance, they identify its components. As a speaker you go through a similar process of analysis when you break up a topic to find all the issues within it. An issue is a question that you must answer to assure the adequate development of your speech. Consider this thesis sentence: "We need to increase our aid to the *Contras* in Nicaragua to block the growing threat of Soviet influence in Latin America." There are four questions that come immediately to mind. (1) Is there a threat of Soviet influence in Latin America? (2) Is it growing? (3) Does this threat include Nicaragua? (4) Would aid to the *Contras* be an effective response to this threat? If you do not address all these questions as you put your speech together, you may overlook some logical and structural flaws.

For certain persuasive speeches, you will be fortunate enough to have lists of stock issues to use as your questions. For most informative and evocative speeches, and many persuasive speeches, such formal requirements are not prescribed, so you must find and define your own issues. In any event, becoming familiar with the strictures of the most-prescribed form will help you make all your speeches, in whatever category, more coherent of purpose.

2a. Use stock issues, when possible, to help you analyze your topic.

Drawing on preestablished, "stock" issues can save you time and effort in preparing a speech. For the standard argumentative problem-solving

approach, there is no need to reinvent the wheel. Central to understanding stock issue analysis is the concept of burden of proof drawn from the
legal system and from formal debate. The individual or side which
advocates change has specific responsibilities. For an extreme example,
consider all the burdens on the British prosecutor in a murder case. In
British law, "murder" is defined as:

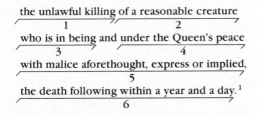

We have underlined and numbered each of the six issues a prosecutor
must prove. To lose even one issue is to lose the case. If the defense can
show that any *one* of the conditions was not present — for instance: that
there was no malice aforethought, *or* that the killing was not unlawful (as
in self-defense), *or* that the victim survived a year and two days after the
alleged act — then murder has not occurred. The burdens on the prosecutor are great, but they are publicly acknowledged and agreed to. Some
kinds of speeches have such well-defined lists of requirements, or stock
issues, that guide the speaker.

(1) Stock debate issues

In a formal debate on a proposition of policy, the speaker advocating a
change is required to provide the audience with satisfactory answers to
all the following questions:

Is there a compelling need for change?
Is that need inherent in the very structure of the present system?
Will the proposed solution meet the need presented?
Is the proposed solution workable and practical?
Do the advantages of the proposed solution outweigh the disadvantages?

You do not have to be a debater to use these stock issues — they serve as
helpful guidelines in analyzing any persuasive topic.

---

[1]F. T. Giles, *The Criminal Law: A Short Introduction* (Harmondsworth, Middlesex: Penguin Books,
1967), 197.

(2) Stock problem-solving issues

Another useful checklist for a problem-solving speech is found in the steps of critical thinking. The following questions may be used as stock issues to analyze a proposition of policy:

Is there a problem?
    What are the symptoms?
    How serious is it?
    What has caused the problem?
What are the appropriate criteria by which to evaluate a solution?
What are all the possible solutions to the problem?
Which of these solutions best fits the criteria established?
How can the solution selected be put into effect?

(3) Stock issues against a change

The examples in **2a(1)** and **2a(2)** apply to persuasive speeches where the primary objective is adoption. In a speech that argues against a policy — where deterrence or discontinuance is the goal — these lists of stock issues can be turned around. Because burden of proof lies with the advocates of change, an opponent of change can succeed by establishing a negative answer to just one key issue. A defense attorney in a slander case can grant that the defendant made statements that were untrue and known to be untrue, but argue that no injury resulted. A negative debater can rest his or her entire case on the issue of the unworkability of a proposed plan. A speaker opposing a change can argue that the wrong criteria have been set for evaluating solutions. However, when you rest an entire argument on a single issue, you must take care to demonstrate how a negative answer to that single question is sufficient to discredit the entire opposing position.

Of course, a speech against a policy is stronger if several of the issues are addressed: 'There is no need for this change; but even if there were, this plan is unworkable; but even if it worked, it would bring about so many undesirable side effects . . ." and so forth.

☐ **Exercise 1.** Which stock debate issue is being addressed in each of the following points?

1. Putting more money into the welfare program will not get at its underlying problems.

2. Adopting a voucher system for the financing of education will allow parents to choose the educational approach that is best for their children.

3. Violent crime has gotten out of control in our cities.

2b. Break your thesis sentence into a list of questions to be answered.

Stock issues apply to fairly stylized speeches, such as legal argument and formal debates, which place very rigorous demands on a speaker. For most speeches, though, the issues you must address have to be drawn out of your topic. Break the thesis sentence down into its components to discover what you must prove or explain.

(1) Find both explicit and implicit issues.

Do not be restricted by the wording of your thesis. In analyzing the grammatical structure of a sentence, you probably learned to fill in understood subjects and predicates. "Pick up that book and then let go" has to be seen as "(You) pick up that book and then (you) let go (of it)." Consider this thesis: *Like other industrialized nations, the United States has a castelike social system based on race, sex, and age.* Imbedded in this thesis are five questions you must discuss:

Does the United States have a castelike system?
Is the stratification based on race?
Is the stratification based on sex?
Is the stratification based on age?
Are these characteristics shared by other industrialized nations?

Sometimes, more than one issue is implicit in a single phrase, as in this example:

Because of her unique qualifications, Ms. Thompson would
         1   2
be a popular and effective principal.
            3

This looks like a sentence with three issues, but really there are four. To establish that Ms. Thompson is *uniquely* qualified, you would have to prove (1) that she has the relevant qualifications, and (2) that no one else has these qualifications. Then you can proceed to prove that (3) she would be a popular principal and (4) she would be an effective principal.

(2) Add or delete issues if audience analysis suggests either action.

Sometimes the list of issues that are logically inherent in a topic is modified in terms of your knowledge of the audience. This is where audience analysis (see **3**) and topic analysis come together. The issue of the need for change can be waived with an audience that is gathered because they are concerned about that problem.

On the other hand, there are issues that are not stated directly in your thesis sentence but are so important to your audience that you must deal with them. "We need to turn to the federal government to finance health care because state and local governments are unable to provide adequate funding." If you know that your audience challenges the assumption that government at any level ought to provide health care for all citizens, then you have another major issue to cover. These understood issues, like understood words in sentences, must be identified.

(3) Find the questions you must answer to develop informative and evocative theses.

Although issue analysis is most often used with argumentative or persuasive speaking, the same principles can guide you in thinking about a speech to inform or to evoke. If you wanted to speak about comic books, you might develop the following thesis sentence:

> With their scope, history, and influence, comic books are an
>   1   2   3
> interesting component of American popular culture.
>   4

Although the parts identified above are not issues in the most technical sense, they serve the same analytical function — they point you toward the questions you need to answer.

In a speech at a retirement dinner, you might capsulize your speech into this thesis sentence:

> Because of Braulio Fuentes's contributions to our organiza-
> tion and his qualities as a human being, we will miss him but
> wish him well in his retirement years.

As you think about developing this talk, you will find that there are four questions you ought to investigate:

Exactly what contributions has he made?
What personal qualities do we value in him?
In what ways will he be missed?
What specific good wishes do we have for his retirement?

To answer these, you can look into Mr. Fuentes's history with your organization. Ask those who work with him what they will miss most, and find out if he plans to travel, raise rare orchids, or start a consulting firm.

The answers to these questions will not necessarily be the main points of your speech, and you might not develop your ideas in this order. However, the analysis serves to direct your research and prevents you from being guilty of any glaring oversights.

☐ **Exercise 2.**   Look at the thesis sentence in each of the speeches in the **Appendix**. Identify the issues implicit in each. Do the speakers address each issue?

☐ **Exercise 3.**   Identify the issues in each of these thesis sentences:

Grading on the curve is inaccurate, unfair, and elitist.
A cruise is an educational way to relax, make friends, and see the world.
Because the property tax is essentially regressive, it is an uncertain and inequitable source of revenue for the city.

3

Audience Analysis

Base your speech preparation on thorough audience analysis.

No speech occurs in a vacuum. You speak to a particular group of people because you want a certain response from them. If you do not know the composition of that group, you cannot make intelligent decisions about what to include, what to emphasize, how best to arrange and present your ideas. Research your audience thoroughly. Their age, sex, attitudes, expectations are all relevant to your planning.

The composition of audiences varies. The members of one may have many similarities; the majority of another, little in common. Within a given audience the degree of homogeneity or heterogeneity can differ for each of the characteristics discussed in this chapter. For instance, an audience can be fairly homogeneous in terms of sex — predominantly female, say — and heterogeneous in its composition of people who agree or disagree with your position.

We approach each of these characteristics as a discrete factor and describe the techniques to be used with various kinds of homogeneous audiences. *You* will have to "mix and match" these techniques as you uncover the actual composition of your potential audience.

Later in the process of preparing your speech, you will use the information to adapt your materials to the audience, following the guidelines in **19**.

3a. Seek information about your audience through as many channels as possible.

Do not limit yourself to any one of the following:

DIRECT OBSERVATION. This is the most reliable source of information about an audience. The easiest audience to analyze is a group of which you are a member. You know what will interest them, convince them, or make them laugh. With an unknown audience try, if you have enough lead time, to observe them either functioning as a group or functioning as an audience. Observation of a group's business meeting, or watching how they respond to another speaker, can tell you a great deal about them.

SYSTEMATIC DATA COLLECTION. One excellent way to become informed about your audience is to ask them about themselves. Politicians and advertisers spend millions on public opinion and market surveys. Such research reveals who their audiences are and how they feel. Do not discount even a simple form of data gathering like having a three- or four-item questionnaire distributed at a meeting before the one where you will speak. You might arouse interest and curiosity while you gain information.

SELECTED INTERVIEWS. When you cannot get information on the whole audience, then arrange to talk to one or two members of the group. If that is not possible, talk to someone who shares characteristics with your potential listeners. For a speech to a group of teenagers, talking to one teenager — even if he or she is not going to be a member of that audience — can provide you with useful information. The same applies to interviewing someone who manages a department at IBM other than the one to which you will speak; and, similarly, you will benefit from conversing with your friend Renea, active in the local chapter of the National Organization for Women, at whose regional conference you will speak.

THE CONTACT PERSON. The person who asked you to speak has certain expectations about the interaction between you and the audience, otherwise you would not have been invited. Ask this contact person to elaborate on his or her perceptions of the audience. Do not be reluctant to ask as many specific questions as occur to you; both you and the contact person have a stake in the success of your speech.

INTELLIGENT INFERENCE AND EMPATHY. When you do not have any specific information about an audience, draw on your general knowledge of human behavior and groups. What are reasonable assumptions about an audience that would be found at a Fourth of July block party, or about those at an open seminar on investment strategies? These need not be obscure; certain intelligent inferences could easily be made about the audience at National Abortion Rights League conference.

Do not use just your reasoning powers; let empathy round out the image. Get outside yourself and adopt your listeners' frame of reference.

Even if you cannot relate to the specific details, try to recall a situation in your life when the same underlying emotion was present. With all the big issues you face as a city councilperson, it can be hard to see why this neighborhood homeowners' group to which you will speak is so upset about changing one-way streets to two-way streets. Stop and remember those times when you perceived something in *your* neighborhood as a threat to your property value and the security of your family. It may not always be relevant to say: when have I been in this situation? But you can usually say: when have I felt this kind of feeling?

3b. Analyze the demographic characteristics of your audience as an aid to predicting their orientation.

There is no such thing as an average audience. A speaker would be more than a little surprised to stand before a group of listeners whose composition followed exactly the distribution of the last census in regard to age, sex, race, socioeconomic status, and religion. Obtaining each audience's vital statistics will enable you to make certain general predictions about their responses. Some pertinent questions might be:

What is the average age of the audience members?
What is the age range?
What is the sexual breakdown of the audience?
What racial and ethnic groups are represented, in about what proportions?
What is the socioeconomic composition of the group?
What occupations are represented?
What religious groups are represented?
What is the political orientation of the group?
How homogeneous (similar) or heterogeneous (diverse) are the audience members for each of the above characteristics?

Obviously, all of these demographic characteristics are not equally important for any given speech. The religious configuration of your audience would be important to have while preparing a speech on abortion. The age distribution would similarly be important for a speech on Social Security reform. Or, religion and age might have no bearing whatsoever on a third topic. Despite differences in relative importance to a particular topic, each demographic characteristics should be noted, if only to give you a general picture. It is disconcerting to face a roomful of minority teenagers when you expected middle-aged, white professionals.

Holding an image of your audience in mind as you prepare and practice your speech will affect dozens of minor decisions not related to your overall strategy. Just on the basis of your general cultural awareness, you will adapt your language usage, humor, and style of delivery to what you know about your audience. Section **19** will help you plan more specific adaptations.

CAVEAT: Very few generalizations can be made on the basis of demographic factors. The studies from which evidence is drawn are often flawed. Also, social change occurs so rapidly that by the time this research is reported the situation has changed. By the time the findings have reached the average layperson through synthesis or summaries, even more time has elapsed. Social science research, even when carefully controlled and well designed, tells us how one group *on the average* differs from another group *on the average*. For example, with respect to almost any trait you might select, the differences among individual women and among individual men are far greater than the differences between the average man and the average woman.

Still, it is naive to say that because people are individuals group data tells us nothing. If you know that an audience is all female or all over sixty-five or all Asian-American, you do know more than if you had no information about the audience at all. Demographic data lets you make some *probability statements*. You can say that many people in an audience are likely to respond in a certain way. You cannot say that any individual in that audienne definitely *will* respond in a given way.

Understanding the limitations of such analysis, you should be aware of various demographic characteristics that may affect your audience's response — including the following:

(1) Age

Maxims like "you're as young as you feel" and "age is a state of mind" tell us to be careful when we make assumptions based on chronological age. Most of us have been exposed to octogenarians who routinely question authority and are open to new experiences, and to eighteen-year-olds who have already ossified their thought patterns. Despite these exceptions, some generalizations can be justified. Current theory holds that psychological development does not stop at the threshold of adulthood, but continues through life in fairly predictable stages. Works by Erikson and Sheehy can offer insight into the most common crises and value realignments of people in their twenties, thirties, forties, and so on.[1] For our purposes, "younger" refers generally to people going through adolescence, formal education, or the early phases of establishing career direction and of confirming life goals.

Younger people tend to be idealistic. They respond positively to arguments based on change and innovation. They are impatient about social change and want to see results in the near future.

They are strongly affected by the values of their peers.

Young people like a speech to be organized in a fluid, narrative fashion. They prefer a rapid, exciting tempo of delivery, employing several media or channels of communication.

Older people are more conservative. They are responsive to appeals to traditional values. They tend to have a stake in the status quo and are reluctant to risk major changes. They are more patient in waiting for results.

When listening to a speech, they prefer a linear, highly structured organization with clear previews, transitions, and summaries. They are most comfortable with a slow, deliberate style of delivery.

(2) Sex

Traditionally, women were socialized to be nurturant, sensitive, compassionate, and emotional. So, in the past, appeals to home, family, and the safety of loved ones have usually been effective with traditional women. Traditionally, men were socialized to be dominant, aggressive, ambitious, and unemotional (except when it came to sports). So a speech to a predominantly traditional male group used appeals to power, success, competitive values, and cold, hard logic.

In the 1970s and 1980s many more women and men have come to a new consciousness of the way sex-role socialization has limited their avenues of expression and growth. They are experimenting with new roles and divisions of labor in public and private life. Both men and

---

[1]See, for example, Erik Erikson, *Identity and the Life Cycle* (New York: Norton, 1980) and Gail Sheehy, *Passages: Predictable Crises of Adult Life* (New York: Dutton, 1976).

women undergoing this process bridle when presented with stereotypical assumptions about roles and power matrices.

As a speaker you are well advised to avoid statements that may offend a sizable portion of your audience. Women, especially as they become aware of past oppression, are very sensitive to slights to their dignity and their role as autonomous adults. Many object to being referred to as girls, gals, or ladies — or by overly cute forms of address like "distaff side" or "the fairer sex" — which tends to trivialize their status. Many women believe that references to their clothes and appearance, however complimentary and well meant, focus on women as sex objects or decorative accessories. To be on the safe side with any audience, avoid such comments as:

> I was chatting at dinner with your lovely vice-president, Professor Ruhly. Now why didn't they have teachers like that when I was in school?

> To Mr. Davis's left, the charming young lady in the pretty blue dress is our regional sales manager, Linda.

Avoid examples that assume everyone fits into traditional roles.

> Tomorrow morning as your wife serves you breakfast, ask her about the prices she finds at the grocery store. [In some households men cook breakfast and shop for groceries.]

> If you had a son about to take over your business, wouldn't you tell him . . . [Why not a daughter?]

Do not perpetuate myths of female incompetence.

> Now, about the direction of market trends. [Giggle] I'm not very good with figures, but I'm sure you men can make some sense out of these charts.

(3) Race/Ethnicity

As with women and men, the attitudinal differences between ethnic groups are not innate. The differences that do exist result from variations in socialization and experience. There are no prescriptions for how to relate to predominantly white, black, Hispanic, or Asian audiences, other than to familiarize yourself with the experiences of that group. The common experience of nonwhite racial groups and most other ethnic minorities in the United States has included discrimination and oppression. Members of these groups, like women, are justifiably sensitive to any communication that reduces their status or reflects old stereotypes. Forms of address, both collective and individual, are very important. Never refer to people by first names, diminutives, or nicknames unless invited to do so. Especially, do not address white males by titles such as Mr., Dr., or Colonel while addressing anyone else more casually. Find out what group designations your audience prefers and respect their wishes.

3c.   Determine the audience's attitudes toward your topic.

If you were to think of every possible reaction that a person might have to the thesis of your speech, you could spread those reactions across a continuum that ranges from extreme disagreement to extreme agreement. Much social science research is based on asking people to classify their attitudes on scales like this one:

DISAGREE   AGREE

Strongly Moderately Slightly Neither Slightly Moderately Strongly
                                 agree nor
                                 disagree

If your goal were to bring about some specific act, your listeners' responses would range across these categories:

Opposed   Inactive   Ready   Taking
to action   to act   action

If the majority of your audience falls on the left of either continuum, that audience should be considered a *hostile* audience. If at the middle, they should be termed *neutral*. To the right, *favorable*. Most speakers would agree that knowing the audience's predisposition toward the topic is the single most important bit of information in planning their speech strategy. When you find out whether your audience is favorable, neutral, or hostile, you will be able to follow the specific suggestions offered in **19**. Although attitudes toward your topic are most obviously relevant to persuasive speaking, they can influence the speech to inform or evoke as well.

3d. Anticipate your audience's expectations by gathering details about the specific speech situation.

We have stressed the importance of knowing your purpose in speaking, but what is your audience's purpose in listening? Why are they sitting there giving you their valuable time? Perhaps they are required to as part of a class or part of a job assignment. Maybe they are present voluntarily, but for a reason unrelated to you or your topic — for example, they enjoy the social contacts of an organization and tolerate a speech as part of the meeting. Or perhaps, if you are very fortunate, they are there because of an interest in what you have to say. In any audience, you will find combinations of these and other motivations. Knowing the predominant audience expectation is vital to the preparation of your speech. An excellent speech can fail miserably if the audience expected a different sort of talk altogether.

This is not to say that you must be bound by the audience's expectations. You can lead them to a new mental set; but to do that successfully you need to discover what they know and expect to begin with. Start with these questions about your listeners and the occasion:

What do they know about your topic?

Overestimating or underestimating the sophistication of your audience can be disastrous. No one likes to be "talked down to" or to waste time listening to what she or he already knows. It is equally frustrating for an audience to try to follow a technical or complicated talk that assumes a background and vocabulary they do not have. In both cases your listeners will first become irritated and then tune out. People listen best and learn best when exposed to information that is just beyond their current level of understanding. Then they are neither bored nor overwhelmed. Make no blanket assumptions about that level, use the techniques of audience analysis to find it.

What do they think about you?

Learn what your audience has heard, read, or assumed about you. If they believe you are an unquestioned expert, a misguided fanatic, or the funniest speaker their program chair has ever met, it will surely influence how they listen to you. You will want to build on their positive expectations and overcome their negative ones. As **17a** explains, knowing what your credibility is before the speech helps you decide how much you need to do to bolster it during the speech.

What is the history of your audience as a group?

Audiences come in many different forms, with varied levels of group cohesion. An example of an audience with a low level of group cohesion would be the people who showed up after reading about your speech in the coming events section of the newspaper. Most audiences, though, have some common history, which may vary from a long association in a business or club to a few weeks together in a classroom. Learn all you can about this collective history. What projects have they undertaken? What lighter, social events have they shared? What problems do they face? What have they accomplished as a group? What other speakers have they heard? You may find possible connections to your speech topic.

What is the program surrounding your speech?

To understand an audience's expectations of you, it is essential to learn your speech's place in the context of their immediate situation. Whether you are part of a three-day conference or a high school assembly, familiarize yourself with the agenda and where you fit into it. Did your listeners just arrive from home, or have they been sitting in session since eight this morning? How long a speech do they expect? Have they had a cocktail hour or eaten a big meal? The overly relaxed or sated audience can be a challenge to a speaker, but so can the thirsty or hungry one. Have they just listened to a long treasurer's report, endless head table introductions, or a stand-up comedian? Is your speech the main event, or are they anticipating the election of officers, the juggling act, or the speaker to follow?

You obviously cannot have control over these conditions, but that makes it all the more important to get answers to as many of your questions as possible beforehand. Then you can direct your time to preparing a speech ideally suited to the occasion.

☐ **Exercise 1.** Suppose you are the contact person for a speaker who will talk about defense spending. Prepare an audience profile at least two paragraphs in length that summarizes the most relevant demographic and attitudinal data. If you are enrolled in a speech class, use the class as the audience you will describe. Otherwise, describe a group you know well, such as your department at work or an organization you belong to.

Research

Research your topic.

Say that you are gratified to have been asked to give a talk on your life history. Pretty easy to do, you think; who knows you better than you? Just a matter of spinning off tales as they come to you: "And then, in the summer of '56 — or was it '55?" Start again with a different supposition: A professional biographer has become interested in your life and wants to include it in her lecture tour repertoire. She would interview you and find out what happened in the summer of '56 — or was it '55 — and then also interview your parents, siblings, children, professors, friends, and colleagues and pore over files in the library. Granting that you and the biographer have equal speaking skills, which speech would give the audience more accurate information and analysis? Which would have a more balanced perspective? This facetious example is put forward to demonstrate that there really is not a speech topic, no matter how close to your heart, that could not benefit from research.

There are two basic sources to tap for research: other humans and recorded information. Ordinarily it is best to start with the recorded information and perhaps then seek additional information, clarification, and guidance from a person knowledgeable about your topic.

> In some circumstances, particularly with an obscure subject or recently articulated problem, you might be best advised to contact an authority to ask for basic sources of information. This should be a last resort, after exhausting the potential of the library and similar public resources.

4a. Use the library.

It can be argued that Benjamin Franklin's greatest contribution was the establishment of the first lending library in America. For all the decades since then, libraries have existed to provide clarification to those who wish to know more about any topic. Even the smallest library usually has a connection to a larger system through which it can order what you need. In addition to the standard lending libraries there are special libraries or collections that have a particular theme as a focus. You can get more information about these from the *Directory of Special Libraries and Information Centers* published by Gale Research Company or from *Special Collections*, published by the R. R. Bowker Company. The American Library Association's *American Library Directory* also lists these special libraries along with the standard ones.

Contrary to the image presented in cartoons, movies, and television, librarians are not there merely to shush people who forget to whisper. They are there to help you find the materials you need. Do not hesitate to ask them questions, they want the challenge of understanding your requirements and directing you to the answers you seek.

If the library gives tours of the facility, be sure that you go on one.

(1) Use the card catalog to locate books on your topic.

The banks of drawers that constitute the card catalog are the first stop for anyone doing research. In them are small cards listing the books available to the general public (special collections usually have a separate catalog). A book will be cited alphabetically in at least three places: by *author*, by *title*, and by variations of its *subject*. Each card will have the book's *call number*, which gives you the location of the book in the library stacks (see Figure 4-1).

Some of the larger libraries also have computer terminals in the card catalog area, which will give you the location of the book by shelf number.

(2) Use the appropriate indexes to locate magazine, journal, and newspaper articles on your topic.

The library will have a number of periodical indexes through which you can find information. These are usually bound volumes, but in some libraries you can also scan a microfilm magazine index. Most common of

FIGURE 4-1

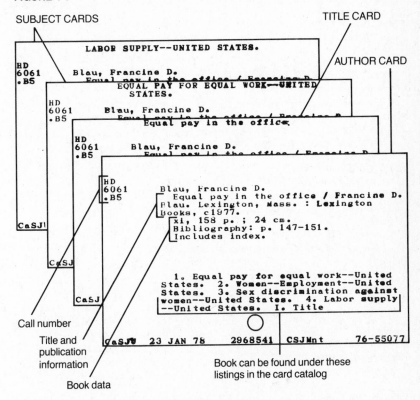

SUBJECT CARDS   TITLE CARD

AUTHOR CARD

Call number

Title and
publication
information

Book data

Book can be found under these
listings in the card catalog

the indexes is the *Reader's Guide to Periodical Literature*, which catalogs
the articles in such magazines as *Time*, *National Geographic Magazine*,
The New Republic, *World Tennis*, and *Technology Review*. A complete list
of the publications covered can be found in the front of the guide.

For many topics the sources included in the *Readers' Guide* will be
too general, in which case you need to examine specific indexes for
journals devoted to a certain field. Some of these more specialized
indexes are:

Government and Public Affairs
    Index to U.S. Government Periodicals
    Congressional Tax Record
    Public Affairs Information Service (PAIS)
    Index to Legal Periodicals
    Criminal Justice Periodical Index

Medicine
  Index Medicus
Humanities and Social Science
  Art Index
  Music Index
  Social Sciences Index
  Essay and General Literature Index
  Biography Index
  Religion Index (One and Two)
Science and Technology
  Applied Science and Technology Index
  Biological and Agricultural Index
  Engineering Index
  Industrial Arts Index
Business and Economics
  Business Periodicals Index
  Journal of Economic Literature
Education
  Current Index to Journals in Education
  Educational Resources Information Center (ERIC)
General
  Popular Periodical Index
  Canadian Periodical Index

There also are indexes for many major newspapers. For example:

The New York Times Index
The Times (London) *Index*
Los Angeles Times Index

Indexes for many other major city newspapers exist. Size of the library and closeness of the major city are usually the factors determining the availability of such indexes.

(3) Use abstracts, special dictionaries, encyclopedias, and similar resources to locate information on your topic.

Abstracts are similar to journal indexes and are specific to a field or discipline. Whereas the indexes give only title and author, abstracts also contain a short summary of the article's content. Some of the abstracts are:

Abstracts of English Studies
Abstracts of Folklore Studies
Abstracts of Police Science

Biological Abstracts
Chemical Abstracts
Economic Abstracts
Excerpta Medica
Geographical Abstracts
Historical Abstracts
International Political Science Abstracts
Physics Abstracts
Psychological Abstracts
Religious and Theological Abstracts
Sociological Abstracts

Special dictionaries and encyclopedias are useful tools, especially for clarifying terms and concepts as they are used in fields of which you may have little knowledge:

Black's Law Dictionary
Chambers Dictionary of Science and Technology
Harper Bible Dictionary (Miller and Lane)
Encyclopedia of Sociology
Encyclopedia of Psychology (Eysensck)
McGraw-Hill Encyclopedia of Science and Technology

These are among many such reference works covering world history, finance, medicine, philosophy, music, literature, and other subjects of significance.

Most libraries will have a copy of *Books in Print*, which lists all currently published books by subject, in a format similar to that of the *Reader's Guide*.

Depending on its size, the library may have many other possible sources of information available: including film strips, microform, records, cassettes, film, and videotapes.

(4) Approach your topic so that you progress from the general to the specific.

One of the most useful talents to have in the early stages of research is the ability to skim read. Even if you had unlimited time to prepare, it would not make sense to grab the books whose authors names begin with A and read them cover to cover, then go to the Bs, and so on. Before checking out any books, look through a number of them. Since you will not have time to read everything, try to get a feel for the most important approaches and theories. To do this, look at the tables of contents, skim the first and last chapters of a book, or read the first and last paragraphs of a chapter or article. Notice recurring names, concepts, and studies. Do not feel obligated to read every single sentence.

When you seek out a particular book, also scan titles around it on the shelves. Books are grouped by general subject, alphabetized by author within the group. You may spot a useful source that was not readily apparent in the card catalog.

In the beginning look for summary or state-of-the-art articles and books that synthesize current thought on your subject. Pieces that trace the history of your topic are also useful. Quite often these sources are readily identifiable by their titles:

"The lasting changes brought by women workers"]Business Week, March 15, 1982]

The Working Mother: A Survey of Problems and Progress in Nine Countries [Alice H. Cook, New York School of Industrial Relations, 1978]

Women in the American Economy: A Look to the 1980's [Juanita M. Kreps, Prentice-Hall, 1976]

"Employment gains of women by industry, 1968–78" [H. Davis, *Monthly Labor Review*, June 1980]

Beginning your research by skimming several sources and reading a few general ones will give you a good overview of your topic. It will help you further narrow your topic and focus the remainder of your search.

4b.   Use electronic information retrieval services.

The advances in computer technology make quick and extensive information retrieval available to an ever-growing number of people. This information retrieval is often called an *online search*. The researcher can modify and focus his or her search strategy while connected to the computer. In the past such spontaneous modifications were not possible. It is from this immediate, *on* the *line*, interaction that the online search gets it name.

There are a number of services that provide information retrieval. DIALOG, BRS (Bibliographic Retrieval Service), and ORBIT (Online Retrieval of Bibliographic Information Timeshared) are well established and useful. "The Source" is an information service geared more toward home computer use, having UPI wire service, stock market quotations, and an airline schedule review besides a "customized information research service." With the exponential growth of computer use in homes and businesses, there is no doubt that there will be many more services on the market. The system you use can depend on your topic and which system is subscribed to by the search service you deal with. You can get access to one of these systems in a number of ways. Many of the larger public libraries now subscribe to at least one and can be used by anyone who makes an appointment. College and university libraries are likely to have a search service, usually available only to students, staff, and faculty. Many companies, unknown to most of their employees, have access to at least one of the major systems. It would be to your advantage to investigate the computer capability of your company, community and friends.

A service like DIALOG can have more than a hundred databases to choose from, a spectrum which encompasses the COMPREHENSIVE DISSERTATION INDEX (University Microfilms), RAPRA ABSTRACTS (Ruber and Plastics Research Association of Great Britain), CHILD ABUSE AND NEGLECT (National Center for Child Abuse and Neglect), FOREIGN TRADERS INDEX (U.S. Department of Commerce), and PHILOSOPHER'S INDEX (Philosophy Documentation Center). Congressional information, magazine indexes, and medical studies all have their own databases. Each of the databases can cover more than a hundred thousand separate articles and papers.

An online search is a labor-saving device, but it does not and should not save you from having to *think*. Online connect costs make fishing expeditions expensive. Most search operators will advise you first to do a manual search in the traditional way: card catalogs and periodical indexes. You must create a concise search strategy by narrowing your topic after considering different avenues of approach. Then you can decide what are the most likely categories used to file and cross-reference the information. These categories are designated by words or short phrases called *descriptors*. After you have done that, you can turn to the computer and exploit its electronic capability.

The online search shines in instances where the traditional search has turned up nothing concrete for the researcher. If you have been frustrated in your labors with the card catalog and the periodical indexes, a *free text* online search can ferret out the more obscure sources. In a free text search the computer does not limit itself to authors, titles, and preestablished descriptors of the subject. You can ask it to scan for any word or combinations of words in the article summaries themselves.

Look at how a computer search might unfold. In the beginning you acquaint the search operator with the subject of your research and the sources you have already investigated. After some discussion, you and the operator decide which database or bases will have information pertinent to your topic. For instance, if you are interested in the subject of equal pay for work of comparable worth, you might run the following search. You and the operator decide that of the DIALOG databases, ABI/Inform, the business management and administration information source, will be most useful since it abstracts from articles from over 400 business publications. You ask the computer for the number of articles with descriptors or titles that include "women," "sex discrimination," and "affirmative action." Figure 4-2 shows what the computer prints out.

At this point you ask the computer for the number of articles that combine all three descriptors, and request a full or partial listing on the basis of that information (see Figure 4-3). You can either call up title, author, and publication information or ask for all of those and also an abstract of any given article.

Figure 4-4 is an example of a free text search for "equal pay for comparable work," along with an abstract called up for consideration.

The usual procedure is to call up a few abstracts online to make certain that they are pertinent to your research, and then order the remainder of the abstracts "offline" to be delivered to you by mail, saving you the extra expense of having them all transmitted over the computer terminal. The search winds up with the computer calculating how much time was used during the search and displaying the amount charged for that time after you log off.

FIGURE 4-2

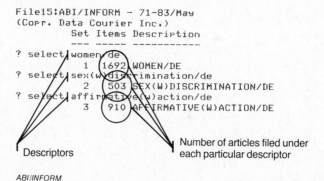

```
File15:ABI/INFORM -- 71-83/May
(Copr. Data Courier Inc.)
        Set Items Description
?  select women/de
        1   1692  WOMEN/DE
?  select sex(w)discrimination/de
        2    503  SEX(W)DISCRIMINATION/DE
?  select affirmative(w)action/de
        3    910  AFFIRMATIVE(W)ACTION/DE
```

Descriptors   Number of articles filed under
                                     each particular descriptor

ABI/INFORM

FIGURE 4-3

Number of articles sharing
all three descriptors

```
? combine 1and2and3
        4  (38)  1AND2AND3

4/2/3
82017059
The Impact of Equal Opportunity Policy on Sex Differentials in Earnings and
Occupations
   Beller, Andrea H.
   American  Economic  Review  v72n2  PP:  171-175  May 1982  CODEN:  AENRAA
ISSN: 0002-8282  JRNL CODE: AER
   DOC TYPE: Journal Paper  LANGUAGE: English  LENGTH: 5 Pages
   AVAILABILITY: ABI/INFORM
   DESCRIPTORS: Sex discrimination; EEOC;  Affirmative action;  Civil Rights
Act 1964-US; Women; Education; Differentials; Earnings
   CLASSIFICATION   CODES:   6100   (CN=Human  resource  planning);   6200
(CN=Training & development); 4320  (CN=Legislation)
```

One printed sample of title,
author, publication information

ABI/INFORM

FIGURE 4-4

Number of articles found through
"free-text" method

```
   select equal(w)pay(1w)comparable(w)work
        5  (9) EQUAL(W)PAY(1W)COMPARABLE(W)WORK
? type5/5/1-3
5/5/1
83007260
Systematic  Bias  in Job Evaluation and Market Wages:  Implications for the
Comparable Worth Debate
   Schwab, Donald P.; Wichern, Dean W.
   Jrnl of Applied Psychology v68n1 PP:  60-69 Feb 1983  CODEN:  JAPGBP
ISSN: 0021-9010  JRNL CODE: JAP
   DOC TYPE: Journal Paper  LANGUAGE: English  LENGTH: 10 Pages
   AVAILABILITY: ABI/INFORM
   The  concept  of  equal  pay  for  comparable work has been proposed as a
possible solution to continuing wage  differentials  between  work  groups.
However,  the validation criteria used to determine the comparable worth of
jobs have been subject to  systematic  measurement  errors.   In  the  job
evaluation  phase,   typically  female  jobs  may  be  systematically
underevaluated,  increasing the wage differential between male  and  female
workers,   and  the wage distributions used to validate job evaluations may
reflect sex-based discrimination.  The consequences of measurement bias in
job  evaluations  and  wage  distributions  are  investigated.   Systematic
measurement errors can be identified by using reverse regression along with
conventional regression techniques.   Systematic measurement error  in  the
evaluation of female jobs does not necessarily result in wage disadvantages
for all job categories.  However, wage distribution bias serves to increase
the wage differentials between male and female jobs.  Graphs.  Equations.
References.
   DESCRIPTORS:  Job  evaluation;  Validation;  Systematic;  Bias;  Wage
differential; Men; Women; Sex discrimination; Comparable worth
   CLASSIFICATION   CODES:   2500   (CN=Organizational   behavior);   9130
(CN=Experimental/Theoretical)
```

Sample of a complete abstract

ABI/INFORM

4c. Seek information directly from other people.

Research is more than delving into piles of books and papers. You are surrounded by potential sources of information in the form of other people—either as individuals or as members of informal or formal information networks. These sources can complement and supplement your library research. They are not a substitute for it. No matter how compelling any single narrative, you do not want to be completely seduced away from those piles of books and papers. The speech you give must still be *your synthesis* of ideas and facts from many sources—not just a report of someone else's ideas.

(1) Finding human resources

Your acquaintances, family, and co-workers can be sources of information.

As you start developing ideas on your topic, begin to talk about them with the people you come in contact with every day. You may encounter surprising sources of expertise. The person with whom you play tennis may turn out to know quite a bit about computers, or your dentist may have gone to China last summer. On many topics, what these people can offer you is not so much expertise as a lay perspective that you will not find in any book. Talk to any five friends and you can compile a list of amazing computer foul-ups. Did any of your acquaintances ever find someone worth dating in a singles bar? What do they think is the most urgent economic problem the country faces?

You might turn this into an informal survey, or even go a step further and develop a brief written questionnaire.

> If you choose to employ a questionnaire, be sure that you do not use leading questions ("Should we continue the cowardly, defeatist policies of the last administration?"). Also be sure that you qualify in your speech any conclusions you may draw, explaining the limitations of an informal, unscientific survey.

Seek out experts.

In every community there are people with specialized expertise in your topic. They can make a significant contribution to your research in that they often can tell you of unpublished data, of local applications or examples of your subject, or direct you to obscure sources.

Try:

EDUCATORS. At whatever level — high school, trade school, college, or university — educators are usually very approachable experts. Dissemination of information is their business. If you do not already have a specific person in mind after your research to this point, call the appropriate department or school. They will direct you to someone knowledgeable.

PUBLIC OFFICIALS AND AGENCIES. People elected to public office consider it one of their duties to make information available to their constituents. Most have staffs whose job it is to locate and send out government documents, copies of bills pending, and so on. In addition, scores of public agencies are staffed by experts who are ready to help you. If you do not know where to start, call the main switchboard of the local or regional government and outline the direction of your research. They can tell you the department with which to begin.

INDEPENDENT AGENCIES AND SPECIAL INTEREST GROUPS. Groups such as the American Cancer Society, Planned Parenthood, and the National Hot Rod Association can be excellent sources of information. Be aware that such groups often represent a limited perspective. Talk to a spokesperson from the National Rifle Assocation, or the Sierra Club, but weigh the information you receive against the standard of objectivity that you have developed (it is hoped) through previous comprehensive research. When possible, interview experts with differing orientations toward your subject, especially if the subject is controversial.

POTPOURRI. Judges, athletes, businesspeople, police officers, doctors, merchants, accountants can all be experts. If you do not know a person in the particular field, see if you have a one-step link to one through a colleague or friend. Failing that, be alert to people mentioned in the newspapers. Chances are that if they were interviewed once, they would be willing to answer other questions. If you have no contacts in a monolithic organization, start with the public relations officer. However, when you know whom you want to talk to, there is no harm in calling that person's office and explaining your request. Maybe you will not get an appointment with the mayor, the chief of police, or the coach of the football team, but you may be able to meet with a top aide or assistant.

(2) Interviewing

Prepare for the interview.

Do not go into an interview cold. Analyze who the person is and ask yourself in what ways she or he can best contribute to your research. If the person has written an article or book on the subject, read it. You should devise a list of questions that are specific enough that you will not be wasting this person's time by asking for information that you could have gotten out of the encyclopedia. You want to prepare open-ended questions, rather than yes-no questions or simple factual queries, but at the same time you do not want to be so vague that you give the person no starting place. For instance, you are studying the history and present condition of women in the labor force and you are directing your questions to the chair of the County Commission on the Status of Women:

NOT: "How many women are there in the work force in this county?" [The figure could have been looked up before.]

NOT: "What are the problems working women encounter?" [Too vague.]

BUT: "I've read that in this county the average woman's salary is 32 percent less than the average man's. To what do you attribute this?"

During the interview

Spend the first few minutes establishing rapport and setting a context for the interview. Explain who you are, why you need the information, and how far you have gotten. Also, confirm your understanding of the time available. This may be a recapitulation of your initial phone call or letter. If you wish to tape the interview, ask permission at this point, but be ready with a notepad in case you do not get it. At any rate, you ought to take notes even if you do tape. Notes will help you keep track of potential questions and needed clarifications as you go along, and you will have a written record to assist you in finding important points when you later go over the tape.

When you begin to ask questions be sure to let the expert do most of the talking. Do not interrupt, disagree or hold forth on your opinions. Be supportive verbally and nonverbally: nod, smile, express interest and concern with your posture and facial expression. Encourage the person with short noninterruptive comments, such as "mm-hmm," "I see," "that's interesting," "then what happened?" and so on.

Check your understanding of the points being made by paraphrasing and clarifying: "In other words, what you are saying is . . ." "Would this be an example of what you are talking about? . . ." "Are you using the term 'discrimination' with the connotation of conscious intent?"

As the expert answers the open-ended questions, follow up with more specific questions in response to those answers: "You said a minute ago that the issue of comparable pay for women may be more important in the long run than the Equal Rights Amendment. Why do you say that?"

Also, use questions to summarize and direct the interview: "So far you've talked about four problems working women face — unequal pay, lack of training, sexual harassment, and inadequate child care. Are there others?"

Allow for a closing phase for the interview. Respect the interviewee's time limit, and if you are approaching it, stop — even if you have gone through only half of your questions. Summarize your perspective of the interview. Often it is productive to ask if the person would like to make a wrap-up statement. In some cases you can ask "what's the question I haven't asked that you wish I had?" And, of course, thank him or her.

4d. Record all information and sources on notecards. Use a separate card for each idea and each bibliographic entry to facilitate retrieval and organization.

Form the habit of identifying the source for every piece of data you use and of recording complete bibliographic information for each source. Think about the battering your credibility will take if you are questioned about a bit of evidence and your only reply is "I found this in my research, but I don't remember exactly where." Writing down volume numbers of journals or the city of publication, details that you will never mention in your speech, may seem like unnecessary work, but routinely recording all information will help you retrieve sources if you need to check them again. If you later develop your speech into a written report or article, your research notes will be priceless.

Have a stack of 4″ x 6″ notecards with you as you go through the card catalog or periodical indexes. For each promising source, write the author's last name. Below that write a few key words of the book's title or the name and date of the periodical, and to the left write the call numbers. Visualize how much room the full names, titles, and publishing data would take, and leave gaps to fill in later as needed (see Figure 4-5).

When you have several of these, go to the stacks, skim through them, and select those sources that you will want to peruse more closely. Fill in the bibliography cards of these books and articles with the full information as in Figure 4-6.

This system may waste a few notecards, but in the long run you will save time by not having to copy information from scribbled jottings onto new notecards and by avoiding return trips to the library later to fill in the gaps. One other benefit of this system is that under it you will never experience the following trauma: Finding an old notecard on which is written the one bit of information that you now see is pivotal, you turn the card around and over fruitlessly as you moan, "This is great! Where'd I get it?"

For each source, select a one- or two-word identification code that

FIGURE 4-5

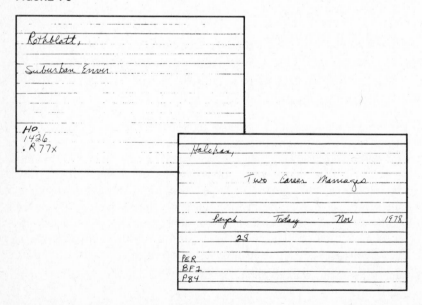

FIGURE 4-6

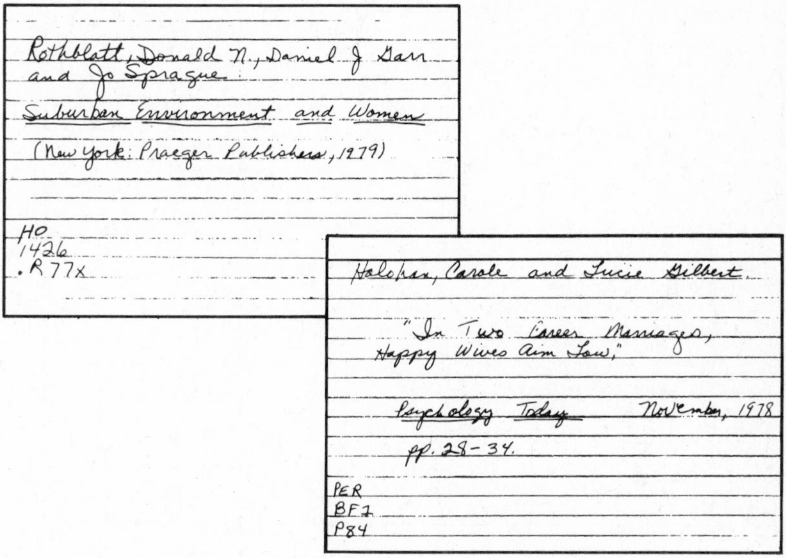

refers to that source and no other. Usually the author's last name is sufficient. "Rothblatt." If there is another book by Rothblatt among your references, you may need to use "Rothblatt, 1980," "Rothblatt, 1979." Or if there are two sources from that author and year: "Rothblatt, *Suburbia*," "Rothblatt, *Urban Development*." Or, of course, if you have different authors with the same last name: "Rothblatt, D.," "Rothblatt, M."

As you read the book or article, jot down each discrete idea or bit of information on a separate card, being sure you add the identifying code and page number. Use only one side of each card. There are three kinds of data you might record:

Direct quotations or citations (Figure 4-7).

Paraphrased ideas (Figure 4-8)

References for later use (Figure 4-9).

If you decide now or later that the table mentioned in Figure 4-9 is valuable, you may want to photocopy it rather than tediously transcribe it

FIGURE 4-7

> Rothblatt, p. 51
>
> " The working wife and mother may have some sources of satisfaction outside the home and some additional power in the home but she is not fundamentally different from the housewife. Rather, she is a housewife with another job. In her own consciousness and in her family's she is still the primary guardian of the home."

FIGURE 4-8

> Rothblatt, p. 52-53.
>
> Cites several studies that show that married women who work, though they spend less time on housework than women not employed, still do much more than half the housework.

FIGURE 4-9

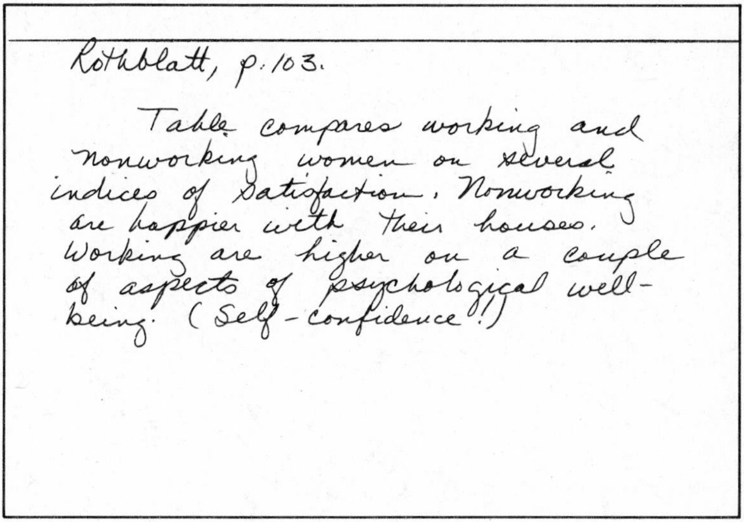

> Rothblatt, p. 103.
>
> Table compares working and nonworking women on several indices of Satisfaction. Nonworking are happier with their houses. Working are higher on a couple of aspects of psychological well-being. (Self-confidence!)

by hand. When you photocopy lists, diagrams, tables, and other technical material, immediately head the sheet as you would a notecard (see Figure 4-10).

If you copy entire articles or chapters, be sure to make a bibliography card for each. Many people find it helpful to photocopy the title page and copyright page of the book or periodical.

When you have gathered many notecards, you may want to stack them under cover cards with titles such as *history*, *causes*, *solutions*, or you may decide to put these key words in the upper right corner. As you will see in the section on organizing, this grouping of ideas and naming of categories usually occurs later in the process of preparing your speech.

These suggestions relate primarily to printed information, but are easily adapted to information acquired through interviews and surveys. Make a bibliography card for each interview, citing the person interviewed, his or her qualifications, and the date of the interview. As you listen to the tape or go over your notes, transcribe the information on cards.

FIGURE 4-10

Rothblatt, p.103.

TABLE 4.5

Mean Scores of Indexes of Satisfaction for
Women's Occupational Status

	Satisfaction Scores[a]	
Satisfaction Index	Non working (n=405)	Working (n=420)
Housing environment	5.64[b]	5.54
Privacy	5.85	5.80
House and lot	5.61	5.52
Homeownership responsibilities	5.33[c]	5.10
Appearance	5.79	5.74
Community services	5.10	5.10
Parks	4.97	4.98
Schools	5.19	5.16
Security	5.26	5.22
Child care	4.18	4.20
Transportation	5.40	5.42
Entertainment	5.48	5.49
Social patterns	5.35	5.30
Friendships	5.64	5.68
Group activities	5.22	5.29
Sense of belonging	5.13[b]	4.95
Psychological well-being	6.92	7.07
Fullness vs. emptiness of life	7.15	7.12
Receptivity towards the world	6.92	7.06
Social respect	7.44	7.83
Personal freedom	6.76	7.04
Sociability	7.06	6.99
Companionship	7.49	7.58
Work satisfaction	7.23	7.53
Tranquility vs. anxiety	6.28	6.27
Self approving vs. guilty	6.65	6.85[c]
Self confidence	7.02	7.27[d]
Energy vs. fatigue	6.48	6.58
Elation vs. depression	6.68	6.67

[a] two-tailed t-test for all score differences yields $p > 0.100$ unless otherwise noted
[b] t-test for score difference yields $p < 0.100$
[c] t-test for score difference yields $p < 0.050$
[d] t-test for score difference yields $p < 0.010$
[e] t-test for score difference yields $p < 0.005$
Source: Compiled by the authors.

103

56

Take care to cite evidence accurately; avoid distorting data or taking it out of context. See **12f**. Be especially clear about what is yours and what is not. Give credit not only for direct quotations, but also for ideas that you paraphrase. Avoid the slightest hint of plagiarism.

ORGANIZATION

INTRODUCTION

Of the four phases of the creative process, most speech training emphasizes preparation and refinement, because these are logical, rule-bound
processes. Incubation and illumination are rarely mentioned, because
they do not lend themselves to systemization. These middle steps touch
the emotions. The process of creating a poem, a story, a painting, a
symphony, or a speech produces intense feelings of discouragement
and excitement. After you have analyzed your audience and topic, and
have throroughly researched your subject, you discover when you start
to outline and organize your ideas that composing a speech is not
always straightforward and systematic. Even with adequate preparation,
you will find yourself pacing the floor, staring into space, filling your
wastebasket with false starts. Rest assured that you are not the only one
to whom this happens.

In writing this book, we did not roll a piece of paper into a typewriter, begin by typing *The Speaker's Handbook*, and then proceed unerringly through to the last page. The naming and arranging of categories took hours: Should practice be dealt with as an aspect of preparation? Can style be separated from content? Does the motivated sequence fit under patterns of organization or under motivational appeals? Even when we had settled on a general outline, the details of that outline were altered again and again as the actual writing progressed. At times the topics seemed so interconnected that we felt we were trying to untangle a skein of yarn rescued from the attentions of the cat. Would it ever come out in one straight line?

This frustration is an inherent part of the creative process. When you have read only one article on a topic, it is easy to write a summary of it. When you have researched and analyzed a topic fully, you begin to suffer from information overload. First, you are overwhelmed by the amount of information; second, you see so many connections among the facets of the topic that you have trouble dividing it. See this frustration as a sign that you have gone beyond the "book report" stage and are beginning to impose your own creative structure on the topic. In effect, you are saving your audience from the agony of information overload by experiencing it yourself and then struggling until you have drawn something clear and meaningful out of the morass.

The analysis and synthesis of information has appropriately been called *invention*. Analysis is the taking apart of a topic, a process that follows specified rules. Synthesis is the remolding of the parts into a new whole — truly creating or inventing an interpretation that did not exist before. There are no set rules for synthesis. While many people could collect the same information and divide a topic into certain logical parts, no two people could prepare the same speech. The synthesis that you create reflects your personality, your values, and your individual approach to life.

The synthesis process cannot be rushed. Too often speakers "prepare" by gathering materials right up to the last minute, postponing the awful inevitability of facing a blank sheet of paper. If all you feel you need to do is write a simple précis or summary, you might plan merely to sit down and do it. If you are going to *create* a speech, a synthesis of your unique understandings, you must set aside plenty of time for incubation and refinement. You have to live with your topic, letting it mature, ripen, ferment. When setting a timetable for preparing your speech, always provide extra time to allow for emergencies. Speech research and rehearsal can go on when you have a headache or when you are in an emotional funk, but the creative aspects of speech organization require physical and psychological alertness.

If you are giving a speech at noon on Friday and have collected all the information, do not plan on putting it together from eight to twelve Friday morning. Although four hours may suffice in this hypothetical situation, it would be best to schedule an hour a day Monday through Thursday. If you spend the time on Monday covering pages with hopeless scribblings, you need not panic. Tuesday things may fall into place, leaving Wednesday and Thursday for refinement.

One successful speaker reports that if she knows in January that she will give a graduation speech in June she tries to put in one work session in February or March. She may not actually word the speech until a week or two before the presentation, but after developing that very sketchy first outline in February she will begin to notice little things in conversation, in reading, on television that relate to her theme. It is as though the first commitment of time activates the incubation process and gives her unconscious mind an assignment to get to work on the problem.

Sections **5–10** suggest ways to organize and structure your material to provide a unified speech. The speech *outline* is not just an arbitrary and tiresome exercise imposed by teachers. Preparation of a complete outline gives you a logical blueprint for your speech. Out of the many ideas you encounter in your research, it is necessary to *select a few main points* that best reflect your purpose in speaking. A set of parallel, clearly stated, mutually exclusive main points will be easy for you and your audience to remember. There are several effective ways to *arrange these points*. Also important are the *transitions* that form the bridges between the parts of the speech. When the body of your speech is structured, you will want to devise an *introduction* to lead your listeners into your topic and, later, wrap it up for them with a *conclusion*.

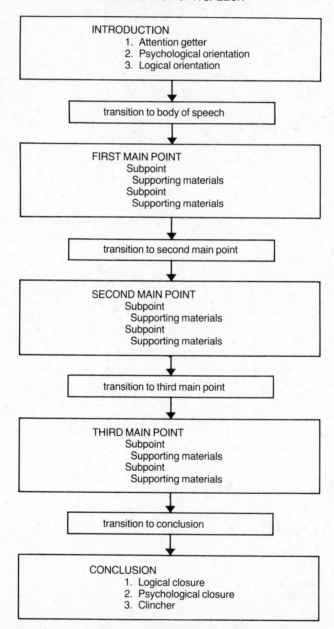

FLOWCHART FOR THE
ORGANIZATION OF A SPEECH

INTRODUCTION
1. Attention getter
2. Psychological orientation
3. Logical orientation

transition to body of speech

FIRST MAIN POINT
Subpoint
Supporting materials
Subpoint
Supporting materials

transition to second main point

SECOND MAIN POINT
Subpoint
Supporting materials
Subpoint
Supporting materials

transition to third main point

THIRD MAIN POINT
Subpoint
Supporting materials
Subpoint
Supporting materials

transition to conclusion

CONCLUSION
1. Logical closure
2. Psychological closure
3. Clincher

5

Outlining

Use an outline as an organizational tool.

The speech outline is an indispensable tool of speech organization. A clear outline will help you keep track of the points you want to cover; using one will also increase the chances that your audience will retain the gist of your message. The act of outlining, laying your ideas out on paper, forces you to select the points that support your thesis and to demonstrate how they fit together. Until you have something concrete in front of you, how can you say you truly know what you are going to talk about? Once you have an outline, you are in a better position to receive assistance and suggestions from friends, teachers, and colleagues, and from your own introspection.

There are two traps you can fall into: either overestimating your preparedness or underestimating it. In the first case you might say, "I've researched this subject so much that I've got it down cold." Until you give the speech—or begin writing down your ideas—how can you be sure? Better to discover your mistakes with your pen as your only audience. In the second case you might say, "I'll never understand this topic, even though I've spent weeks in the library!" A session at the writing table could surprise you by making evident your unconscious understanding of the subject.

NOTE: It is important that you understand the concept of outlining that appears in sections 5–7. Some outline formats include the introduction and conclusion as main points of the speech. We do not recommend this. Rather, outlining as used here refers to the ordering of the *basic* ideas in the body of the speech. Also, do not confuse the formal speech outline with informal research notes, see **4d**, or speaking notes, see **21e**. While either of these may take an outline form, the *outline* referred to in the following sections is a detailed, logical plan of the speech.

5a. Use the conventional outline format.

By following these rules of outlining, you will be able to visualize the relationships among the ideas of your speech:

(1) Follow a consistent set of symbols.

It is conventional to use roman numerals to label the main ideas of the speech and to alternate from letters to numbers for each successive level of subordination, in this manner:

> I. Main point
>   A. First level of subordination
>   1. Second level of subordination
>   a. Third level of subordination
>   (1) Fourth level of subordination
>   (a) Fifth level of subordination

Do not skip levels. If your speech has only main points and one level of subpoints, use I, II, III and A, B, C. If your outline includes a second level of subordination, you must also use 1, 2, 3. Do not indulge in idiosyncratic systems of labeling levels such as:

> 1—Dogs
>   •Hunters
> a: Spaniels
>   b—Retrievers

Dashes, colons and inversions of the standard progression may make sense to you. It would be to your benefit, however, to get into the habit of using the universally accepted format. Not only is this format simple (though still allowing you to go to the fifth level of subordination), most people find it familiar and easy to understand because of its long, widespread use.

(2) Show the logical relationship of ideas through proper indention.

Each subordinate idea should be indented several spaces to align with the first word—not the labeling numeral or letter—of the point it supports. This makes the relationship among ideas visually obvious.

WRONG

I. Bagpipes are not solely a Scottish
instrument.
  A. Bagpipes originated in Asia
Minor.
  B. There are various forms of
bagpipes in Ireland and Spain, for
example.
    1. Spanish bagpipes are
similar in construction to Scottish
pipes, with the sizes of the parts
different
    2. Uilleann bagpipes in
Ireland differ from Scottish pipes in
that the piper uses bellows under the
arm to keep the bag full rather than
blowing into the bag.

WRONG

I. Bagpipes are not solely a Scottish
instrument.
A. Bagpipes originated in Asia Minor.
B. There are various forms of bagpipes in
Ireland and Spain, for example.
1. Spanish bagpipes are similar in
construction to Scottish pipes, with
the sizes of the parts different.
2. Uilleann bagpipes in Ireland differ
from Scottish pipes in that the piper
uses bellows under the arm to keep the
bag full rather than blowing into the
bag.

RIGHT

I. Bagpipes are not solely a Scottish instrument
  A. Bagpipes originated in Asia Minor.
  B. There are various forms of bagpipes in Ireland and Spain, for example.
    1. Spanish bagpipes are similar in construction to Scottish pipes, with
       the sizes of the parts different.
    2. Uilleann bagpipes in Ireland differ from Scottish pipes in that the
       piper uses bellows under the arm to keep the bag full rather than
       blowing into the bag.

Note how in the last example your eye was directed down the levels of subordination. Your outline should not look like a piece of prose. Your outline exists only to illuminate and clarify the structure of your ideas.

(3) As a general rule, each level of subordination should be developed with two or more parts.

English teachers are fond of saying "never have a *1* without a *2*, or an *A* without a *B*." Generally this is good advice. The concept of dividing an idea into parts — subordination — becomes nonsensical if a major point is "divided" into only one subpoint. Categories are useful because they encompass several related things. Suppose a main point of your speech were outlined as follows:

    I. Redwood City is the best California city in which to live.
      A. It has the best climate.
    II. ....

If Redwood City's climate were your only example, you would be in trouble. A good climate is hardly enough to justify the conclusion you have drawn. You might be guilty of hasty generalization. To avoid this fallacy, outline your speech following the rule of having *at least* two supporting points at each level of subordination. It is far better to develop a few points fully than to cover many points superficially. The rule *no 1 without a 2, no A without a B* is a good one to insure depth of analysis.

(4) Each symbol should designate *one* point only.

Do not combine two or more ideas in any point of your outline. Give each separate idea its own logical heading. By the same token, your outline should not contain any free-floating words or phrases. Every idea should be firmly anchored to a symbol in the hierarchy of points.

WRONG

CAUSES

    A. Both economic and sociological factors contribute significantly to urban decay.
    B. Political factors are of minor importance.

RIGHT

      I. Urban decay has a number of causes.
         A. Economic factors are the major cause.
         B. Sociological factors are also significant.
         C. Political factors are relatively minor.

☐ **Exercise 1.** Outline one of the speeches in the **Appendix**. How many levels of subordination does the speaker use? Are there cases of a 1 without a 2, or an A without a B?

5b. Use a full-sentence outline to insure coherent development of your speech.

The thesis statement (see **1d**), the main points, and at least the first level of subpoints should be stated as declarative sentences. See also **6e**. The declarative sentence is, in effect, a proposition. As such it can be proved or disproved, accepted, or rejected.

    Look at the following sentence:

I. Secondhand smoke harms nonsmokers.

If this sentence were presented to you on a true-false test, you could, with adequate knowledge, answer one way or the other. It is the black or white condition of the declarative sentence that makes it such a useful tool.

    What would you do if you read this item on a true-false test?

I. Nonsmoker's rights

OR THIS:

I. What is the effect of secondhand smoke on nonsmokers?

Obviously an answer of true or false to either of these examples would be impossible. It would be equally absurd if a stranger approached you and asked, "Do you agree with me about the growth of the Welfare State?" Your inevitable retort would be, "Well, what *do* you think about the growth of the Welfare State?"

    Far too many speeches are constructed around just such vague phrases, questions, and uncompleted ideas. The listener knows the speaker's general topic, but cannot always recognize the specific points the speaker is trying to make. Besides rendering the speech more coherent for your audience, the use of declarative sentences in your outline forces you to become conscious of the exact points you want to make and forces you to frame them explicitly.

Once the thesis and main points are stated in propositional form, they will provide a basis against which you can test all other speech content. Section **2** discusses how to identify the issues inherent in your thesis statement. These issues essentially dictate what the main points should be. See **6a**. Each main point can be analyzed in a similar manner to discover what subpoints are logically required to prove or amplify it.

As you begin to research any topic, you will find scores of interesting details and perspectives. How do you decide which ones to include in your speech and which ones to leave out?

The following outlines deal with a topic — The History of Women in the U.S. Labor Force — that could fill, and has filled, many volumes. Observe how the use of a thesis sentence and full-sentence main and secondary points in the first outline provides a basis for the speaker to decide what to include.

FULL-SENTENCE OUTLINE

Thesis: Since the beginning of the Industrial Revolution, women in the United States have been exploited as a cheap and expendable source of labor.

I. In preindustrial colonial settings, the boundaries between men's and women's spheres were indistinct.
   A. Colonial women ran self-sufficient domestic factories.
      1. Women produced the major source of artificial light, candles.
      2. Clothing and bedding were manufactured.
      3. The making of soap was a major contribution.
   B. The rigors of frontier life decreed a more equal division of labor between women and men than found on the rapidly industrializing eastern seaboard.
      1. Men and women shared long hours of joint farm work.
      2. Women were often left alone for long periods to run the farm.
II. Between the Revolution and the Civil War, increased industrialization led to increased exploitation of women workers.
   A. Factories undercut home production.
   B. When the western migration caused shortages of male workers, women became a cheap source of labor for the factories.

      1. The percentage of women in the work force increased.

      2. Women, in 1829, earned one-quarter of what men did.

   C. Women workers' efforts to improve their lot were not successful.

      1. The first women's strike was in 1824, but poor organization made it and others ineffective.

      2. Associations of women workers failed because of the women's isolation and inexperience.

III. In spite of increasing unionization between the Civil War and World War II, women's position in the work force remained inferior.

   A. Women were an unwelcome minority in trade organizations.

      1. Male union leaders did not believe in equal pay for equal work.

      2. Women were barred from union offices, men said, because "no conveniences were available."

   B. Attempts by women before 1900 to organize among themselves met with failure.

      1. Women's unions were not taken seriously.

      2. Women workers were usually too impoverished to strike successfully.

   C. Important gains by women workers in the first decades of the 20th century yielded little net improvement.

      1. Women's situation had improved in some areas.

         a. Unionization of the garment industry was successful.

         b. New job classifications were opened to women during World War I.

      2. Women workers still had neither security nor equality.

         a. Men got their jobs back after the war.

         b. Women received one-half comparable men's pay.

IV. During World War II and after, women were used as a dispensable and secondary source of labor.

   A. Traditional views of femininity were conveniently set aside according to economic needs.

      1. Three million women were recruited to replace our fighting men.

      2. "Rosie the Riveter" became a mythic ideal.

   B. After the war, labor, government, and industry cooperated to push women out of their new jobs.

      1. Although most women wanted to keep working, by 1946 four million were gone from the work force.

      2. When plants began to rehire men, women's seniority was often ignored.

      3. With the unions' tacit approval, many jobs held by women during the war were reclassified as men's jobs.

      4. Many of the laid-off women were denied unemployment insurance.

      5. Articles and pamphlets exhorted women to return to their "primary role."

         a. Women were needed to provide a haven for returning men.

         b. Women were needed to nurture the nuclear family.

Here is a *topic outline* on the same subject.

TOPIC OUTLINE

Topic: Working Women in the United States
I. Preindustrial
  A. Colonial women
    1. Soap
    2. Clothing
  B. Frontier women
    1. Indian attacks
    2. Farm work
II. Increased industrialization to Civil War
  A. Women in factories
    1. Smaller hands suited to weaving
    2. One dollar per week, less lodging
  B. First union attempts
    1. 1824
    2. Lady Shoe Binders, Lynn, Mass.
III. Post-Civil War to pre-World War II
  A. Growth
    1. 225,922 in 1850
    2. 323,370 in 1870
  B. Conflicts
    1. Male union leaders
    2. Strikes
  C. The struggle for suffrage
    1. Elizabeth Cady Stanton
    2. Susan B. Anthony
  D. World War I
    1. New jobs
    2. Department of Labor Women's Bureau
IV. World War II era
  A. Rosie the Riveter
    1. Three million women
    2. Patriotic appeals
  B. Women in the military
    1. WASPS
    2. Army nurses
  C. The feminine mystique
    1. Home as haven
    2. Rise of suburbia

At first glance the topic outline seems to be a coherent, tidy arrangement of points. All the main points appear to relate to the topic and all the subpoints appear to relate to the main points, but can you form a sharp image of what the speaker is saying about working women in the

United States? For example, the first main point of the speech is "Preindustrial." Preindustrial what? The preindustrial *era*, presumably. Yet the term "preindustrial" is so broad that it could include the first humans to appear in America, thousands of years ago. In fact, this point will probably deal with the work women did between the first European colonization and the advent of the Industrial Revolution, but it ought to be phrased to leave no doubt. This is only half the job, though. No matter how refined, a subject still needs a predicate. Although a speaker can delimit a subject with precision, using sufficient modifiers and qualifiers, it will not be clear what she or he means to *say* about that subject. Even if the speaker refines point I of the second outline to describe a specific group of women in a specific era (e.g., "Colonial life for women, 1620–1783"), you cannot pinpoint what idea is being developed: that there were many working women? that their lives were hard? or that they participated in all spheres of work? As these questions are raised and answered, the speaker transforms a loose phrase into a full sentence. If it turns into something like main point I in the first outline, the speaker would probably decide that stories about Indian attacks, however interesting, do not belong in this speech.

☐ **Exercise 2.** Now compare the remaining main points of the two outlines and specify which subpoints are extraneous and which need to be modified.

The use of a full-sentence outline is important in informative and evocative speeches as well as in argumentative and persuasive speeches. In a speech to evoke or to inform, you do not literally *prove* a thesis or its main points, but you do have an obligation to cover topics fully. Using sentences rather than phrases will focus your speech development and will provide you with clearer criteria for deciding what points to include and what ones to leave out. Full-sentence outlines are not extra work, they are a needed tool to demonstrate logical relationships in the speech structure.

NOTE: Lincoln may have made notes on the back of an envelope in preparing the Gettysburg Address, but he had years of experience as a lawyer and legislator in a society much more oral than ours has come to be. Even today, though, you may know speakers who seem to talk fluently without preparing full-sentence outlines. These people are probably speakers with a lot of experience and who have such familiarity with their topic that they understand all the relationships among the aspects of it.

When they jot down a few key words or phrases, they recall entire lines of argument they have discussed many times. Moreover, these speakers are usually very relaxed in front of an audience and can concentrate on developing a complex chain of thought. If *you* meet both of these criteria — either by extensive successful experience or through certification by an expert speech instructor — you might choose to use a keyword outline on the back of an envelope. Otherwise, it is safest to give yourself the confidence that comes with writing out a full-sentence outline.

5c. Supplement your logical outline with marginal notations of the rhetorical devices used.

Every speech has a psychological as well as a logical structure. A formalized content outline helps you to crystallize the relationships between propositions and support. You can also use the outline to chart the relationships between speaker and audience. Sections **11 – 19** explain how to use many rhetorical devices to enhance your speech. Make marginal notations on your outline, showing where you plan to use various rhetorical devices. This will help you see what you are doing so you can improve the audience appeal of your speech. Is all the humor clustered at the beginning and end of an hour-long lecture? Perhaps some humor can be shifted to the middle. Do you support every main point with a fact followed by a hypothetical example? Perhaps you can vary the forms of support.

6

Selecting Points

Partition your speech into a few major components of equal importance and then select appropriate subpoints to develop each component.

6a. **Choose main points which taken together correspond exactly to your thesis statement.** *See also* **1d**, **2a**, **2b**, *and* **5b**.

To decide what main points to include in your speech, first look at the issues implicit in the thesis sentence. Follow the steps discussed in **2b** to identify the essential questions you must answer. Once you know what a complete development of your topic requires, use the thesis sentence as a standard against which to test your main points. Ask yourself:

Is there any part of my thesis not developed in the speech?

Is there any main idea of the speech that is not reflected in the thesis?

Look at the following thesis sentence and the main points selected to develop it.

Thesis statement: The jojoba plant is an effective energy source capable of eliminating U.S. dependence on foreign oil.

I. The jojoba plant is a virtually untapped source of energy.
II. Energy can be produced from the jojoba plant efficiently and safely.
III. Given an adequate educational program, the public would come to accept jojoba plant energy.

Obviously something is missing. Either the thesis sentence should be changed by deleting the last phrase or another main point should be added establishing the ability of jojoba plant energy to eliminate U.S. dependence on foreign oil.

Here is another set of main points developed from the same thesis sentence.

Thesis statement: The jojoba plant is an effective energy source capable of eliminating U.S. dependency on foreign oil.

    I. The jojoba plant is a safe, efficient, marketable source of energy.
    II. The jojoba plant could create sufficient energy to eliminate U.S. dependence on foreign oil.
    III. The jojoba plant can be used as a source of protein.

In this case the final main point has nothing to do with the thesis sentence. This idea might be mentioned in passing as a part of the introduction or conclusion, but should not be a main point unless the thesis sentence were broadened to include the jojoba's value as a food source.

The following set of main points correspond exactly to the thesis sentence; nothing essential is missing, nothing superfluous is included.

Thesis statement: The jojoba plant is an effective energy source capable of eliminating U.S. dependence on foreign oil.

    I. The jojoba plant is a virtually untapped source of energy.
    II. The jojoba plant is a safe, efficient, and marketable source of energy.
    III. The jojoba plant could create sufficient energy to eliminate U.S. dependence on foreign oil.

☐ **Exercise 1.** Do the following sets of main points correspond to the thesis sentence? If not, rewrite the outline and/or thesis sentence so that the correspondence is exact.

Thesis: Cats make better pets than dogs.

    I. Cats are neater than dogs.
    II. Cats are more independent than dogs.
    III. Cats have an interesting life history in mythology and literature.
    IV. Cats are loyal and affectionate.

Thesis: A four-day work week would be beneficial to our company.

    I. Employees will enjoy longer weekends.
    II. Employees will miss rush hour traffic jams.
    III. Employees can share child care more equitably.

Thesis: Homosexuals are discriminated against in every area of their lives.

I. Homosexuals are victims of discrimination in housing.
II. Homosexuals are victims of discrimination in employment.
III. Homosexuals have made valuable cultural contributions throughout history.

6b. Have at least two, but not more than five, main points in the average speech.

Although this rule sounds arbitrary, it is not as restricting as you may think. As a speaker, you should be able to cluster your ideas around a few main themes. If every thought is treated as a main point, there will be no opportunity left to *develop* any of them.

When you begin to prepare a speech, do not limit yourself. Begin to jot down every idea you might possibly cover in your speech. Follow the techniques of brainstorming: go for quantity rather than quality at this point. Do not judge or dismiss any idea. Write it down. Write quickly and do not worry if some ideas are variations on the same theme or wildly divergent. You cannot start the process of organizing until you have some raw material to organize.

Suppose you were going to give a speech on factors affecting the health of a marriage. If you started to jot down ideas, you might end up with a list similar to this:

Factors affecting the health of a marriage.

1. sexual attraction
2. like interests
3. congenial in-laws
4. sleep patterns
5. alpha rhythms
6. zodiac signs
7. earning power
8. politics
9. religious beliefs
10. cultural backgrounds
11. family incomes
12. approve of each other's friends
13. sense of humor
14. wanting offspring
15. proximity to parents' home
16. occupational goals
17. relative maturity
18. energy levels

If you started to structure your speech straight from this list, you would have eighteen main points. But can you really say that zodiacal signs are as important as shared interests, or that alpha rhythms are as important as the relative maturity of the partners? As a speaker, you would never remember eighteen points and, thinking back on the speech, neither would your audience. Maybe, in frustration, you could say: "There's only one factor in a healthy marriage: Love." To build a speech around one main point called "Love" is potentially no more informative: either you are so general that you tell your audience nothing that they do not already know, or, with eighteen random subpoints, you never extract meaning from an unorganized barrage of information.

Look back over the list and consider how you might cluster these factors. Are there any that stand out as possible main points? Are there any that seem obviously to fit together? Are there any that fall naturally under others? Write down your ideas for organizing these factors.

There is no one correct way to group ideas. Your authors, who generated the above list, later grouped the ideas quite differently. One of us came up with

   I. Givens (3, 10, 11, 15)
  II. Emotional and Psychic factors (1, 4, 5, 9, 13, 14, 17, 18)
 III. Rational negotiable issues (2, 7, 8, 12, 16)
     omit (6)

and the other

   I. Similarity of past experience (3, 10, 11, 15)
  II. Compatibility of present interests and future goals (2, 7, 8, 9, 12, 14, 16, 17)
 III. Chemistry of the relationship (1, 4, 5, 6, 13, 18)

Undoubtedly your headings and groupings were different from ours. Almost certainly there were a few items left over which you omitted altogether or which had to be forced a bit to fit into any category. You may note that points that were grouped together were not all of equal importance within their group. Sometimes one or more of the ideas from your brainstorming list serves as a category under which to group lesser points. Sometimes, as the authors did in the example, you will group several minor ideas first and then devise a superordinate heading.

This process is the essence of organizing:

1. generating many ideas
2. grouping them into clusters
3. labelling each cluster
4. reworking, adjusting, culling the ideas until you have two to five major groupings that cover the most important ideas and that can be developed in your allotted time

6c. Select main points that are mutually exclusive.

Main points should be mutually exclusive for maximum clarity. Each category should exclude the ideas that are subsumed by any other category. Put more simply, this rule is a version of the maxim "a place for everything and everything in its place." The challenge for the speaker lies in finding a scheme where each idea fits in just *one* place.

Sometimes when you are grouping ideas under potential main points, as in **6b**, you will find that many will fit into two or more categories. When this overlapping occurs, you know that you have not yet found an effective system for classifying your ideas. Settling on a single organizational pattern is essential. If you do not know where an idea fits, your audience certainly will not. If you were unsure of your pattern, the result might be an outline like this:

Topic: Wines

    I. Red wines
       A. Bordeaux/Médoc
       B. Burgundy/Côte de Beaune
       C. Côtes-du-Rhône
       D. Chianti
   II. White wines
       A. Bordeaux/Graves
       B. Burgundy/Chablis
       C. Loire Valley
       D. German
III.California wines
       A. Claret
       B. Burgundy
       C. Chablis
       D. Zinfandel

It appears that the topic was not completely thought through before the speaker began to lay out the structure of the speech. The speaker has not yet been able to decide whether the kinds of wine shall be divided geographically or divided by color. Since California makes both red and white wines, the three main points are not distinct categories. Ideally, with a system of mutually exclusive main points, you would know how to classify any kind of wine. Yet, with this outline, where would you put Chenin Blanc? It fits legitimately under either white or California. There is no basis to exclude it from either category. Each main point, taken alone, seems a plausible way to classify some wines. But the three points taken together do not constitute a sensible way to look at the topic. It is like trying to add fractions to decimals.

Here is another example of an outline on the same topic:

Topic: Wines

    I. Red wines
      A. European
        1. Bordeaux
        2. Burgundy
        3. Côtes-du-Rhône
        4. Chianti
      B. Californian
        1. Cabernet Sauvignon
        2. Pinot Noir
        3. Petit Sirah
        4. Zinfandel
   II. White wines
      A. European
        1. Bordeaux
        2. Burgundy
        3. Loire
        4. Mosel
      B. Californian
        1. Sauvignon Blanc
        2. Chardonnay
        3. Chenin Blanc
        4. Grey Riesling

In the preceding example the topic is divided into main points along a single dimension: the color of the wine. These main points are each broken down into two geographical regions. At the second level of subordination the speaker classifies European wines by region and California wines by the type of grape, since this is the custom in labeling wines from these areas.

This same topic could be divided many other ways. European wines and California wines might be the main points with Red and White as subpoints under each. The main points might also be styles of wine like:

    I. Burgundy
      A. Red
        1. European
        2. Californian
       B. White
        1. European
        2. Californian
   II. Bordeaux, etc.

or particular grapes like:

    I. Gewürztraminer
       A. Alsatian
       B. Californian
    II. Merlot
       A. French
       B. Californian, etc.

or Dry wines and Sweet wines, Cheap wines and Expensive wines, and so forth.

What is so important is that you choose *one* classification scheme for your main points that gives you a rule by which to include each item under one and only one main point.

NOTE: There will often be a few cases that fall between categories or are difficult to classify. For a general audience it is usually best to narrow your topic to exclude these unusual cases and discuss them in the question and answer period if necessary. Be sure in laying out your categories to use such language as "the most popular wines can generally be classified . . ." or "with a few exceptions . . ."

For a technical topic with a sophisticated audience, you may discuss the borderline cases in your introduction, conclusion, or transitions or by creating a catchall category:

Theories of Language Development.
    I. Chomsky's Linguistic Competence Theory
    II. Skinner's Behavioral Theory
    III. Other theories

> If something goes in two places, your points
> are not mutually exclusive. If it goes nowhere,
> it is a borderline case.

6d. Arrange main points and subpoints to express coordinate and subordinate relationships.

Ideas of equal importance or of parallel logical function are called coordinate points. Points of lesser significance which support, explain, or contribute steps of logical development to other ideas are called subordinate points.

It is no accident that *main* points are so labeled. As explained in **6a** and **6b**, they are those few ideas that are central and indispensable to the development of the thesis. The audience may not remember every word or turn of phrase, but you undoubtedly want your listeners to remember the essence of your message. Far too often a speech is just a blurred series of examples, questions, facts, statistics, arguments, jokes. No ideas stand out from the rest; everything seems to be of equal importance. It is easy to confuse the support and development of a point with the point itself. If we could graph the emphasis or impact of the ideas of this kind of speech there would be little variation between the peaks and troughs of the line:

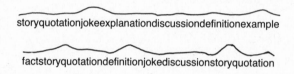

storyquotationjokeexplanationdiscussiondefinitionexample

factstoryquotationdefinitionjokediscussionstoryquotation

Of course the audience cannot retain all of these ideas. Probably they will remember five to nine points. If we could graph their retention it might look like:

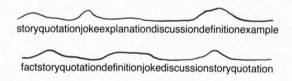

storyquotationjokeexplanationdiscussiondefinitionexample

factstoryquotationdefinitionjokediscussionstoryquotation

When teachers give tests, they often discover that students have remembered the teacher's stories and examples but not their major points. Preachers lament the fact that congregations wake up for their jokes and doze through the rest of the sermon. Ideally, you want the retention of ideas to parallel their significance in the overall speech structure, as in the graph on recall.

By mastering techniques of support **(12)**, attention and interest **(15)**, style **(18)**, and effective delivery **(23)**, you can insure that your audience will remember the points you think are most important.

First, however, the relative importance of these points must be very clear in your own mind. Every point in the speech is subordinate, coordinate, or superordinate to every other.

COMPLETE RECALL

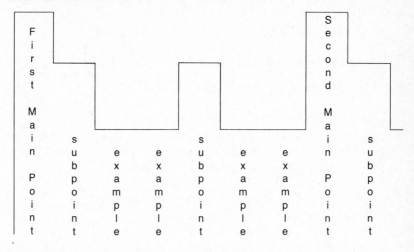

NO RECALL

If you were to classify methods of transporting goods you might come up with:

Transportation of goods
    Trains
    Trucks
    Airplanes
    Ships

In this example, trains, trucks, airplanes, and ships bear a coordinate relationship to each other and a subordinate relationship to the larger, or superordinate, category Transportation of goods. Each mode of transportation in turn may have more-specific divisions. For instance:

Types of trucks
    Tractors
    Vans
    Dumps
    Tankers
    Flatbeds

Here each type of truck bears a subordinate relationship to the heading Types of trucks and a coordinate relationship to each other type.

Logical relationships are similarly shown through subordination and coordination, as in this example:

Trucks are an efficient means of transporting goods.
[because]
They have a wide network of destinations.
[because]
They have a great versatility of design.
[and because]
They are relatively cheap to operate.

It is evident that the reasons are subordinate to the points they establish. *Never arrange a speech so that an assertion and the proof for that assertion appear to be of coordinate or equal importance.*

(1) All main points should be of equal importance in relation to the thesis of the speech.

In the following outline the main points are not coordinate:

Thesis: Catherine Johnson would make an excellent U.S. Senator.

I. She has proven skill as a lawmaker in her state legislature.
II. She has firsthand knowledge of foreign policy issues.
III. She won the confidence of several important constituent groups.
IV. She is a good wife and mother.

Point IV jars as much as if it had been stated that "She is a Libra," or "She is a good driver." Such points may have validity, but they are not important, or even relevant, qualifications for the U.S. Senate. The last point could be omitted (probably best), mentioned in passing in the introduction, or incorporated into a more substantial main point, such as: She has the personal qualities of an effective leader.

> If you have one main idea that seems much less important than the others, (1) omit it, (2) rephrase another main point so this less-important idea can become a subpoint, (3) mention the idea as part of the introduction or conclusion, (4) occasionally consider a catch-all main point, such as: There are several other factors . . .

(2) Each subpoint should directly relate to the point it supports. At each level of subordination, subpoints should be of equal importance.

Do not group unrelated subpoints. Consider the following example from a speech on the role of aircraft carriers in the Second World War.

I. Aircraft carriers were instrumental in winning the war in the Pacific.
   A. The successful use of aircraft carriers at the Battle of Midway blunted the Japanese drive across the Pacific.
   B. The F4F fighter was redesigned to have folding wings so that aircraft carriers could carry more planes.
   C. Planes launched from aircraft carriers were able to inflict damage to enemy bases out of the range of land-based aircraft.

Subpoint B is interesting and probably appropriate as a subpoint somewhere in this speech, perhaps supporting a superordinate point dealing with steps that were taken to make the carrier forces more efficient. Clearly though, subpoint B has no *direct* relationship to the point about the war in the Pacific.

Consider now another set of subpoints in support of that main point.

I. Aircraft carriers were instrumental in winning the war in the Pacific.
   A. The successful use of aircraft carriers at the battles of the Coral Sea and Midway blunted the Japanese drive across the Pacific.
   B. Planes launched from aircraft carriers were able to inflict damage to enemy bases out of the range of land-based aircraft.
   C. Antisubmarine warfare was the major use of aircraft carriers in the Atlantic.

In this case subpoint C is not related to the major idea nor is it subordinate in importance. The use of aircraft carriers in the Atlantic does not fit under their use in the Pacific. The two ideas bear a coordinate relationship and the statement in subpoint C should probably be main point II.

6e. In a formal outline, phrase main points as single declarative sentences. *See also* **1d** and **5b**.

Writing main points as phrases, questions, or groups of sentences does not provide an adequate basis to allow you to test the relevance of your supporting material. Think of main points as miniature thesis sentences, and apply the principles from **1d** and **5b**.

WRONG: I. What are the causes of crime?
RIGHT: I. Crime is cause by a combination of sociological and psychological factors.

WRONG: I. History of the feminist movement in the United States
RIGHT: I. U.S. feminism can be divided into four historical periods.

WRONG: I. Buying a house will have tax advantages. You will also build equity. House ownership is fun and fosters pride.
RIGHT: I. House ownership builds equity, provides tax benefits, and gives pleasure.

OR

I. There are both economic and emotional benefits to owning a house.

6f. Phrase main points and subpoints in clear, effective, and parallel language.

Once you have framed your main ideas so they are logically and grammatically complete according to **6a–e**, take time to recast your points in language that will highlight them for your audience. When you express your main points in parallel language — that is, when you present them in sentences that repeat a certain syntactic structure or repeat a particular grammatical form — you make them more easily identifiable. This augments the techniques of signposting, previews, and reviews covered in Section **8**, all of which you use to make your organization clear to your listeners.

Ideas that are phrased in concise, colorful, parallel language are more likely to be remembered both by speaker and by listeners. *See also* **18**. Look at the following main points from a speech on higher education:

WORDY AND UNPARALLEL

I. The skills you will learn in college will add to the probability of your earning more money, not only in your first job, but throughout your entire lifetime.

II. Through higher education one can also gain a perspective on many aspects of life, to enrich the nonworking hours and provide for a more creative use of leisure time.

III. While they are in college, most students have a variety of social and interpersonal experiences and make new friends through extra-curricular activities and informal exchanges.

These are declarative sentences, as they ought to be, and they do show three separate, important arguments in favor of the thesis that a college education is valuable. The points, though, are too wordy and redundant to stand out clearly from the general flow of the speech.

Here they are made considerably more concise without sacrificing their basic meaning:

MORE CONCISE

I. Your earning power will be increased by a college education.
II. One can prepare for a richer use of leisure time by attending college.
III. In college, students meet new friends and enjoy worthwhile social experiences.

Still, these main points can be made more memorable and effective. The sentences lack parallelism; One is in the passive voice, two are in the active voice; one is in the second person, two are in the third person; one is plural, two are singular. Listeners are not as quick to see the relationships between the points when the perspective and the focus keep changing like this. Whenever possible, strive for grammatical consistency of structure, person, number, and voice:

CONCISE AND PARALLEL

I. A college education will enhance your earning power.
II. A college education will enrich your use of leisure time.
III. A college education will expose you to new people and social experiences.

☐ **Exercise 2.** Rephrase the following main points so that they are concise and parallel.

Thesis: The United Nations is essential to world peace and harmony.

I. The United Nations serves the useful function of providing all countries with a place where they might air their grievances or propose courses of action they consider desirable.
II. It would be better if all countries could articulate their hopes for the future and use the United Nations to direct their energies toward a common goal.

III. With the world "getting smaller," everybody is beginning to realize that we are all one big, human family and that we need the United Nations to help us keep in touch with other "family members."

Thesis: Purchasing a photocopy machine will make your office more efficient.

   I. No longer will you waste time going out to a copying service.
  II. Unit cost of copies is less on your own machine.
III. People report that photocopy machines are easy to operate and maintain.

7

Arranging Points

When you arrange your points, consider the traditional patterns of speech organization, but also be aware of how the sequence of ideas will affect your audience psychologically.

When the main ideas of a speech are selected, it is necessary to arrange them in the order that will maximize effectiveness. In some cases the decision is virtually made for made for you. Debate speeches or closing arguments to juries, for example, have such strict requirements that they almost always unfold according to stock patterns, as shown in **2a**. Many ceremonial or special occasion speeches are so stylized that they follow a formula. See Section **27**. One can expect a commencement speaker to begin by congratulating the graduates and their parents and then move to enunciating a challenge for the future. And it is safe to predict that at a retirement dinner the speaker will begin by summarizing the honoree's achievements and subsequently be speculating humorously about the honoree's coming leisure time. For the usual informative or persuasive speech, though, there is no given pattern. You, as a speaker, must select the best arrangement of ideas.

7a. Arrange main points in a pattern that arises inherently from the subject matter.

There are several traditional patterns of speech arrangement: chronological, spatial, cause-effect, problem-solution, and topical.

(1) The chronological pattern orders ideas in a time sequence.

Historical development is the most common chronological pattern. If you were giving a speech on the course of European music 1600–1900, you might arrange it this way:

    I. The Baroque period (1600–1750)
    II. The Classical period (1720–1810)
    III. The Romantic period (1800–1900)

Also look back to the outline on women workers in **5b**.

Another chronological pattern divides a topic into *past-present-future*. In a speech on automobile propulsion, you might arrange your ideas in this manner:

    I. In the days of cheap oil, auto engines did not need to be energy efficient.
    II. Today, stopgap attachments are being used to upgrade engine efficiency.
    III. We can look forward to new technologies that may even replace the need for fossil-fuel-burning engines.

A third way of looking at a subject chronologically is to analyze a process *step by step*. The topic "How to keep fit through aerobic exercise" could generate this outline:

    I. Determine the resting and working heart rate for your age.
    II. Begin each session with stretching exercises and low-level cardiovascular warm-up.
    III. Through vigorous exercise maintain your working heart rate for thirty to forty minutes.
    IV. Allow at least ten minutes for cool-down and stretching exercises.

(2) The spatial pattern arranges points by location.

The spatial pattern is often based on geography. This can encompass the globe or the two blocks around your house.

    Topic: Crime

    I. Crime on the Eastern seaboard
    II. Crime in the Midwest
    III. Crime on the Pacific Coast

Other geographical arrangements might divide this topic into Crime in Europe, Crime in Asia, Crime in Latin America; or Crime in Manhattan, Crime in Brooklyn, Crime in the Bronx.

Geography need not refer just to areas on a map but can show up as other ways of dividing the world spatially.

Topic: Crime

   I. Rural Crime
  II. Urban Crime
 III. Suburban Crime

The spatial pattern might also be applied to much smaller areas, such as the floor plan of a house or the arrangement of a library. The following example of a spatial pattern describes a very small area indeed:

Topic: An aircraft instrument panel

   I. Instruments needed to maintain controlled flight are on the left side of the panel.
     A. Compass
     B. Altimeter
     C. Artificial horizon
     D. Turn and bank indicator
     E. Air speed indicator
  II. Instruments providing information on the operating condition of the aircraft are on the right side.
     A. Tachometer
     B. Manifold pressure gauge
     C. Oil temperature gauge
     D. Oil pressure gauge
     E. Fuel gauge

(3) In the cause-effect pattern, the speaker moves from a discussion of the origins of a condition to the ways it manifests itself.

This pattern is used to show that events which occur in sequence are in fact causally related. A cause-effect structure is well suited to a speech where the goal is to achieve either understanding or agreement rather than overt action.

   I. There has been a sharp increase in housing costs and interest rates over the last decade.
     [as a result]
  II. It is extremely difficult for a one– income family to purchase a house.

Occasionally the pattern may be reversed to an effect-cause sequence.

    I. It is extremely difficult for a one-income family to purchase a house.
       [this is because]
    II. There has been a sharp increase in housing costs and interest rates over the last decade.

Of course, when using the cause-effect pattern, you must be sure that the causal relationship you propose is a valid one. See **11c**.

(4) The problem-solution pattern examines the symptoms of a problem and then suggests a remedy.

This pattern is used in persuasive speeches that advocate a new policy or a specific course of action.

    I. The current system of financing health care in the United States is inadequate.
       [to remedy this]
    II. A system of national health insurance would provide medical care to all citizens.

On rare occasions a speaker might choose a solution-problem pattern.

    I. A system of national health care insurance would provide adequate medical care to all citizens.
       [this is necessary because]
    II. The current system of financing health care in the United States is inadequate.

The psychological and stylistic weaknesses of this pattern should be evident. Most audiences would resist accepting a program of change before hearing the justification for that change.

(5) The topical pattern of organization divides a speech into elements that have no pattern exclusive of their relationship to the topic itself.

This is the most frequently used speech pattern. It is also the most difficult in that you cannot rely on a predetermined structure, but must understand the range and limitations of the subject itself in order to select an effective pattern. Some topics obviously fit a time or space sequence; many subjects, however, do not lend themselves readily to any of the arrangements discussed so far. In these cases you need to generate an original system for structuring the speech. Since a pattern intrinsic to one subject will not work with another, the application of any topical pattern you select will be unique to that one speech.

Often the best structure for a speech is the listing of the components of a whole or the listing of reasons that add up to the thesis sentence. The final outline on wine in **6c** is an example of the part-to-whole relationship. The following is an example of a topical pattern that lists reasons for a conclusion.

Thesis: Capital punishment should be abolished.

   I. Capital punishment does not deter crime.
  II. Capital punishment is ultimately more costly than life imprisonment.
 III. The risk of executing an innocent person is morally unacceptable.

Sometimes topical patterns may combine aspects of other organizational patterns. For instance, A *cause* leads to an *effect*, which is seen as a *problem* and therefore requires a *solution*.

   I. Children watch a great deal of television.
      [therefore]
  II. Children are not developing skills in reading and creative play.
      [and this is a problem; so to remedy it]
 III. Parents should limit children's viewing time.

Still another topical pattern may be based on a logical argument. The entire speech might be a deductive syllogism. See **11b**.

   I. The United States cannot recognize both the traditional regime and the current military junta in Ruritania. [Major premise]
  II. It is essential to our national interest that we recognize the military junta. [Minor premise]
 III. The United States cannot continue to recognize the traditional regime. [logical conclusion]

A speech might also follow an inductive format. See **11a**.

   I. The city council keeps cutting police and fire department budgets.
      [and]
  II. There are potholes in the streets.
      [and]

   III. Municipal buses are out of service continuously.
      [and]
   IV. City parks are poorly maintained.
      [therefore]
   [Logical conclusion] Our local government is not providing adequate services to the citizens.

NOTE: Sometimes two or more organizational patterns will seem to fit your topic equally well. In that case try to understand your audience's frame of reference to determine which sequence will be clearest and most persuasive to them. Suppose, for instance, you were giving an informative speech on a vegetable processing plant. You could arrange the speech chronologically from when the produce arrives to when the cartons of packaged food are shipped away. Or you could arrange the speech spatially, leading the audience through the front offices and around the floor of the plant. For an audience familiar with food processing, either sequence might be fine. For an uninformed audience, though, the spatial arrangement, which might start out in the quality control section, could be confusing. The chronological pattern, starting with the vegetables arriving from the fields, would be preferable.

☐ **Exercise 1.** By generating separate sets of main points, show how each of these topics could be presented in three different organizational patterns.

Smoking and Lung Cancer
Backgammon
Racial Discrimination in the United States
Airline Hijacking
Oriental Cooking

7b. Group subpoints according to a pattern, but do not feel compelled to echo the pattern of the main points.

After your main ideas are set, look at the subpoints under each. These too need to be arranged in some effective order — topical, chronological, whatever. You do not have to repeat the pattern used for the main points; you can choose the format that makes the most sense for each set of subpoints. Notice the different arrangements in the detailed outline that follows:

   Thesis: With their scope, history, and influence, comic books are an interesting component of American popular culture.

I. Comic books are not merely "comic," but explore a range of subject matter.

TOPICAL

   A. Funny Animal comics and Kid comics are parables and parodies of the human condition.
     1. Elmer Fudd and Bugs: Tradition vs. the pioneering spirit.
     2. Barks' ducks: Epic adventure and human foibles.
     3. Harvey's rich kids: Capitalism with a human face.

   B. True Love and Teen comics present a hackneyed, boring, and sometimes disturbing picture of male/female relationships.
     1. True Love girl meets, loses, gets, marries boy (and vows never to be so stupid as to put her needs above his again).
     2. Teen comic girl fights other girls for the favors of a jerk male like Archie, who her father thinks is a twerp.
     3. True Love and Teen comics foster the Us vs. Them view of the male/female world.

   C. Western and Adventure comics concentrate on the triumph of good over evil.
     1. Western cattle barons learn that six-gun-slinging saviors arise naturally from oppressed common folk.
     2. Adventure stories pit virtuous types against the blind malice of uncaring nature.

   D. Horror and Mystery comics investigate ethics and morality while titillating and scaring readers.
     1. Eternal punishment for an unethical choice is a recurring theme of Horror comics.
     2. The tempting hedonism of wrongdoers is graphically displayed in Mystery comics—until the ironic twist of fate on the last page.

   E. Superhero comics manifest the unspoken and sometimes frightening fantasies and aspirations of the American people.
     1. Superman is the supremely powerful spokesman and policeman for the American definition of the "right way."
     2. The jackbooted hero, Blackhawk, was created in World War II to fight totalitarianism fire with fire.
     3. Mar-Vell personifies the desire for total knowledge and the wisdom needed to use it.
     4. Spider-Man is the embodiment of the perennial underdog triumphant.

II. Comic books started as anthologies of another medium but soon grew into a separate art form developing along a path of its own.

CHRONOLOGICAL

   A. Early comic books were mostly reprints of Sunday newspaper comic strip sections.
     1. "Foxy Granpa" was reprinted in a number of comic books just after the turn of the century.
     2. The following decades saw strips like "Mutt & Jeff," "Little Orphan Annie," and "Moon Mullins" reprinted.
     3. Reprint books in the thirties included such titles as "Tarzan" in *Tip Top Comics* and "Terry and the Pirates" in *Popular Comics*.

   B. By 1938 the majority of comic books contained original work and, with the appearance of Superman, the Golden Age of comics began.

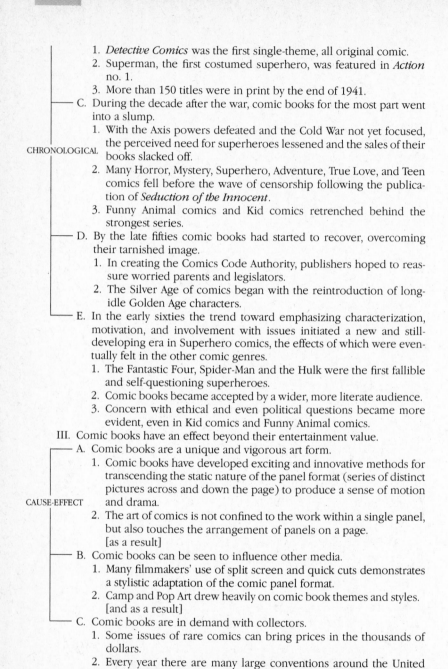

CHRONOLOGICAL

1. *Detective Comics* was the first single-theme, all original comic.
2. Superman, the first costumed superhero, was featured in *Action* no. 1.
3. More than 150 titles were in print by the end of 1941.

C. During the decade after the war, comic books for the most part went into a slump.
  1. With the Axis powers defeated and the Cold War not yet focused, the perceived need for superheroes lessened and the sales of their books slacked off.
  2. Many Horror, Mystery, Superhero, Adventure, True Love, and Teen comics fell before the wave of censorship following the publication of *Seduction of the Innocent*.
  3. Funny Animal comics and Kid comics retrenched behind the strongest series.

D. By the late fifties comic books had started to recover, overcoming their tarnished image.
  1. In creating the Comics Code Authority, publishers hoped to reassure worried parents and legislators.
  2. The Silver Age of comics began with the reintroduction of long-idle Golden Age characters.

E. In the early sixties the trend toward emphasizing characterization, motivation, and involvement with issues initiated a new and still-developing era in Superhero comics, the effects of which were eventually felt in the other comic genres.
  1. The Fantastic Four, Spider-Man and the Hulk were the first fallible and self-questioning superheroes.
  2. Comic books became accepted by a wider, more literate audience.
  3. Concern with ethical and even political questions became more evident, even in Kid comics and Funny Animal comics.

III. Comic books have an effect beyond their entertainment value.

CAUSE-EFFECT

A. Comic books are a unique and vigorous art form.
  1. Comic books have developed exciting and innovative methods for transcending the static nature of the panel format (series of distinct pictures across and down the page) to produce a sense of motion and drama.
  2. The art of comics is not confined to the work within a single panel, but also touches the arrangement of panels on a page. [as a result]

B. Comic books can be seen to influence other media.
  1. Many filmmakers' use of split screen and quick cuts demonstrates a stylistic adaptation of the comic panel format.
  2. Camp and Pop Art drew heavily on comic book themes and styles. [and as a result]

C. Comic books are in demand with collectors.
  1. Some issues of rare comics can bring prices in the thousands of dollars.
  2. Every year there are many large conventions around the United States where comics can be bought, sold, and traded.

8

Transitions

Transitions should link points to provide unity and express relationships among ideas.

Transitional sentences, phrases, and words serve as bridges between points. They also signal to the listener how two ideas are related. The connective words can completely change the impact of a message. Observe the not-so-subtle differences in these three sentences:

He plays the piano, *and* I invited him to my party.

He plays the piano, *so* I invited him to my party.

He plays the piano, *but* I invited him to my party.

Clear and evocative transitions are more important in speaking than in writing, because the spoken message is ephemeral (see **18a**). In this book, for example, we show you the relationships among ideas by indenting, capitalizing, and using different punctuation and typefaces. But, as a speaker, you do not have access to these devices. You need to use verbal signposting techniques to show how your points relate. Keep your listeners informed about the overall structure of your speech by the generous use of phrases like

My next major point is . . .
The third cause of inflation is . . .
To show you what I mean, let me tell you three stories.
In summarizing this entire argument . . .
The final point we should consider is . . .
What, then, is the solution to this three-part problem I have outlined?

Do not worry about using too many signposts. Your audience will appreciate them.

8a. Select transitions that reflect the logical relationships among ideas.

The transitions you choose should illuminate the basic organizational structure of the speech. Without even seeing their content you can tell what pattern these speeches follow:

Thesis: . . . .

    I say that for three reasons. First,
  I. . . . .
    This situation is also due to
  II. . . . .
    Last of all, we can attribute the problem to
  III. . . . .

OR

Thesis: . . . .

    Initially,
  I. . . . .
    Next,
  II. . . . .
    Finally,
  III. . . . .

The transitions alone tell you that you are hearing an effect-to-cause speech in the first case and a chronologically arranged speech in the second.

Points can be related in a number of ways. Crystallizing those relationships and expressing them through appropriate transitional phrases will enhance your clarity. Try to use a variety of transitions, do not get in a habit of linking all your ideas with "OK, now let's look at . . ." or "First of all," "Second of all," "Third of all," and "Last of all." The following list provides examples of the many transitional words that can be used to tie main points to one another, main points to subpoints, subpoints to one another, supporting evidence to arguments, or introductions and conclusions to the body of the speech. Transitions are needed in all these places.

Relationship	Transitional words
Chronological	First, second, third, Next, then After . . . Following . . .
Cause-effect	So, since, thus, Therefore, hence, Consequently, as a result, Due to . . . Because . . .
Part-to-whole	One such . . . Another . . . The first (second or third) of these . . . For instance, for example, Illustrative of this, A case in point: Let me give you an example . . .
Equality	Similarly, additionally, Another . . . Of equal importance . . . Also, Moreover,
Opposition	But, though, however, On the other hand, Conversely, on the contrary, Yet . . . In spite of . . . Nonetheless, nevertheless,

8b. Make use of internal previews and summaries.

The importance of previews in speech introductions and of summaries in conclusions is emphasized elsewhere (see **9** and **10**). Sometimes transitions between main points should take the form of internal summaries or internal previews that pull together two or three main points.

INTERNAL PREVIEW

Once your résumé is prepared, the next step in job seeking is to prepare a list of specific job openings. The three best sources here are newspaper listings, your campus placement service, and word-of-mouth recommendations. We will examine the pros and cons of each of these.

INTERNAL SUMMARY

Since the problems in our department were affecting morale and since we had found they were caused by poor communication, we instituted an unusual training program. Let me tell you about it.

INTERNAL SUMMARY AND PREVIEW

I've told you why we need to reduce our dependence on the automobile, and I hope I've convinced you that a light rail system is the best alternative for our city. Now, you're probably asking two questions: "What will it cost?" and "How will it work?" I want to answer both these questions. First, the question of cost.

CAVEAT: Do not forecast the end of your speech prematurely by bluntly saying "In summary," anywhere but in the conclusion. See **10d**. Carefully qualify your internal summaries by using phrases like, "So, to summarize this first idea," or "Let me review the points so far."

☐ **Exercise 1.** Write transitions to connect the main points of the women workers outline in **5b**, and of the comic book outline in **7b**.

Identify the transitional sentences, phrases, and words in one or more of the speeches in the **Appendix**.

9

Introductions

Use an introduction to establish a relationship with your audience and to orient them to your topic.

After you have outlined the body of the speech according to the organizational techniques described in the previous sections, compose an introduction that will prepare your listeners to deal with you and your topic. Both the speaker and the audience need a period of adjustment before getting to the meat of the speech.

It is important to realize that your speech really starts before you utter the first word and that *that* first word is crucial to the success of the speech. The moment the attention shifts to you — whether you are sitting at the head table or in the first row of seats or standing to the side of the boardroom — you need to begin to develop a rapport and prepare your audience to listen to you. For the most part they want to like you and want to listen, and there is some tension as a result. Because you know how important these initial moments are, you will have planned your first few sentences very carefully. Your listeners will relax when they see you know what you are doing, that you are obviously in control.

Engage the audience.

Perhaps you have witnessed speakers who start talking halfway up from their seats, continue talking while walking to the podium, and *then* notice the audience. When *you* become the center of attention, stand up and, if necessary, move confidently to the position from which you will speak; then pause to *engage the audience*. Look at them and acknowledge nonverbally the fact that you and they are together.

The main thing you want to do in these first few moments is to survive them. You know from experience as an audience member how long it takes to get used to a speaker's appearance, style of talking, and mannerisms. If you are feeling self-conscious during this part of the speech, it is probably appropriate: chances are the audience is paying more attention to you personally than to your ideas. Your task is to shift their attention from you to the topic.

This section identifies and explains the important features of an introduction that will propel you through the uncomfortable moments and into the body of your speech.

9a. Frame your opening sentences carefully to engage your audience's attention.

Even experienced speakers who do not worry beforehand about the exact wording of the body of their speech tend to plan and prepare their introduction carefully. Because you will be occupied with all the things that are going on at the beginning of your speech, do not risk leaving your opening sentences to the inspiration of the moment. You need strong and basic material that will carry the speech forward.

Start with a sentence that leaves no doubt that you are beginning. Avoid false starts, apologetic or tentative phrases: "Is the mike on?" "Well, here goes nothing," or "Let's see, where shall I start?" Tone is almost as important as content here. Your immediate purpose is to command the attention of your audience. Several methods of gaining attention are discussed in **15a**. Techniques such as suspense, novelty, humor, and conflict are effective and you will probably use them throughout your speech; they are almost mandatory in your introduction.

You may begin the attention-getting phase of your introduction by telling a joke, relating a story, citing an apt quotation, making a startling statement, or asking a provocative question. Be imaginative; it is even all right to be a little dramatic; but do not go too far. An attention getter should emerge logically from your topic and have at least a reasonable connection. Avoid a contrived and gimmicky opening such as flicking off the room lights and asking, "Are you in the dark about?..." Your attention getter should be consistent with your personality and the situation. What is perfectly normal for someone else may seem unnatural from you. Adopting an unnatural style is doubly troublesome: not only are you uncomfortable, but your audience will sense that you are not yourself.

With this in mind, consider the following possible attention getters for the comic book speech in **7b**.

A humorous or light way of introducing the topic may suit you best:

> Did you ever want to leap a tall building in a single bound? I
> did. Did you ever want to be more powerful than a locomo-
> tive? I did. Did you ever want to be faster than a speeding
> bullet? I did. As you can tell, I was warped early by the
> influence of comic books . . .

Or perhaps you are more comfortable with a dramatic attention
getter:

> On a May afternoon in Washington, Frank Salacuse and John
> Snyder wrapped up their negotiations and shook hands. Both
> were happy with the result. Snyder walked away with $17,500,
> and Salacuse's syndicate now had a mint copy of *Marvel
> Comics* No. 1, a comic book with the 1939 price of 10¢ on its
> cover.

A straightforward conversational aproach to the topic can still get
attention:

> In the ten years I've been collecting comic books, I've learned
> that they are more than escape or entertainment. As I read the
> 13,000 comics in my collection, their contribution to popular
> culture has become clearer and clearer.

As this third example illustrates, attention getters need not be unduly
catchy or clever. However, it is essential that you begin your speech with
a few well-planned sentences that say, in effect: I know where I'm going
and I want you to come with me — it will be worth your while.

☐ **Exercise 1.**   Do all four speeches in the **Appendix** have clear attention-
getting steps? What devices are used?

☐ **Exercise 2.**   Write an engaging attention getter for the speech on women
in the labor force in **5b**.

9b. Provide a psychological orientation.

Attention, once gained, must be transformed into interest. Before you can
ask your audience to concentrate on the substance of your message, you
need to orient them psychologically. This orientation has two parts:
establishing a good relationship with your listeners and interesting them
in what you have to say.

(1) Establish a relationship with your audience.

When deciding how to build a positive relationship with your audience, you should ask two questions:

What relationship do I have with these people now?

AND

What relationship do I need to have in order to accomplish my speech purpose?

In effect, you are conducting one of the phases of audience analysis described in **3d**. The answers to these questions will help you decide what combination of the following techniques can be used in your introduction to build rapport with your listeners.

Establish credibility.

The judgments the members of the audience make about you as a person influence the judgments they make about your topic. Section **17** on credibility says that to be respected and believable a speaker should be perceived as having good sense, good will, and good character. The chairperson's glowing introduction may leave no doubt about your expertise on law enforcement, but to meet your goal of persuading these students to consider careers as police officers you need to establish your good will. On the other hand, you may be speaking to a group of friends who like and trust you but wonder: what does good old Joe know about nuclear energy? In this case, you would use the introduction to bolster your credibility in the area of good sense.

Establish common ground.

Emphasize similar background, experience, interests, goals to show what you and your audience share. Observe how John H. Hanley, president of the St. Louis-based Monsanto Company, builds common ground with members of the Houston Club:

> Seeing many people here today with whom Monsanto has a business and professional relationship reinforces my belief that we in St. Louis and you in Houston have a great deal in common.
>   Cynics might say, "Yes, both places are hotter than soup in the summer." They might add that our two baseball teams are not so hot.

But I shrug off those disrespectful comments and point to our mutual good sense in promoting an aggressive, diversified business community in our respective home towns.

I applaud our mutual good taste in covering two of the world's greatest sports emporia — the Astrodome and Busch Stadium — with Monsanto's Astroturf.[1]

Refer to the setting or occasion.

This is one way to show your listeners that you are not giving a canned speech.

Lyndon Johnson used this technique at a ceremony celebrating the seventy-fifth anniversary of Scott and White Hospital, where he had often been a patient.

> Whenever I am in the presence of so many doctors and nurses and technicians, I am somewhat more accustomed to being spoken to than in having much chance to speak myself. As a matter of fact, when that fine introduction was completed and I heard my name called, force of habit almost caused me to lean back in my chair, stick out my tongue and say, Aah."
>
> Needless to say, I am very grateful to your fellow practitioners who attend me, from time to time, for making it possible for me to keep this engagement today. It is an occasion I did not want to miss.[2]

Flatter your audience.

Everyone likes to be complimented, as long as it is personalized and not too heavy-handed. An audience that perceives that you like and admire them is more likely to reciprocate.

In a speech presented at a workshop for teachers, one of the authors used this approach:

> Those of you who gave up your Saturday morning to be here are not a typical group of teachers. Study after study reveals that the teachers who show up voluntarily to in-service workshops on teaching skills are the very best teachers. Just look around you. The ones who most need this workshop aren't here today, are they? But a brush-up is always helpful. "A" teachers want to learn to be "A+" teachers. And maybe together we can find some ways to reach those "C−" teachers who didn't come.

[1]*Vital Speeches of the Day* 45, no. 2 (Nov. 1, 1978): 55.
[2]*Representative American Speeches* 45, no. 4 (1972–73): 140.

Refer to the person who introduced you or some other person present.

One good way to build a relationship with a group is to demonstrate that you relate successfully to one of its popular members.

> Thank you, Jack, for that very flattering introduction. You know, it's said of some speakers "this person needs no introduction." I'm not one of those. I need all the introduction I can get. Recognizing that, Jack was kind enough not to mention that he's had to bail me out, both figuratively and literally, many times in the fifteen years we've known each other.

Use humor.

A similar sense of humor is a good basis for a relationship, both interpersonally and on a larger scale. Show your audience that you and they laugh at the same things. However, this is a particularly perilous technique. See **16c** for cautions about its use.

In a business communications course, Ellen Watrous started her speech on historical cost accounting versus replacement cost accounting in this fashion:

> A French balloonist once floated across the English Channel and landed in a field of wheat. He spotted an Englishman and said, "Excuse me, sir. Can you tell me where I am?" The Englishman replied, "Certainly. You are in a basket in a field of wheat." "You must be an accountant," said the balloonist. "Amazing," said the Englishman. "How did you know?" "Easy," replied the balloonist. "Your information is typical: totally accurate but absolutely useless."

Speakers can seem remote and aloof, cut off from the audience by role and status. Use your introduction to create a personal bond with your listeners. You can do this with references to folksy, everyday, common occurrences. If your audience can visualize you going to the dentist, walking the dog, losing your car keys, or fixing the plumbing, they will be conscious of you as a human being, not just a dispenser of information.

CAVEAT: Some speakers are so intent on seeming human that they become gratingly humble. They lose credibility altogether by such bumbling comments as: "I'm a little nervous being up here," "Now, where are my notes?" or "I'm not really the one who is qualified to be telling you this."

In addition to establishing a relationship that is warm and friendly, you want the introduction to set a tone of collaboration with your audience. There are some extremely passive and dependent people who, rather than collaborating, prefer to give themselves over to the power of a charismatic speaker. (If you have this sort of audience, there are ethical concerns implicit in perpetuating such a speaker-listener relationship. Do you choose to be a Hitler or Jim Jones!) For the most part, though, people learn better when they are active than when they are passive, and they have more of a commitment to a decision in which they have participated. You can therefore appreciate that a collaborative tone will aid you in achieving your speech goals. Here are some ways to create a sense of dialogue even in a speech that is primarily a monologue:

- Acknowledge your audience's expertise. "As managers, you could give me a dozen examples of what I've just said."
- Admit your own fallibility. "One issue I'm still struggling with is . . ."
- Ask for their help. "I hope that during the discussion period later you'll share some of the solutions you've found to these problems."

In general, the idea you are trying to project is: "Although I'm doing the talking now, I'm here to learn from you as well as instruct you. I hope to influence your thinking, but I'm willing to have you influence mine."

(2) Motivate your audience toward your topic.

This motivational step is one of those most often overlooked in speechmaking, but it is *the* pivotal step of the introduction. Your speech, in spite of the enthusiasm you hold for the topic, can be derailed by your audience's what's-it-to-me? attitude. This attitude is not limited to the hostile audience; it is characteristic of nearly all audiences. You need to reassure your listeners that there are good reasons for them to be warming seats, that your topic — whether it be of an informative, persuasive, or evocative nature — has a link with their own experiences and is thereby worthy of their attention. The speech on accounting, cited above, was presented to a class of undergraduate students in various fields of business. The speaker went on to say:

> Everyone here destined to work for business enterprises is in the same basket with the lost balloonist. In fact, many of you will become the balloonist himself. He's the person who makes investment and credit decisions through which busi-

105

ness enterprises obtain financing, accumulating capital for production and marketing of goods and services. And he depends on information provided by financial statements to make those investment and credit decisions which will inevitably affect your working lives. Yet financial accounting suffers from the same malady that the Englishman in our story suffers. That is, accounting fails to provide relevant information about the effects of inflation and price changes on the financial statements of business enterprises.

Sometimes a two-step link is necessary—not every speech topic can be sold to your audience on the grounds that it will make them rich, save them time, help them succeed, or make them popular. When you cannot make a direct link to a basic need, motivating your audience depends on a step-by-step exposure of connections that lead from your topic to some core value. At the outset of your speech, your listeners may not be immediately stimulated by your topic of African Firewalking. They may not care about foreign cultures as such, but you can make a two-step link. Step one: Explain firewalking so that your audience understands its place in African culture. Step two: Show the audience that the world is changing and that they will need to understand diverse cultures (like African culture) so that they can learn how to deal productively with people coming from backgrounds that vary from the audience's own.

Understanding the information in **14** (Motivational Appeals) and **15** (Attention and Interest) will be especially useful.

☐ **Exercise 3.** Analyze how psychological orientation is provided in each speech in the **Appendix**. What steps, if any, do the speakers take to establish a relationship? To motivate the audience?

☐ **Exercise 4.** Suppose you were speaking to the following audiences on the topics indicated. How would you go about building a positive relationship? How would you motivate them to listen further?

a. A Jewish women's group about the importance of wearing seat belts
b. A group of fire fighters about public speaking
c. A college speech course about kinds of running shoes

9c. Provide a logical orientation.

Now that your audience is motivated to listen, you must be sure they are prepared to listen. In the logical orientation you show your listeners how you will approach and develop your topic—in effect, giving them an intellectual road map.

"Logical" is used here, in its broadest sense, in contrast to "psychological" as used in **9b**. The emphasis has shifted from an orientation generated by consideration of the audience, to one that grows from your subject. The essence of logic is part/whole relationships. In this phase of your introduction you show the larger whole into which your speech fits and how you have partitioned your topic.

(1) Establish a context for your speech.

Give your audience a perspective on your topic by using one or more of the following:

Fit your topic into a familiar framework.

> San Jose is located fifty miles south of Oakland and fifty-four miles southeast of San Francisco, about thirty miles inland from the Pacific Ocean.

Here we are relating the unknown in terms of the known, in a geographical sense. You can also relate your topic to some schema, chart, organizational structure, or process with which your audience is already familiar. In this case, if your listeners know where the Pacific Ocean and San Francisco are, they can start to think about San Jose.

In the next example the speaker places the object of discussion in its relationship to a known organic structure:

> As you know, the federal government is divided into three branches: the Legislative, the Judicial, and the Executive. When we think of the Legislative branch we think of the Congress. However, there are several other parts of this branch. Today I want to describe to you the workings of the Speech Writing Division of the Legislative Reference Service, part of the Library of Congress.

The speaker can also connect an unfamiliar topic to the familiar by using analogy:

> When the traffic lights break down on a busy corner, you see a traffic cop standing in the middle of the intersection, blowing a whistle and telling impatient motorists where to go. In effect, that is what I do as Crisis Manager at the Metacom Corporation.

Place your topic historically.

Another way to provide perspective on your topic is to describe its historical context. It helps listeners to know the background and what events led up to the situation as it stands at the time of your speech. The Reverend James G. Harris, of the University Baptist Church of Fort Worth, introduces his sermon against the prayer amendment in just such a manner.

> On November 8, [1971] just one week from tomorrow, House Joint Resolution 191 will be introduced on the floor of Congress. It shall be subject to a vote without passing through the Judiciary Committee, where hearings could have cleared the air and where opponents to this bill would have had a chance to be heard in reasons for their vigorous opposition.
>
> In 1964, three months were spent in hearings when a so-called prayer amendment, the Becker Amendment, was proposed. As a result of these hearings, the overwhelming evidence presented to the Committee was so convincing that the effort was abandoned. At that time, to avoid such a hearing, the so-called prayer lobbyists sought to get the necessary 218 signatures of congressmen that would have made it possible to bypass the Judiciary Committee and eliminate the hearings that are so necessary for a thorough study of a bill. Only 170 signatures could be obtained in 1964.
>
> The champions of freedom won a great victory and we relaxed. But the other side did not relax. For seven years they have lobbied and worked. After these intervening years, a discharge petition was signed a few days ago by the required 218 congressmen, and within a matter of days this bill will be presented on the floor of the House. We who are concerned and alarmed have little time to turn the tide around. I bring this message to inform you of what I believe is a grave peril to our liberty and to share with you my own convictions.[3]

You might also want to place your topic is a broader historical context. For example, in the introduction of a speech dealing with some aspect of the French Revolution, mention can be made of what was happening in America, the rest of Europe, or the Far East at that time in history, thereby providing the listeners with the larger picture.

CAVEAT: We are talking here about a brief historical recapitulation. In many speeches a fairly extended narration of past events is important,

---

[3]*Representative American Speeches* 44, no. 4 (1971–72): 145.

and in such a case "History" should be a main point of the speech. Look at your thesis sentence and see what it dictates. It might state: "Past injustices require us to provide compensatory educational experiences for minorities." That would demand a main point dealing with the history of the particular minorities.

Place your topic conceptually.

Just as you can place your topic in time or space, so can you locate it in the world of ideas. By showing your listeners how your speech fits in with certain familiar theories, concepts, and definitions, you help them prepare to listen. For example:

> You're familiar with the law of supply and demand as it relates to goods and services. Let me review this basic market mechanism with you, because I want to ask you to apply these same essential principles to our system of information exchange.

And:

> Since the publication of Eric Berne's *Games People Play*, psychologists have applied the ego states—"parent," "child," "adult"—to their analysis of a variety of human relationships. I'd like you to consider how that paradigm serves to explain many of the communication problems that arise between supervisors and the employees they supervise.

Provide new definitions and concepts.

If you are going to use unfamiliar terms and concepts in your speech, or familiar terms in unfamiliar ways, prepare your audience. Related to this, if you feel the need to use a term or phrase that has been co-opted as a slogan or rallying cry by some group, with all the attendant distortion of meaning, you had better be sure to define early and exactly how you plan to use it.

> *Firmware* describes a semipermanent programming feature that has some characteristics of hardware, some of software. It is best described as software that is not modifiable by the user.

Define a familiar term used in an unfamiliar way:

> Often when people speak of a system of restitution for criminals, they refer to a program where prisoners contribute

> wages to a collective pool of some sort. The restitution system
> I will be talking about involves direct compensation for indi-
> vidual criminals to their victims.

Former Secretary of Defense Harold Brown takes care to define a
potential "buzzword" in this speech:

> What we mean by the term "National security" needs to be
> defined periodically by those of us who use it often. Let me
> offer a working definition for the purposes of this talk. Most of
> us — having given up missionary zeal — would consider the
> United States reasonably secure if we were able to go about
> our business without major external infringement on our
> internal affairs, and without damage to our society as a whole
> from the outside.[4]

(2) Orient the audience to your approach to the topic.

The second step in a logical orientation — once you have shown how
your speech fits into some larger context — is to preview the structure of
your speech. If your listeners have been given a framework on which to
attach your points as your speech unfolds, their comprehension of your
topic and thesis is made that much easier.

Reassuring your audience of what you are going to cover will reduce
anxiety and internal counterarguing. Suppose you declare, "I will discuss
the background of the problem, and discuss my solutions to it, and then I
will answer those objections most often raised against my position."
Hearing this, your audience will be more patient, not raising those
arguments in their minds to block out your position before you have
stated it.

In most introductions you will explicitly state one or more of the
following: your topic, thesis, title, or purpose. For example: "I would like
to persuade you to change your vote on this bond issue." The circumstances that would make this strategically *not* the thing to do are
discussed in Section **19** on persuasive strategies. At times you also want
to tell what you are *not* talking about — essentially explaining to your
audience how you have narrowed your topic.

Observe how, in paragraphs 3 through 6 of her speech in the

---

[4]"Our National Security Position: Training, Material Readiness and Mobility," *Vital Speeches of the
Day* 45, no. 1 (Oct. 5, 1978): 27.

Appendix, Mary Cunningham spells out in detail what the speech will not cover.

Another choice you have is whether to give an exact preview of the points you are going to cover or just a much more general sketch of your topic. Explicit previews are useful in the majority of speeches and absolutely essential for speeches with fairly technical or complex topics. The speaker gives his or her listeners a reassuring road map to carry through the speech, one that they can refer to if they start to get lost. When should you not use an explicit preview? If your speech is built around a dramatic, climactic sequence, you should not ruin the effect by giving it away in a preview. Rather, summarize your ideas in the conclusion. In a case where each point builds on the audience's understanding of the previous points, a detailed preview might do more harm than good. Very short, simple speeches rarely need previewing.

□ **Exercise 5.** What methods are used by the speakers in the **Appendix** to provide logical orientation? Would any of these speeches be more effective if they did or did not include a specific preview?

□ **Exercise 6.** Write a logical orientation for either the comic book outline in **7b** or the outline on women in the labor force in **5b**. Include a specific preview of the main points. Rewrite it, substituting a more general preview that paraphrases and capsulizes the main points. Under what circumstances would each form be most effective?

9d. Make your introduction as compact as possible by combining or omitting steps when appropriate.

Generally, plan an introduction that is between 10 and 15 percent of your speaking time. If your introduction included all the steps in **9a**, **b**, and **c** as discrete units, it would be longer than the speech itself. Do not progress mechanically through these steps; your introduction will be choppy, disjointed, and overlong. Organize the introduction in a natural narrative style, keeping in mind the *functions* of getting attention and providing psychological and logical orientation. Whenever possible, select material that fulfills several of the functions of an introduction.

In addition to combining parts of the introduction, it is often appropriate to omit steps altogether. A presidential speech can begin, "My fellow Americans, tonight I want to talk about the serious problem of inflation." Attention, credibility, and motivation to listen are assumed.

When attention is already riveted on you — as when you are about to announce the long-awaited results of a competition — a lengthy opening story is out of place, maybe even hazardous to your health. Likewise:

- If you are a minister speaking to your own congregation, or a candidate addressing a rally of your campaign workers, you certainly do not need to waste time building a relationship.
- With a group of angry property owners gathered to protest a tax increase, it serves no real purpose to tell them how important the topic is.
- A study group that meets regularly to hear lectures on a certain topic needs very little logical orientation. You can jump quite directly into the substance of your speech.

Examine your audience, the occasion and your speech purpose to see what aspects of an introduction can be combined, handled with a passing sentence or indirect reference, or omitted altogether. Just be sure that, by the time you begin your first main point, you can answer all these questions in the affirmative:

Are they listening?
Do they want to keep listening to me?
Do they want to know more about this topic?
Do they understand where I'm coming from?
Do they understand where I'm going?

☐ **Exercise 7.** Examine each of the speeches in the **Appendix**. Are all of the steps of an introduction present in each? What steps are omitted? Do you think the omissions are justified? What functions are combined?

9e. Avoid these introduction pitfalls:

Don't begin with, "Before I start I'd like to say . . ." You have already started. See opening paragraphs of **9**.

Don't ever begin with an apology like: "I'm not really prepared" or "I don't know much about this, but . . ." See **9a**.

Don't be dramatic to the point of assuming a whole new identity or persona. Leave that to the cabaret impersonators and give *your* speech as *yourself*. See **9a** and **18c**.

Don't use an attention getter that has no real link to your topic. Avoid the temptation to stretch a point so you can start with an unrelated joke you think is hilarious. Similarly, firing a starter's pistol in the air at the beginning of a speech on "How To Get a Running Start on your Competition" would do more to distract than attract your audience. See **9a**.

Don't make your introduction seem disproportionately long. See **9d**.

Don't use stock phrases like "Unaccustomed as I am to public speaking" or overworked apocryphal stories. Ask a friend to give a brutal critique of your trove of expressions and stories. See **18d**.

Don't name-drop in building your credibility. You do not want your audience to think that you are just gratifying your ego. See **17c**.

Don't startle your audience by coming out of a yogalike trance into an explosion of oral energy. This is a favorite of high school orators. Engage your audience before your start. See opening paragraphs of **9**.

Don't start with a long quotation that leaves your audience wondering where the quotation ends and your words begin.

10

Conclusions

Use a conclusion to provide logical and psychological closure.

Many speakers make the common mistake of not leaving enough time for a proper conclusion. It is not enough to finish developing your last main point and them mumble, "I guess that's all I wanted to say." Just as you led your audience into your topic step by step in the introduction, so must you lead them out again in a conclusion, tying all the threads together, leaving your audience with a sense of completeness or closure. Like the introduction, the conclusion should be precisely planned, almost to the point of memorization. You should choose your words carefully: social scientists tell us that people are most likely to remember what they hear last.

10a. Provide logical closure.

Although you have already demonstrated the interconnectedness of your points and ideas in the body of the speech by the use of transitions and internal previews and summaries, you still need to tie it all together for your audience at the end.

(1) Summarize the main ideas of the speech.

In all but the shortest of speeches you are well advised to include a fairly explicit restatement of your thesis and main ideas. Most of the reasons you might be reluctant to state your thesis and main points in your introduction do not apply to the conclusion. For instance, at the end of your speech even a hostile audience may as well know that your intent has been to persuade them. The argument or dramatic sequence you did not want to reveal at first has now been unfolded and it will be helpful to recapitulate.

In a technical or argumentative speech it can be particularly useful to restate your thesis and main points exactly. For instance:

> So, today I have tried to show you that conjugal visits should be allowed in prisons. I first explained the system of conjugal visits that has been adopted successfully in some penal institutions. Second, I made the point that conjugal visits contribute directly to the morale and rehabilitation of prisoners. Finally, I documented that the visitation system is beneficial to society as a whole.

In some speeches you may think this is too mechanical. You may then choose to paraphrase rather than restate exactly, summing up the content, but not in the identical words.

> To summarize — meaning is in the head of the listener. You cannot stir up what is not already there. You communicate through all the senses. Often the where and the when may influence those that listen to you. If you can't put your message in the language of your listener, you are likely to fail.[1]

Only in a short, one-point speech can you safely omit a summary. Otherwise, there is no reason not to summarize — you have nothing to lose and only clarity to gain.

(2) Reestablish the connection of your topic to a larger context.

There can be an integration of the parts of a speech that goes beyond mere summary. In some cases, a conclusion serves to pull together several ideas into a pattern that has been implicit all along. This can be true for either inductive or deductive lines of reasoning, where the final relationship among points needs to be spelled out. See **11**. In other cases, you will want to build on the points you have established to refer to broader implications or ramifications of your topic. There may not be time to address these topics in your speech, but you want to raise the issues for your audience to think about.

---

[1]Waldo W. Braden, "In the Heads of the Listeners," *Vital Speeches of the Day* 44, no. 2 (Nov. 1, 1977): 44.

In the introduction, you drew your speech topic out of some broader context. After developing your ideas, you may want to show how they tie back to the original larger picture. A speech on the training of teachers may have such a format, as shown graphically in Figure 10-1.

If you have introduced new definitions and concepts, or familiar definitions and concepts in unfamiliar ways, use the conclusion to reinforce your use of them.

☐ **Exercise 1.** How do the speeches in the **Appendix** provide logical closure? Do you approve of the speakers' decisions to summarize explicitly, generally, or not at all?

☐ **Exercise 2.** Write a logical wrap-up for either the comic book outline in **7b** or the outline on women in the labor force in **5b**.

10b. Provide psychological closure.

Making your topic fit together logically for your audience is not enough. They have to go out psychologically satisfied with your speech—you

FIGURE 10-1

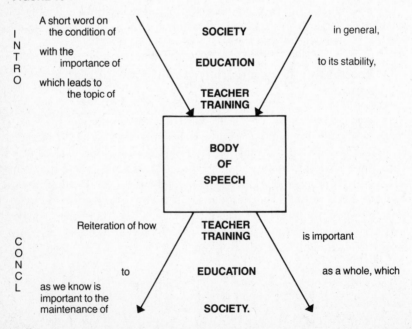

need to have touched them. When you plan your conclusion, think not only about what you want your listeners to understand and agree with, but also about how you want them to be feeling at the end of the speech.

(1) Remind the audience how the topic affects their lives.

In the introduction, you made the topic personal to your audience. During the speech itself, you implicitly sustained that orientation by making your examples and manner of speaking appropriately personal. At the end you must bring the topic home again and show your listeners why it should be of more than academic interest to them — that they have a stake in what you have described.

This process can be diagrammed as in Figure 10-2.

The financial accounting speech referred to in **9b** moved away from the audience's immediate concerns right after the introduction. The body of the speech consisted of a rather technical comparison of historical cost accounting and replacement cost accounting. However, in the conclusion the speaker returned the spotlight to her listeners:

> Whether you work for a large organization or have your own small business, whether you keep your own books or deal with a cadre of accountants, these two systems will affect you. Understanding the basic logic of each is necessary if you are to make sound decisions.

(2) Make an appeal.

Part of the psychological wrap-up of a speech can be a direct appeal to your audience, especially in a speech to persuade. Ask them directly to behave in a certain way (through adoption, deterrence, discontinuance, or continuance) or ask them to change their attitudes. Robert Kennedy, in a speech to the Democratic legislative dinner, shortly after the Watts riots of 1967, ended his speech this way:

> For us as Democrats the responsibility is clear. We must reject the council of those willing to pass laws against violence while refusing to help eliminate rats . . .
> We must offer that leadership — in every legislature and school board and city hall — which dares to speak out *before* it

117

tests the shifting wind of popular anger and confusion; that leadership which prefers facts to illusions, actions to sullen withdrawal, sacrifice and effort to indulgence and ease.[2]

An appeal can be strengthened by a statement of your own intent: "I plan to give blood tomorrow morning and I hope to see you down there."

FIGURE 10-2

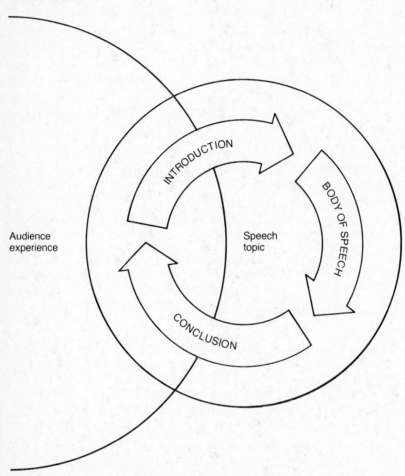

Audience experience

INTRODUCTION

BODY OF SPEECH

Speech topic

CONCLUSION

---

[2]*Congressional Record*, August 7, 1967.

☐ **Exercise 3.** What do the speeches in the **Appendix** do to provide psychological closure? Are they effective?

10c. End your speech with a clincher.

It is as important to plan your last sentence as it is your first. Every speech needs a sentence that leaves no doubt that the speech is finished. Speakers who have not prepared this clincher tend to keep summarizing while trying to devise a good exit line. As a result, many of them taper off in dismay and defeat with such frail endings as:

"I guess that's all I wanted to say."
"Oops! My time is up, I'd better stop now."
"Well, I'd like to say more, but I ought to take questions."

Other speakers do not taper, they just stop short, leaving the audience to decide whether the blank air is a pause or the real ending.

One type of effective clincher for a speech ties back to the attention getter used in the introduction: answer definitively that provocative question you asked initially; reintroduce your opening joke or story and take it one step further — or twist it in the light of your thesis.

> Frank Salacuse's syndicate spent $17,500 for its comic book, but all *you* need is a pocket full of change and transportation to the nearest newsstand or grocery store to rediscover a unique facet of Americana.

Also consider clinching your speech with a proverb, aphorism, quotation, or snatch of poetry.

> The needs of blacks and whites are too strongly intwined to separate. As Whitney Young used to say, "We may have come here on different ships, but we're in the same boat now."
> So white Americans must join with black people to rekindle the American Dream, and to sing, in the words of Langston Hughes:
>> O, let America be America again —
>> The land that never has been yet —
>> and yet must be.[3]

When long, complex sentences are used to build up to a finish, the clincher itself should be a short sentence. Even a sentence fragment.

---

[3]Vernon E. Jordan, "Blacks and the Nixon Administration: The Next Four Years," *Representative American Speeches* 45 no. 4 (1972–73): 48–49.

> Your ability to make sense of the world which you now enter
> will depend on your determination to retain your own integ-
> rity. If you do that, the rest will follow. Yours may not be what
> is often called a happy life; it may be battered by adversity. But
> it will be a life of purpose, of dignity, and of meaning. And that
> should be enough for anyone.[4]

Or vice versa: the last paragraph may have a few short sentences in rapid succession that lead to the ending complex sentence, as in "How to Lose a Sale" in the **Appendix**. Notice how the long/short contrast augments the finality both of Sprague's last sentence and of Silber's clincher.

Do not use "thank you" as a substitute for a clincher. It is not customary to thank your audience after a classroom speech or a business presentation, but only when you have been honored by a special invitation to speak. In which case, "thank you" can be the transition from the other parts of your conclusion into your clincher.

> And so, for all these reasons, I hope you agree that govern-
> ment regulation must be checked.
>   Thank you for inviting me to be here and for your kind
> attention. As you seek solutions to the complex problems of
> your industry, I hope that you will remember the words of
> Thomas Jefferson: "The price of liberty is eternal vigilance."

The delivery of your clincher is as important as its content. Do not mumble your last sentence in a throwaway voice or spend the last few speaking moments gathering up your notes and slinking away. Be familiar enough with your clincher that you can deliver it while maintaining eye contact with your listeners. When you finish, drop your eyes briefly, then reestablish contact to indicate willingness to answer questions, or to acknowledge applause. Inevitably, just as in the beginning, you will be self-conscious at this point. You will feel the focus changing from your message back to you. Remind yourself to project a confident image here so that you do not undo the effect of your clincher.

☐ **Exercise 4.** Evaluate the last few sentences of each speech in the **Appendix**. Does the final sentence of each successfully serve the functions of a clincher?

☐ **Exercise 5.** Write a clincher for either the outline on comic books in **7b** or the outline on women in the labor force in **5b**.

---

[4]John R. Silber, "Beyond the Real World Integrity," *Vital Speeches of the Day* 45, no. 19 (July 15, 1979): 604–606.

10d. Avoid these conclusion pitfalls:

Don't end with an apology:
>"I guess I've rambled on long enough."
>"I don't know if I've made this clear."
>"I'm not usually this hyper; it must be the coffee."

Don't trail off. Do your audience the courtesy of wrapping things up and using a clincher. See **10c**.

Don't introduce a whole new idea in your conclusion. The body of your speech is the place for that. See **6a**.

Don't make the conclusion disproportionately long. It is a summary and ending.

Don't end a speech in a style or mood that is at odds with the tenor of the rest of the speech. You do your listeners a disservice if you have kept them laughing up to the very end only to hit them with a stark recitation of doom. See **18c**.

Don't use the phrases "in conclusion" or "in summary" in any part of the speech other than the actual conclusion. You will lose part of your audience while they reorient themselves to the fact that the speech is continuing even though they thought it was winding down.

CONTENT

INTRODUCTION

In talking about the power of words, VerLynn Sprague, the father of one of the authors, customarily gave this rebuttal to an old cliché:

> It's been said that a picture is worth a thousand words. Well, I'm not sure how true that is. Some pictures are worth a million words. It depends on the words. Let me choose the words for you: the Twenty-third Psalm, the Lord's Prayer, the preamble to the Constitution, the introduction to the Declara-

tion of Independence, the Gettysburg Address and Shakespeare's Sonnet 18. A person would be hard-pressed to find a picture that means as much to me as those thousand words do.

The next nine sections deal with words and pictures, and the pictures we draw with words. Of all the choices you make as a speaker, by far the most important is your choice of the message you will send.

Too often people tend to think of a speaking assignment as a burden, a block of time to be filled. Approach it more positively! Here is a chance to share something you really believe in. Have you ever thought about the potential power a public speaker has? Look at just one dimension of that power—the amount of time you control as a speaker. If you give an eight-minute speech in a class, that does not seem like much—until you consider that with an audience of thirty people you have been granted four hours of human time and attention. If you give a two-hour training workshop to a dozen co-workers, that is twenty-four human hours—one full day. Or, if you deliver a one-hour keynote address to one hundred fifty people at a conference, you have consumed one hundred fifty human hours—*almost a week*. This view of the speaking situation dramatizes your tremendous opportunity and responsibility.

Being entrusted with these precious hours of human time motivates you to prepare extensively. You will not want to waste your listeners' time by underestimating their intelligence, stating the obvious, boring them, or taking twice as long as necessary to make a point. Remember, you are not doing all this work for an eight-minute result, you are getting set for four hours of potential influence.

It probably took VerLynn Sprague at least an hour to select and count the thousand words that would best illustrate the point about their power. He knew his ratio of preparation time to speaking time was going to be 60 to 1, but he felt it was worth it to formulate the material that was original, effective, and memorable.

We believe that a speaker, to show good faith with an audience, has an ethical obligation to respect their interests as well as his or her own. Of course, the speaker has a purpose in speaking, but the power of the platform should not be abused. If you are very skilled, you can use personal charisma, emotional appeals, and loaded language to have an almost hypnotic effect on some listeners. We cannot say that these techniques are ineffective. We do make the judgment that they are unethical.

A good speech should never substitute emotion for reason. When you presume to command people's time and attention, you owe it to them to know what you are talking about. Your message should be logical, factual, and coherent. Only after developing the sound rational base should you move on to making the message personal and palatable. The concepts in Sections **11** and **12** are the essential ingredients of all speech content. The materials in Section **13 – 19**, used appropriately, supplement and complement the substantive message.

Familiarity with basic principles of *reasoning* helps you develop logical patterns of thought and avoid fallacies. Selecting the proper *supporting materials* provides proof and amplification for your ideas. Though much support is verbal, *visual aids* further enhance your meaning. There is a psychological component to speech content; it comes into play through *motivational appeals* to listener needs and values, through sparking their *attention and interest*, and through evoking their delight in *humor*. Your effectiveness as a speaker is determined to a great extent by your *credibility* and by your choice of words: your *style*. For the speaker who attempts to influence attitudes and behavior, a special challenge arises in combining all the factors of content into *persuasive strategies*.

11

Reasoning

Use sound reasoning to develop your speech. Avoid logical fallacies.

Reasoning is the process by which we come to understand something previously unknown, through analyzing and integrating those things we already know. Your goal in a public speech is to share your insights with your listeners by "thinking" out loud, retracing for them the steps that led you to your conclusions. If you have not fully reasoned out your conclusions, or if you have made gross logical missteps in reaching them, their chances of being accepted by an audience become exceedingly slim. Any remotely intelligent group of listeners will not be moved by *what* you think; they will want to know *why* you think it. Consequently, the reasoning that should be the foundation of every speech can also be seen as "the giving of *good* reasons."

To develop a logical line of thought and test its validity, you will need to become familiar with standard patterns of reasoning and with a few of the most common fallacies.

11a. Use an inductive pattern of reasoning when your argument consists of combining a series of observations to lead to a probable conclusion.

The simplest and most common kind of reasoning is *induction*. Dozens of times a day we draw inferences that go beyond what we observe directly. Induction assumes an orderly universe. We could not function unless we trusted regularities in events, unless we believed that much of what has happened before will happen again. We step in front of oncoming traffic because we believe from previous experience that the cars will obey the traffic signals. After several sleepless nights we stop drinking coffee at bedtime.

Inductive reasoning consists of collecting enough instances to establish a pattern. A typical line of inductive thought can be portrayed as follows:

Orchid$_1$ has no fragrance.
Orchid$_2$ has no fragrance.
Orchid$_3$ has no fragrance.
. . . .
. . . .
. . . .
Orchid$_n$ has no fragrance.

Therefore, it is probable that all orchids have no fragrance.

The extent to which you can generalize from such observations is linked to the extent of your sampling. If you smelled only the orchids in one corner of one hothouse, you would be less able to make a general conclusion than had you smelled orchids in different hothouses throughout the country.

By far the greatest problem in this kind of reasoning is determining the value of n above. Obviously you want to test several cases before drawing a conclusion, but how many are enough? This is the issue of "enoughness." If you drive five Hupmobiles and they all have mechnical difficulties, is that enough to say that Hupmobiles are bad cars? If a researcher finds that 132 out of 150 soap opera fans surveyed do housework while listening, is that enough to justify a conclusion about that group? At best you can say, "It is likely that Hupmobiles are lemons," and "Soap opera fans probably do housework while listening." The conclusions drawn from induction are always *probable* rather than *absolute*. The only way you could say that *all* Hupmobiles are lemons would be if you had tested every one. This would be counting, not reasoning. Reasoning, as you recall, is defined as drawing conclusions about the unknown.

An inductive conclusion can fall anywhere along this continuum:

possible	plausible	probable	almost certain

The degree of certainty depends on the methods used in making our observations, and on the number of observations made. A conclusion like, "the last two times I've gone to that restaurant the service has been lousy. I'll bet they've changed management," would fall far to the left. Two observations is a very small number, and there are many other viable explanations for the poor service. At the other end of the continuum is a statement like, "Birth control pills prevent fertilization." This conclusion is based on a great many observations collected systematically. We can say we are 99 percent sure it is true, but we still lack complete certainty.

How strong must this probability be before you can consider valid the conclusion of an inductive argument? A 51 percent probability, 75 percent, 99 percent? Unlike deductive reasoning, for which there are agreed-upon tests of validity, the test of an induction varies in every case. There is no mathematical or logical answer to the question. The issue of "enoughness" is more a psychological question of individual perception, as is explained below.

Would you leap off a twenty-foot wall for $1,000? Many would say yes. It is *possible* that you could be killed, but it is probable that you would escape with no worse that a sprained ankle. Would you jump from the roof of a three-story building for $1,000? Most people would say no. It is *possible* you would be unharmed, but not very probable. In both cases you set the acceptable level of probability by weighing the risks against potential gains. Flipping a coin has a 50 percent probability — good enough for a dollar bet, but would you bet your life on a coin toss? When you choose to fly in an airliner, you bet your life, but the probability is 400,000 to one you will arrive safely, and the gains of speedy transportation outweigh the minimal risk.

When induction is used in a public speech, the speaker's task is to convince the audience members that the conclusion arrived at is probable enough to warrant their acceptance. The so-called "inductive leap" is based on an apt image. You lead the listeners to a certain point with the data you have and then ask them to jump across a chasm to the conclusion you see. Here, as in the preceding examples, the level of "enoughness" is contingent on the risks and benefits perceived.

Suppose that you know of a new kind of drug rehabilitation program that has been found to be quite effective in pilot studies in three different communities. In urging its adoption in your city, your line of reasoning might go like this:

The program worked in community A.
The program worked in community B.

The program worked in community C.
Therefore, it is probable that the program is effective and will work here.

Because these other cases were not studied totally systematically (with control groups, random sampling, and follow-up studies, for example), and because there are only three instances, you cannot state your conclusion at a high level of probability. You must recognize that the drug rehabilitation program could fail in your community. Imagine that it were possible to assign concrete levels of probability, and that both proponents and skeptics of the program agreed that there was about a 75 percent chance of its success. A member of your audience might well ask "Why should we spend $650,000 just for a three-out-of-four chance we might help a bunch of junkies?" You cannot change the 75 percent odds, but what you can do is affect your audience's assessment of the costs and rewards. Tell them how the program, if it works, will benefit the whole community: decrease crime, put former addicts back in productive employment, and lower the temptations for adolescent drug use. Also minimize the costs. "$650,000 sounds like a lot, but it's only $.85 per citizen." When the listeners reassess the costs and rewards, and see them as you do, the 75 percent odds may look more attractive.

Consider another example, where the conclusion's probability is very high.

Nuclear power plant A has had no accidents.
Nuclear power plant B has had no accidents.
Nuclear power plant C has had no accidents.
. . . .
Nuclear power plant n has had no accidents.
Therefore, it is probable that nuclear power plants are safe.

Suppose the conclusion could be granted a 95 percent level of probability. Even so, you or someone else might not feel the evidence was sufficient to make the inductive leap. In explaining this to the audience, you would minimize the rewards — most of the energy we would get can be obtained through other sources — and maximize the risks by describing just how awful a nuclear accident could be. Your argument is: "I'm not willing to subject my family to a 5-out-of-100 chance of this sort of destruction just to have a few extra electronic luxuries."

In the case of the drug problem, a low probability met the test of enoughness for the speaker. In the case of the nuclear power plant, even 95 percent was not enough. The difference lies in the perception of risk and reward. No level of enoughness is too high or too low — no inductive argument is innately logical or illogical. The validity is negotiated between you and your audience.

In summary, when you use an inductive pattern of reasoning:

Look before you "leap."

Be cautious in drawing inferences from limited data. How many cases did you examine? Were they selected fairly? Are the contrary instances accounted for? See **11e, 12c**.

Recognize that your conclusions are only probable.

Be aware that you could be wrong, even at 99 percent probability. Use qualifiers like "many," "most," "evidence strongly indicates," "we can say with near certainty." Acknowledge that those who disagree with you are not necessarily wrong or illogical; they have the right to set their "enoughness" level at a place different from yours.

Demonstrate the cost/reward analysis that led you to accept or reject the probable conclusion.

In effect you are explaining a bet you have made: "I think these are good/bad odds because . . ." Do not assume that your audience sees the costs, risks, and rewards as you do. Lay these out as concretely and graphically as possible.

11b.   Use a deductive pattern of reasoning when your argument consists of demonstrating how the relationships among established premises lead to a necessary conclusion.

Unlike induction, where the emphasis is on collecting observable data, deduction consists of manipulating verbal statements, or premises, according to formal rules. Deduction, then, does not really involve bringing new data into play, but just rearranges what you already know. If this is the case, why do we think we can learn anything new through the process of deduction if we are dealing with the known? Bits of data are useless until we can assign meaning to them by discovering how they fit together. From this are derived scientific breakthroughs, brainteasers, gossip, and the English murder mystery. In the obligatory denouement of the last-named, the detective patiently explains to a roomful of suspects the meaning of the details known but not assimilated by the reader:

Since Lord Robert's voice was heard at ten and his body was found at midnight, all of the suspects seem to have alibis. However, only the murderer could know that Lord Robert was drinking cognac that night instead of his habitual port. All of you here heard one person talk about missing "the old fellow smiling over his *snifter*." Yes, the same person who charmed us all yesterday with his impersonations! Colonel Side-bottom — you killed Lord Robert at nine, and returned to fake a conversation to be overheard!

Having the clues is not enough, it takes a supersleuth to find the perfect pattern.

Although all of us have used deduction throughout our lives, most of us first became aware of it in a formalized way in our first algebra class when we confronted:

$$a = b$$
$$b = c$$
$$c = ?$$

We found that the answer, $c = a$, was both simple and inescapable. All deductive arguments (or *syllogisms*, as they are called) are really just variations of the simple equation above. In fact, formal logicians reduce statements they are considering to just such mathematical equations. However, for the purpose of this book we are going to do this only to illustrate the underlying principles of deductive reasoning: if we know how two terms (concepts, events, characteristics) relate to a third term, we can determine how they relate to each other.

Term a is related in a known way to term b.
We know certain things about b.
Therefore, we can draw certain conclusions about term a.

To use deductive reasoning in a speech, you need to transpose this into a series of steps:

Step One: Establish that a relationship exists between two terms.

Step Two: Establish the actual condition/status of one of the terms.

Step Three: Show how a conclusion about the other term necessarily follows.

All kinds of relationships can exist. For example:

One term may be an intrinsic characteristic of the other.
All ducks have webbed feet.
Conflict is inherent in the collective bargaining model.

One term may be a category that includes the other.
All Volkswagens are motor vehicles.
The Food Stamp program is part of the social welfare system.

One term may be inevitably linked to the other.
If you heat water to 212° at sea level, *then* it will boil.
If corporate taxes are cut, *then* investment will increase.

The two terms may be opposite or exclude each other.
Either that fabric is natural or it is synthetic.
Unless we crack down on drunk drivers, fatalities will rise.

When you establish these statements of relationship and then provide one piece of data about one of the terms, your conclusion has to follow.

This is a duck. *Then it definitely has webbed feet.*
We did not crack down on drunk drivers, so *traffic fatalities must have increased.*

The beauty of deduction lies in its certainty. If your listeners accept the premises, they must accept the conclusion.

This seems so attractive one might wonder why a speaker would use any other method. Why waste energy on the probable conclusions of induction, with their floating points of enoughness that allow audiences to capriciously — yet legitimately — reject a 95 percent certain conclusion? Why not stick with deduction, where the rules are clear and the conclusions have to be accepted? The problem with deduction is that in order for its conclusion to be absolute, its premises must be absolute. Unfortunately, most absolute statements of relationships are either untrue or trivial. Who really cares if ducks have webbed feet, or needs to reason about it? The things we do have to reason about, and tend to give speeches about, are complex issues of public policy, human behavior, and social values. In these domains it is rarely possible to find acceptable statements that "*all X* is *Y* or that, "if *X*, then *Y always* follows" or that "either *X* or *Y* and *no other alternative.*"

Does a cut in corporate taxes *absolutely have to* result in increased business investment? A more honest syllogism would be:

It is highly probable that a cut in corporate taxes will increase investment.
Congress is almost certain to cut taxes.
Therefore, it is highly probable that investment will increase.

But now we have lost the tidy inevitability of deduction. No longer do the rules of logic force our listeners to accept our conclusion. We are back to the same kinds of problems we face in induction, persuading the audience to weigh the probabilities as we do. Your appeal to them would be:

If you grant this premise as probable,
and
if you grant this other premise as probable,
then it is logical to grant this conclusion as probable.

When you look at deduction this way, you can, as a speaker, take some liberties not available to the logician. You may build a deductively structured argument with premises that are not absolute, recognizing of course that the conclusions you derive will not be absolute either. Each point needs to be supported sufficiently to persuade a member of the audience to say "I'll grant that point; it's reasonable; it's probable." Thus the degree of probability of any conclusion is a product of the degree of probability granted to each premise. (If quanitification of probabilities were possible, it would work like this: Major premise that is 80 percent probable × minor premise that is 75 percent probable = conclusion that is 60 percent probable.)

The form of a deductive argument is still an elegant way to justify a conclusion, even when it has been modified to lose the clean force of a true syllogism. In its diluted but more realistic form it provides an effective structure for part of a speech, or for the entire speech. When the conclusion you want your audience to reach can be arrived at through many logical channels, seriously consider arranging your points in a deductive format. In the following examples the same conclusion is reached by basically inductive and basically deductive patterns. Compare their effectiveness.

INDUCTIVE

I. The United States responded inappropriately to the British-Argentine conflict over the Falkland Islands.
II. The United States responded inappropriately to the Israeli invasion of Lebanon.
III. The United States mishandled the human rights issue in Afghanistan and Poland.
IV. The United States mishandled arms and technology deals with both Chinas.

V. The United States alienated its European allies with its stand on the Soviet natural gas pipeline.
Therefore, the United States has lacked a good foreign policy for over a decade.

DEDUCTIVE

I. A good foreign, policy should be consistent, credible and ethical.
   A. Quotations from experts
   B. Historical example
II. United States foreign policy in the last ten years has been inconsistent.
   A. Falklands conflict
   B. Lebanon invasion
III. United States foreign policy in the last ten years has lacked credibility with both allies and adversaries.
   A. Soviet natural gas pipeline
   B. People's Republic of China and Taiwan
IV. United States foreign policy in the last ten years has not developed a standard of ethics.
   A. Helsinki agreement and human rights
   B. Aid to totalitarian regimes
Therefore, the United States has lacked a good foreign policy for over a decade.

Observe that the deductive format has more unity, and gives a clearer picture of why the speaker labels United States foreign policy a failure. To the extent that a listener accepts the first deductive premise (I) and the second premise (II, III and IV), the conclusion will receive that level of acceptance. The accumulation of specific examples in the inductive pattern does not offer as clear a focus for why the conclusion might be accepted or rejected. Do you fail to accept the thesis because there were not enough examples? Or because you disagree with the interpretation of these examples? Or because you have no reason to define foreign policy other than as whatever serves a country's immediate self-interest?

One of the real advantages of structuring ideas deductively is that you must state the relationships among the concepts with which you are dealing. When you clearly state the major premise on which your argument rests, you call to your listeners' minds certain values, assumptions, or even logical truisms. The audience can then apply these concepts when you move on to specific cases in developing your minor premise. In the following logical arguments, notice how the major premise serves in each case to direct the listener's awareness to a statement that the speaker might otherwise have taken for granted.

Anyone who has been elected to high political office has had to make a number of compromises along the way.

Candidate J has served as governor and United States senator.
Therefore, candidate J has made a number of political compromises.

A person denied access to the benefits of society will either become embittered or will turn to crime.
Many members of ethnic minorities who are denied access have not committed crimes.
Therefore, many are embittered.

It has always been the goal of our social welfare system to help recipients become self-sufficient.
Certain current programs encourage dependency and discourage initiative.
Therefore, these programs should be changed.

A good friend is a person who helps you reach your potential.
Several people in this organization have helped me strive toward my potential.
Therefore, as I say good-bye, I feel like I am leaving many good friends.

Sometimes speakers have so internalized a point of view that they neglect to lay out parts of their argument they see as obvious. In this respect, the first point in each argument above might have been omitted or tossed in as an aside rather than developed. We find, though, that excellent speeches often take the time to articulate and justify the premises they are based on. If you say "Of course Thompson should be hired, he has the most experience" or "We couldn't possibly pass this bill, it endangers the free enterprise system," you are assuming that your audience accepts your assumption that "the person with the most experience should be hired," or that "anything that endangers the free enterprise system is undesirable." If they do not accept those assumptions, all your efforts to prove Thompson's experience or the bill's effects are wasted. If they do agree, you will not have lost much time by reiterating those points. Listeners will be more likely to remember your specifics if they have a logical framework for them.

Like the detective with the clues, your task is not just to list the facts, but to demonstrate how they fit together and what they ultimately mean. Often the conclusion of the speech is the place to weave together the threads of a deductive argument.

So, I've shown that it is our goal to reach full employment and that the only available paths are through direct provision of public sector jobs or through indirect stimulation of private sector jobs. Since I went on to give you several reasons for rejecting the public sector alternative, there is only one conclusion left. To create full employment the private sector must be stimulated.

☐ **Exercise 1.** Here are some conclusions that could have been reached either inductively or deductively. Briefly lay out an inductive and a deductive argument that leads to each.

Natural childbirth is best for parents and infant.
Motorcyclists should be required to wear helmets.
The Academy Awards are rarely given to the best films.

☐ **Exercise 2.** What costs or risks would you need to minimize and what benefits would you need to maximize in order to establish a high probability of acceptance for these conclusions?

This new treatment for herpes should be marketed.
Every car should be equipped with air bags.
We should hire only college graduates for our sales department.
You should cut animal fat out of your diet.

☐ **Exercise 3.** What unstated assumption or absolute statement of relationship underlies each of these arguments?

She must be doing a good job. She hasn't been fired.
You should buy a condominium. It's cheaper than a house.
Well, it's not a win for labor, so I guess management wins.
I thought he had some self-respect, but now I learn he's on welfare.

☐ **Exercise 4.** Identify the basic reasoning pattern in each speech in the **Appendix**. Are they inductive or deductive? Can you lay out the underlying argument in three or four sentences?

11c. Use causal reasoning to demonstrate that one event results from another.

Causal reasoning is the backbone of all speeches that deal with policy and problem solving. In most cases, if a person says, "I don't favor your policy (or program, or solution)" what they are really saying is "I disagree with you that X causes Y." What this means is that you must carefully scrutinize the relationship that exists between two events to satisfy yourself that it *is* causal, and then you must provide your listeners with information that indicates how thoroughly you tested this relationship.

Of course, in a problem-solving or policy speech there is rarely *one* cause. To assert that there is would be gross oversimplification and would jeopardize the acceptance of your conclusions.

(1) Test the validity of the causal relationships you claim.

A causal relationship is stronger than a mere correlation. It is not coexistence. Two events may occur together or in sequence without one causing the other. For instance, morning sickness and weight gain often occur together, but neither causes the other; they are the result of a third event, pregnancy. To be sure that the relationship is a causal one, apply these tests:

Do the alleged cause and alleged effect always occur together?

To prove that a causal relationship exists, at least two formal comparisons must be made, as with a control group and experimental group. Otherwise mere coincidence or correlation cannot be ruled out. It is not enough to show that the alleged cause is present with the alleged effect, but that also in the absence of the alleged cause the alleged effect does not ever appear.

If a rash appears every time you eat tomatoes, and never appears when you haven't eaten tomatoes, this is strong evidence that tomatoes cause the rash.

There are three groups of arthritis sufferers, matched in all important charcteristics such as age, sex, diet and general health. Group A receives the drug Painaway, Group B receives a placebo, and Group C receives no treatment. Members of Group A experience dramatic relief, and there is no change in the condition of members of Group B and Group C. This supports the claim that Painaway causes a reduction in arthritis symptoms.

To prove a causal relationship, you must show both concurrent presence and concurrent absence. All that is needed to *disprove* a suggested causal relationship is to point to a case where the alleged cause was present without the alleged effect, or vice versa. So, if you found that your rash occurred occasionally when you had not eaten tomatoes, or if you had once eaten tomatoes and not gotten the rash, the causal relationship does not exist.

Classical economic theory suggests that raising tariffs reduces imports. Yet, when we increased the tariff on Argentine beef, imports remained constant.

For years I believed the other teachers who said students would only read the book if they were given weekly quizzes. Then one semester I dropped the quizzes and found that they were as well prepared each week as before.

Do the alleged cause and the alleged effect vary together?

Another test of causation is to determine that the magnitude of change in the cause matches that in the effect.

If one bite of tomato gives you a small rash, and consuming many tomatoes gives you a big rash, this is one more bit of evidence to suggest that tomatoes cause your rash.

High school graduates, on the average, earn more than high school dropouts. People with some college education earn more than high school grads, but less than college graduates. People with advanced degrees, taken as a group, have the highest incomes. Though you can think of individual exceptions, research on groups of people shows that each increment of formal education is accompanied by an equivalent increase in earning power.

(2) Do not oversimplify causal relationship.

In the worlds of physics and chemistry, there are some clear, straightforward causal relationships.

An action results in an equal and opposite reaction.

OR

Adding silver nitrate solution ($AgNO^3$) to sodium chloride (NaCl) will cause silver chloride (AgCl) to precipitate.

These could be represented as

$C \rightarrow E$

However, in the areas of politics, psychology, medicine, economics, and the like, more complex patterns usually exist.

Some effects have multiple causes.

If smoking were the single cause of lung cancer, then every smoker would have lung cancer, and every victim of lung cancer would be a smoker. Obviously, this is not the case. Yet research does show smoking to be one causal factor contributing to lung cancer. The simple tests outlined in **11c(1)** cannot be applied to cases of multiple causation. If you speak of issues like poverty, crime, divorce, economic recession as though they had a single direct cause, you will justifiably lose credibility with your audience.

Some causes are also effects, and some effects are also causes in a long causal chain.

When we designate a cause of a certain event, we can look at the immediate cause or a more distant factor. A doctor might say that the cause of a particular death was a cerebral hemorrhage. What, though, was the cause of that? Perhaps a fractured skull, which was caused by going through a windshield, which was caused by the impact of a car with a tree, which was caused by excessive drinking, which was caused by worry over being unemployed . . .

$$C \rightarrow (E/C) \rightarrow (E/C) \rightarrow (E/C) \rightarrow E$$

In a speech you need to discuss enough of these links to give a realistic picture and to demonstrate to your listeners that you understand the complexity of the process, without going so far back in the chain as to be absurd.

It is sometimes important to point out the cyclical nature of certain causal chains. For example, ignorance about a particular group may lead to prejudice, which in turn results in lack of contact with that group, which perpetuates ignorance. This sort of analysis is far more interesting than positing a single cause of racial disharmony.

Some effects result from a one-time cause, and some from ongoing causes.

Effects that are labeled undesirable can be dealt with in two ways, either by treating the effect directly, or by blocking the cause that produces the effect. To decide which strategy makes the most sense in a given instance, you need to determine whether the cause is one-time or ongoing.

Picture a neighborhood with bare dirt for landscaping, glassless windows, broken furniture in the yards and residents in need of medical care. You are concerned about these symptoms and want to take some action. If you find that a tornado whipped through the area, you may push for emergency relief, rebuilding loans, and intervention by the Corps of Engineers to clear wreckage. However, if you learn that the area is depressed and that poverty is chronic, then you may choose to advocate organizing retraining programs, campaigns to attract large business to the community, or setting up health clinics. A mistake in evaluation, where the effect of an ongoing cause is treated as if it resulted from a one-time cause, will lead to the eventual reappearance of that effect.

To try to remedy problems through minor adjustments in laws and institutions, when the real causes lie in basic attitudes and values, is the worst kind of oversimplification. Nearly as bad is the tendency to advocate "education" as the answer to all social ills. Better to lay out a two-phase solution, with short-range steps to deal with the symptoms, complemented by a long-range attack on the underlying cause.

☐ **Exercise 5.**   Explain two ways you might *disprove* each of the following causal assertions, using principles from **11c(1)**:

Supreme Court rulings on arrest procedures have allowed criminals to go free.
Unfair laws have caused discrimination against women.
Strokes are caused by stress.
Lack of educational expenditure has produced an inferior generation of college students.
Smoking marijuana leads to the use of hard drugs.

☐ **Exercise 6.**   Now, explain how each of the causal statements in Exercise 5 might reflect one or more of the kinds of oversimplification referred to in **11c(2)**.

☐ **Exercise 7.**   Identify at least one instance of causal reasoning in each speech in the **Appendix**. Are the causal links valid?

11d. Use reasoning by analogy to draw conclusions about unknown events, based on what you know about similar events.

When we reason by analogy we compare two things that can be placed in the same category. In the process, we assume that since we know that *A* and *B* have a number of characteristics in common, we can conclude that those things we do not know about *B* are highly likely to resemble their counterparts that we *do* know about in *A*.

> Our sushi bar in Santa Cruz has been so successful that we want to open one in another city. We asked ourselves what it was about Santa Cruz that contributed to our success, so we could choose a city that duplicated those conditions. We credited the coastal location for availability of fresh fish, the proximity to Japanese-American population centers, the presence of relatively affluent, sophisticated, and health-oriented consumers. Based on this analysis we've selected Redondo Beach for our next restaurant.

(1) Be sure that when you reason by analogy the two cases are similar in all relevant and important respects.

Here is the sort of unconscious analogy we all use everyday. Does it meet the test?

> Alternately sulking and throwing tantrums was effective in manipulating my father. Therefore, these same tactics should be effective with my boss, Fred.

There are certain similarities between the father and the boss: both are authority figures, both are male, both are older, both have trouble dealing with emotions. It is also easy to point out differences. Father is tall, Fred is short. Father drives foreign cars, Fred drives a pickup. No cases are identical, and just pointing out differences does not discredit an analogy automatically. Are there relevant and important ways they differ? In this instance, yes. The relationship with the father was a personal one; that with Fred is professional. In one case a child and an adult are relating; in the other, two adults. Major personality differences between the father and Fred may exist. These stated differences are probably important enough to lead the person to reject the conclusion that sulking and throwing tantrums are effective ways of dealing with the boss.

(2) Do not confuse a literal analogy, which is a form of reasoning, with a figurative analogy, which is used only in a descriptive function.

Reasoning by analogy requires a comparison of two members of the same category. Figurative analogy compares the members of different categories.

> Convincing my boss, Fred, to adopt a new procedure takes as much persistence, luck, and timing as starting my 1972 Fiat on a January morning.

This may have a stylistic impact, but it cannot support a conclusion. The example in **(1)**, however flawed in its logic, did compare two human relationships, not a human relationship and a human-machine relationship.

11e. Avoid these reasoning fallacies:

Some people commit reasoning fallacies knowingly, with dishonest intent. Others commit them through lack of practice in doing their own thinking. The good public speaker wants to avoid the appearance of either. Once you have built your speech around sound, logical arguments, go through it to detect any constructions that even hint of sloppy thinking. One glaring fallacy in your speech will make all your other conclusions suspect. It is not necessary to learn all the fallacies — over one hundred have been categorized with Latin names — but you should be familiar with the most common of them.

(1) Attacking the person rather than the argument

This fallacy, traditionally labeled *ad hominem*, substitutes character assassination for solid refutation or persuasion.

> Anyone who advocates abortion on demand is a murderer anyway. It certainly wouldn't surprise me to find them taking kickbacks from the clinics that would receive government funds.

(2) Setting up a straw figure

This fallacy consists of creating a weak argument, attributing it to the opposing side, and then proceeding to demolish it. The false implication is that all the opponents' arguments are as flimsy as the "straw figure," and could be dismissed with equal ease if time permitted. A familiar example was the cry of "unisex toilets!" in every discussion of the Equal Rights Amendment.

Opponents of affirmative action policies are sometimes heard to raise these objections:

> We can't hire people without regard for their qualifications.
> It's not right to hire a mathematician to teach English just because she's a woman.
> It would be terrible to pass over a white man with a Ph.D. and choose a person with a B.A. just to hire a minority.

This is misleading, because proponents of affirmative action do not advocate disregarding qualifications. The speaker has distorted the issue with these extreme examples to avoid confronting the complexity of the problem.

(3) Extending an argument to absurd lengths (*reductio ad absurdum*)

Similar to the straw figure, this fallacy makes a potentially sound argument appear groundless by extending it to a point where it can be ridiculed. Often this extension goes beyond reasonable interpretation of the original point. In challenging current methods of criminal sentencing, a speaker might say:

> The average criminal is condemned to a bleak cell while top government wrongdoers lounge around in "country club" facilities. The logic is that the latter have already been punished considerably by loss of face, prestige, and professional standing. This seems to say that punishments should be harsher on those who have the least to lose. By this reasoning the senator who commits murder might get off with a citation and public embarrassment, while an unemployed ghetto dweller who shoplifts should be put on bread and water, with regular sessions on the rack.

Pointing out these patently outrageous inequities does not constitute a legitimate attack on the basic concept that the impact of punishment on an offender can be one valid criterion for decisions about sentencing. This kind of fallacy relies on the humor of the cockeyed image it creates. Disarmed by a ludicrous example, the listeners lose sight of the real issue.

(4) Circular reasoning

Circular reasoning assumes as one of its premises the very conclusion it sets out to establish. Most of us know the hopeless feeling of trying to deal logically with such dead-end arguments as "you can't get credit unless you have a good credit rating, and you can't have a good credit rating unless you have gotten credit." Often circular reasoning results from granting absolute authority to some source, and thus being blinded to the fact that others might not attribute similar authority to it.

I know that God exists.
It says so repeatedly in the Bible.
And everything in the Bible is true since it's the ordained word of God.

Other instances of circular reasoning come out of definitional word games.

No sane person would consider suicide, because it's insane to want to take your own life.

We need a Court of Equity to resolve labor-management disputes, because collective bargaining results in settlements that aren't equitable. What do I mean by an equitable settlement? I mean the kind of settlement that is arrived at by a Court of Equity.

(5) The semantic fallacy

The rich, connotative nature of words, which so enhances communication, can also abet fuzzy thinking. When midstream shifts of definition are obvious, they can be funny, as in "blackberries are red when they're green," or "not one single burglar was arrested this month; they must all have been married."

More subtle and dangerous shifts in definition can occur in various critical parts of an argument.

The free enterprise system, which we all cherish, could not exist without competition. This bill to protect small businesses threatens our whole economic structure. There can be no true competition when one group is given special protection.

In the underlying value premise, the word *competition* is used in the general sense of a market mechanism. In claiming that the bill endangered *competition* the word is used in a much narrower sense, as in "a specific contest between individuals." The semantic fallacy is especially difficult to identify and is frustrating to respond to, because the syllogistic form of the argument appears to be valid. The problem arises from the slight slippage of definition as a term is used with different meanings in different premises.

(6) False dichotomy

It is fallacious to base reasoning on an *either/or* statement when the two alternatives are not really mutually exclusive, or when other alternatives exist. A cigarette commercial used to ask: "What do you want, good grammar or good taste?" The proper answer to that was: "Why do we have to choose? Nothing prevents us from having both." Many speeches set up equally artificial choices.

> Would you rather have a football program or a band and orchestra at our school?

This can be a false dichotomy. Through careful economic management and marshalling of resources it may be possible to maintain both.

> Either we sell modern jets to Taiwan or we lose the confidence of our allies.

This basic premise so oversimplifies a complex issue that no conclusions can be drawn from it.

(7) Faulty reversal of an if-then statement (affirming the consequent)

One kind of deductive reasoning is based on an If A, then B relationship. A common fallacy is to assume that because B follows A, the reverse is also true: that A follows B.

> *If* I hear voices through the wall, *then* there is someone is the next room.
> I hear voices through the wall.
> Therefore, there is someone is the next room.

This is a valid statement. However, its validity in this form does not mean that its reverse will be also be true. The following cannot be derived from the original If-then statement:

> I don't hear voices, so there must be no one in the next room.

This problem arises from lazy thinking, where a person knows two factors are associated but has not carefully analyzed which follows from the other, if indeed that sort of relationship exists at all. Guilt by association is the most common manifestation of this fallacy.

> If a candidate agrees with all the principles of an organization, then he or she will receive that organization's endorsement.
> The People's Counterinsurgency Brigade endorsed Elizabeth Day.
> Therefore, she must agree with all their principles.

This is a fallacious conclusion, because there is nothing in the first statement that requires an organization to endorse only those candidates who are in 100 percent agreement with its principles. It is entirely possible that Day's opponent shares no values with the PCB, and Day only one, so she receives the endorsement as the lesser of the evils. The conclusion that Day must agree with all PCB principles would be valid only if the original If-then statement were reversed, saying that total agreement necessarily follows from endorsement. That relationship has not been established in this example.

Political candidates so fear this kind of faulty reasoning by voters that they will often publicly repudiate the endorsement of extreme groups and supporters. They cannot count on the electorate to recognize the difference between a group endorsing a candidate and a candidate endorsing a group.

(8) Hasty generalization

This fallacy entails making a premature inductive "leap." See **11a**. It is glorified in the pomp surrounding Ground Hog Day, where data from an isolated event is blindly accepted as gospel in relation to a much wider range of events.

This statement has a faulty leap:

> Abscam proved that every elected official has a price.

Time may not allow you, as a speaker, to include all your data that led you to a conclusion. It is especially important, then, to have the unused data as your fingertips so that you can deflect any accusations of hasty generalization that may come up.

(9) Confusing sequence with cause (*post hoc, ergo propter hoc*)

The Latin label for this fallacy translates as "after the event, therefore because of the event." It is natural to try to understand the world around us by looking for cause-effect patterns wherever possible. So strong is this motivation that we are frequently guilty of imitating Chanticleer the rooster, who firmly believed it was his predawn crowing that caused the sun to rise each day.

Perhaps the most famous example of this fallacy in this century is the "Tut Curse." Five months after he had opened the tomb of the Pharaoh Tutankhamen, Lord Carnarvon died in Cairo from complications following an insect bite. At the moment of his death, Cairo experienced a power blackout, and this was interpreted by many to be a manifestation of an ancient curse. Thereafter, if anyone remotely connected to Egyptology died, it was attributed to the mummy's curse, no matter if the agent of this "curse" were heavy traffic or arteriosclerosis.

To avoid this fallacy, never assume causation based on time sequence alone. Test every causal hypothesis against the criteria in **11c**.

☐ **Exercise 8.**   Identify the fallacy or fallacies in each statement.

I'm surprised you health food nuts eat granola packaged in cellophane bags. Aren't you afraid the synthetic chemicals will poison the contents?

Anyone who wears clothes made out of the American flag doesn't care about this country anyway.

You said you could prove the point by sheer logic. Well, I agree. The logic was pretty sheer.

It always rains on Easter. I remember it has for the last three years.

Well, either you support your country or you are critical of the government. Which is it?

The jury system should be abolished. Last year a jury awarded $3 million to a woman who didn't like the nose job she got. The next month the doctor committed suicide.

☐ **Exercise 9.**   Examine the reasoning in the speeches in the **Appendix**. Do you find any fallacies in reasoning?

12

Supporting Materials

Clarify and justify each of your points with a variety of supporting materials. Be sure these materials meet the tests for valid evidence and are smoothly integrated into the speech.

When you have set up the basic structure of your speech through planning your lines of argument and developing an outline of your points, you then turn to selecting the materials that make up the real building blocks of your speech. The process can be thought of as analogous to "fleshing out" a skeletal drawing of a figure, or to adding the siding to the frame of a building. These supporting materials are crucial to the success of your speech. They are the "stuff" it is made of. They probably determine whether your listeners characterize your utterances as valid or invalid, interesting or boring.

The forms of support you use can only be selected in reference to a basic structure. It is impossible to judge the appropriateness of supporting materials unless you are very clear about what you are supporting. We are appalled to hear some speakers say "my first point is the Chicago example. My next point is the study done by the Harvard sociologist." Example of what? Study proving or explaining what principle? It is extremely important, as we stress in 2 (Topic Analysis) and 6 (Selecting Points), that you measure every component of your speech against a logical outline. If your point is *Crime is on the increase*, then the story of a single crime, however graphic and compelling, should not be chosen for your development. To *support* that point you need comparative data—examples collected from at least two periods of time must be presented to establish a trend.

Supporting materials may take the form of clarification or of proof. Often, especially in speeches to inform or evoke, these materials amplify, clarify, or expand on ideas. In other cases materials are used to bolster controversial claims for which a speaker seeks acceptance. Although the philosophical notion of ever proving a point completely could be questioned, we speak of supporting materials as proof because they can serve to justify an idea, adding to the probability of its acceptance by tending to prove. Frequently a single piece of support, such as a statistic, functions as both clarification and proof of a point. Some kinds of support, though, like hypothetical examples or definitions, can only be used as amplification; they never serve to prove anything.

Select the support for your ideas first on the basis of relevance, then validity, and then interest value. Avoid the rut some speakers fall into when they use mostly examples, or mostly testimony, or mostly explanation. Form the habit of using a variety of the following methods to develop your speech.

12a. Simplify and structure your explanations.

A large part of speaking is merely explanation — stating an idea and then restating it in a way that develops or expands upon the basic notion. Unfortunately some explanations do more to confuse than clarify, usually when the speaker has lost sight of which of the many details of a complex process or idea are the essential ones. It is a real challenge to select the most significant details and present them in the clearest order.

How can you most economically create the mental picture that will aid your listeners' understanding? Generally, clear explanations move from the simple to the complex, from the familiar to the unfamiliar. Even at the risk of temporary oversimplification, it is advisable to lay out the most basic concepts first and later to introduce qualifiers, exceptions, and interesting tangents. Think of each listener as the newcomer to town who would first want to learn the basic route from home to work, and only after mastering that would want to learn about shortcuts and scenic detours.

Try some of the following methods to make your explanations clear.

(1) Start with a simple analogy —

> A nuclear powerplant is like a steam locomotive. The fireman
> shovels coal into the furnace, where the heat it gives off turns

the water in the boiler into steam. The steam travels through pipes to pistons, where the energy is converted and carried by driving rods to the wheels, pulling long trains of cars down the rails. Substitute a nuclear pile for the coal, a turbine for the pistons, and an electrical generator for the drive wheels, and you have a nuclear powerplant.

— then clarify the points of dissimilarity:

Of course, where in the locomotive you'd see a grimy engineer squinting at a pressure gauge with a pop-off valve, in the plant you'd see a large number of scientists and operators presiding over banks of sensors, controls, and computers, each with triple-redundancy safety telltales. The biggest difference, as we know, is that a lump of plutonium contains 240 million times the potential heat energy of a similarly sized lump of coal.

(2) Begin with a simple, even fanciful example —

"Projection" is our unconscious tendency to exaggerate in others those qualities we aren't able to accept in ourselves. An elephant and a pig got in a boat to visit some friends across the lake. Unfortunately, the vessel was too small and sank like a stone. When the wet animals pulled themselves back on shore the elephant turned to the pig and snapped, "I wish you'd lose some weight!"

— move to a more complex and realistic example —

As managers we are often guilty of projection in dealing with our employees. The boss who takes a half-day personal side trip en route to a convention may come down hard on the employee who returns from lunch five minutes late. Lecturing someone else about wasting company time fills the boss's psychological need to censure his or her own conduct.

— and finally to an example sophisticated, subtle, and complex enough for your audience to transfer to situations they may actually encounter:

One company I consulted for had repeated conflicts between the sales manager and young, attractive women he supervised. He seemed to be extremely critical of minor errors they made, while overlooking identical behavior in males and less-attractive females. The situation was dividing the department and creating a major morale problem. When I discussed this with the sales manager, he accused the young women of being "seductive" both with customers and co-workers. Instead of arguing the interpretation, I asked him, "How are *you* seductive on the job?" At first he dismissed the question as absurd, since all his superiors were males. I asked him to tell me how seductive people act. His quick rejoinder was, "They cast a spell. They substitute charm for competence. They get rewards they haven't earned." We then explored his own behavior and presently found that at the executive committee meetings his appealing sales personality often made him stand out over the department heads of accounting and marketing, who he believed worked harder and did more homework for the meetings. He felt guilty about his "undeserved" success, which he attributed to luck and charm. As we explored further the ways he *did* contribute to the executive committee and earn the respect of top management, he lost his need to punish members of his sales staff for being attractive and appealing.

(3) Use organizers to enhance comprehension.

Section **7** emphasizes the importance of systemizing ideas for economy and clarity.

Group and label the material.

The many steps in building an apartment complex can be grouped into these three phases:

One: Finding attractive sites with the proper zoning.
Two: Negotiating for the purchase of a piece of property.
Three: Contracting with architects and builders.

Use previews.

First, I'll show you how to make a simple white sauce, and then move on to three more-elaborate sauces that start with the basic recipe.

Use summaries.

So, from this short description of one novel and three of her poems, you can see once again the two themes that permeate Sylvia Plath's work.

Use acronyms.

> When you want to show empathy through nonverbal cues, remember to SOFTEN your listening style:
>
> **S**mile
> **O**pen posture
> **F**acial expression
> **T**ouch
> **E**ye contact
> **N**odding.

Use slogans, catchwords, and memorable phrases.

> So, look at those files in your drawer that you haven't used in a year, and assess their real value. Keep in mind Peg Bracken's advice about leftover food: "When in doubt, throw it out."
>
> Try to do something decisive with each piece of mail as you open it. Apply the "Four D's": **D**rop the item, **D**elay the item, **D**elegate the item, or **D**o the item.

12b. Define unfamiliar words and concepts.

We have all had the experience of listening to speakers who used so many unfamiliar terms that they might as well have been speaking in a foreign language. Although they sincerely explained the value of "controlling extraneous variance through double blinds, rotating matrices on orthogonal axes, and then storing the data on floppy disks," our minds strained for a bit, skittered across images of venetian blinds, rotating tires, women in floppy hats . . . and then retired to private fantasies. In other cases we may have had a hazy notion of the speaker's meaning but craved reassurance: regressive taxes (*poor people pay more — no — less?*); *left brain function (is that the logical side?*); deglaze the pan (*something like sauté, probably*).

There are many methods of definition you can use to save your audience from this kind of experience. Select one or more of the following, depending on which type best suits your situation.

(1) Logical Definition

Logical definition, also known as genus-species or dictionary definition, has two steps. It first places the concept to be defined into a category;

then it explains the characteristics which distinguish that concept from all other members of the category. For example:

ANTHROPOLOGY is a

Step 1	*formal field of academic study*	[not a religion or a political system or a health food]
Step 2	that studies the human species *as a whole* to develop a *comprehensive understanding of human nature and history.*	[which differentiates it from physics, sociology, biology, psychology]

Some speakers make the mistake of skipping Step 1. Listening to a description of the Spitfire as being "more effective, certainly, than the Boulton Paul Defiant, and faster and more agile than its predecessors and contemporaries," will not be enlightening if the listener is not told that the Spitfire is in the category *WWII British Fighter Aircraft*. Note that the category is fairly specific. It provides a better focus than the less-specific category *Airplane*, which can bring to mind images of everything from the Wright Flyer to a Boeing 747.

(2) Etymological and historical definition

One way to clarify a word's meaning is to explain how the word was derived, either as linked to some historical event or as drawn from root words in an older culture:

ETYMOLOGICAL

Anthropology is drawn from the Greek *anthropos*, meaning "human being," and "ology," meaning "the study of."

HISTORICAL

In 279 B.C., King Pyrrhus of Epirus defeated the Romans in a battle that decimated his forces. Looking over the battlefield afterward, he is said to have proclaimed, "Another such victory and I am undone!" *Pyrrhic victory* has come to mean any victory achieved at too high a cost.

(3) Operational definition

One way to explain a term is to tell how the object or concept referred to works or operates. Such operational definitions may simply indicate the steps that make up a process:

The *mean* is what you get when you add up all the scores and divide by the number of scores.

Logging on to the computer consists of specifying the system, giving your user ID number, and designating the form your data will take.

Social scientists use operational definitions to explain how conceptual terms are measured:

A physically active person will be defined as someone who spends at least six hours a week participating in a vigorous form of exercise.

A good supervisor will be defined as a person receiving a score of 25 or higher on the supervisor rating index.

Returning to the anthropology example, you might define the field by telling what an anthropologist does:

An anthropologist makes systematic observations about past or present human behavior and then synthesizes these observations into generalizations about human nature and history.

(4) Definition by negation

Socrates said "Nobody knows what justice is, but everyone knows what injustice is." In many cases the best way to clarify a term is to explain what it is not. Abstract notions such as fairness, clarity, and power can sometimes be better defined by describing actions that are unfair, relationships that are unclear, or people who are powerless.

Reference to opposites can be used to explain concrete terms too:

Hypogylcemia is something like the opposite of diabetes.

Anthropologists do not amass specialized data on a whim—digging for bones because they need the exercise or living among the natives because the indigenous fish are delicious.

This sort of definition can be powerful and intriguing. For a well-rounded picture, however, negation is best combined with other forms of definition.

(5) Definition by authority

This method of defining is useful for controversial or vague terms where a choice must be made among plausible alternatives. The arbiter of meaning becomes the person with the most credibility or the most power (see also **12e**).

I don't know what *you* mean by "a little late," but the boss says anything over fifteen minutes goes on your record.

Free speech cannot be suppressed unless a "clear and present danger" exists. The Supreme Court has defined it thus: "No danger flowing from speech can be deemed clear and present, unless the incidence of the evil apprehended is so imminent that it may befall before there is opportunity for full discussion. If there be time to expose through discussion the falsehood and fallacies, to avert the evil by the processes of education, the remedy to be applied is more speech, not enforced silence. Only an emergency can justify repression."

In the anthropology speech you could cite the renowned Margaret Mead:

> She characterizes anthropology as a latecomer, and an un-committed discipline that spans several fields: "It does not fall, with relentless traditionalism, into any category of science or of humanities or of social science. . . . It is in this very anomal-ousness that I believe anthropology can make a unique con-tribution to a liberal education."[1]

(6) Definition by example

Among the many supporting roles played by examples (see **12c**), defini-tion by example is a common and effective means to make terms con-crete. The speaker explains something by pointing at it, verbally or literally.

When I talk about a charismatic leader, I mean someone like John Kennedy, Martin Luther King, Jr., or Adolf Hitler.

The weapon used in Kendo is a bamboo practice sword called a *shinai*. Here is one [hefts *shinai*].

There are two basic ways to cause the strings of the guitar to vibrate: strumming, which sounds like this [strums], and picking, which sounds like this [picks].

Anthropology includes such works and studies as L. S. B. Leakey's archeological research in the Olduvai Gorge, Margaret Mead's description of sex roles of the Tchambuli society, Noam Chomsky's treatise on transformation linguistics, and Konrad Lorenz's arguments for the innateness of human aggression.

---

[1]Margaret Mead, "Anthropology and Education for the Future," in *Readings in Anthropology*, 3rd ed. Jesse D. Jennings and E. Adamson Hoebel, eds. (New York, McGraw-Hill Book Co., 1972), 3–6

Observe that the examples chosen to define anthropology were familiar and diverse, representing four distinct areas of anthropological research.

12c. Make frequent use of examples.

Few words can perk up an audience better than "Now let me give you an example." Beyond the universal appeal of a good story, examples provide the audience with a chance to check their perceptions of a speaker's message. When concepts are brought down to actual cases, the listener can see if his or her images coincide with those of the speaker.

(1) Factual examples

A fact is an assertion that is universally accepted. Sometimes it is directly verifiable, as in "Sandra Day O'Connor is a justice of the Supreme Court." Even if you were not at the swearing in, there is enough corroborative evidence from many sources to satisfy you that this is a factual statement. "The earth is 93 million miles from the sun" is another assertion accepted as a fact, although it is not *directly* verifiable through any of the five senses. We do accept it, however, because we have constructed theoretical frameworks around consistent results of observation and can make predictions of near absolute certainty. Knowing the speed of light in Einsteinian space/time, the distance of the earth from the sun can be checked with instruments that extend the senses.

Factual examples in a speech are usually short, since the assumption is that the audience already accepts them. What this means is that you may point quickly to several familiar examples. To clarify an idea you might say: "The employee benefits manager handles all of the forms of reward that are not wages — medical insurance, dental insurance, bonuses, profit-sharing plans, company scholarships, for example." To prove a proposition you would also point to familiar and accepted cases. "In the early campaigns in Virginia, the generals of the Confederacy repeatedly demonstrated superior tactics. Think, for example, of Jackson's Valley Campaign, or Lee and the Seven Days' Battles and Second Bull Run." But, obviously, these brief examples would not be effective with listeners who had never heard of profit sharing or who knew nothing of the Civil War. In such cases more detail would be needed.

(2) Extended examples

When a succession of quick references will not illuminate a point for your listeners, extend the example into an illustration:

Let's look at one example of the tactical superiority of Confederate generals: Lee's Campaign of Second Bull Run. With daring and skill, Lee kept his opponent, Pope, off balance. Lee first sent Jackson around to capture the Union base of supplies twenty miles to Pope's rear. When Pope predictably went after Jackson, Jackson eluded him. During this time Lee moved his army to put it into a position where, when Pope did finally find and attack Jackson, Lee was able to make a devastatingly decisive flank attack.

Though these scenarios take time to develop, they create vivid images that might make the point with more emphasis than shorter examples.

(3) Hypothetical examples

Sometimes, when no factual example quite suits your purpose, or when you are speculating about the future, you may choose a brief or extended hypothetical example:

How should you develop an investment portfolio? Well, let's imagine that you have a monthly household income of $4,000 and that your expenses run about $2,800. Let me show you how to calculate what portion of the remainder should go into fairly liquid low-risk areas like the money markets or short term T-bills, and what portion can go into higher-risk areas like commodities.

Picture a young woman — let's call her Katie — heading toward her car after working overtime. Because she's so tired she doesn't hear the footsteps behind her until she's some distance from the building. Katie quickens her pace . . .

Hypothetical examples do not have to be extended ones:

What would happen if this tax law were to pass? Well, Jim over there couldn't deduct his business lunches. Audrey wouldn't be able to depreciate her buildings. You, Tom, with kids about to start college . . .

Obviously, hypothetical examples cannot *prove* anything. They are useful for clarification, because they can be tailored to fit the subject exactly. Be sure to introduce them, however, so that there is no doubt in your listeners' minds that they are hypothetical.

(4) Examples used in developing an inductive line of reasoning

When examples are used to prove a point rather than just to clarify it, specific logical tests must be met. This is the essence of inductive reasoning as discussed in **11a**.

Are sufficient examples given?

To establish the point that high schools in your county are failing to provide basic literacy skills, it would hardly suffice to tell about a few functionally illiterate graduates you know personally. The more examples you give, the less likely your listeners will dismiss the phenomenon as the product of chance.

Are the examples representative?

Even if you gave a dozen examples of local graduates who were functionally illiterate, the conclusion would be suspect if all the cases were from the remedial class at one school. To be credible, examples should represent a cross section of students in the county.

Are negative instances accounted for?

Your conclusion about the failure of the schools might be countered by someone citing the example of her niece who was a National Merit

> Be aware that the examples you pick reflect a set of assumptions about the world. Be sensitive to racist or sexist implications of your illustrations. Are all the bosses men, the secretaries women; do all the laborers have Polish names and all the drunks Irish? If your examples imply you see the world in these inaccurate stereotypes, understand that some members of your audience will be offended. If, however, you believe we have a pluralistic and rapidly changing society, mix up the names, sexes, races, and roles to reflect that diversity.

Scholar or pointing out that test scores at Arbor Estates High School were above the national average. When you reason by example, you must look into and account for dramatic negative examples. Perhaps the niece has an IQ of 175. Maybe Arbor Estates High School has a cadre of charismatic English teachers. Your obligation, if you wish to carry your point, is to show how these examples are atypical, why they should be excluded from a consideration of the general status of most students in most schools in the county.

☐ **Exercise 1.** Look at the speeches in the **Appendix**. Identify instances of the techniques of clear explanation as put forth in **12a**.

☐ **Exercise 2.** Define each of these terms by at least two different methods.

Love
Collective bargaining
A tachometer
Sibling rivalry

☐ **Exercise 3.** Select two of the terms in Exercise 2 and expand on each by presenting (a) a brief factual example, (b) an extended example, and (c) a hypothetical example.

12d. Use statistical evidence to quantify, clarify, and prove your points.

When examples are systematically collected, amassed, and classified, they are reported as statistics. In the case of the literacy topic discussed in **12c(4)**, it would not be feasible to discuss, by name, all the students who illustrate your point. It would simply take too much time to give enough examples to show the seriousness of the problem. This is when you turn to statistical evidence. By examining test scores, conducting follow-up studies of graduates, or interviewing teachers, you could clarify and support your speech with material such as:

Fifty-eight percent of the seniors in our county high schools did not reach the basic proficiency level on the state reading exams.

One-third of our graduates who went to college failed freshman English.

Teachers report that one out of four students have trouble comprehending material written at the seventh-grade level.

(1) Check the validity of statistical evidence by applying the tests of *who*, *why*, *when*, *how*.

Who collected the data?

Investigate the qualifications and competence of the researchers. Was the work done by a professional pollster or the host of a call-in radio show? A graduate student or a noted scholar? An advertising agency or a government task force?

Why was the data collected?

The motivation behind collecting certain information can make the data suspect. Statistics from research done by a candidate's staff, purporting to show massive support for the candidate, may come more from a need to demoralize the opposition than a need to show a true picture to the public. Most people have more confidence in inquiries that grow out of a drive to advance knowledge. Although not totally free of bias, independent pollsters, investigative journalists, scientists, and academics are seen to be more objective than persons committed to selling a product or promoting a cause.

When was the data collected?

Be sure your evidence is up-to-date. Attitudes change as swiftly as prices these days, and sometimes data is obsolete by the time it is published. If you are dealing with a continuously active subject, like the economy, it would not hurt to consult an expert about a source for the most recent data.

How was the data collected?

Find out as much as you can about the design of the research and the details of how it was executed. If a certain statistical finding supports a key point of your speech, do not settle for a one-paragraph reference from *Psychology Today*. Track it back to the *Journal of Social and Experimental Psychology* and learn more about the original study.

First, compare definitions. You may find the title of the study promising, but a closer reading could show that the investigator defines "part-time workers" or "effective leadership" in ways that do not apply to your speech.

Check how the cases were chosen. Subjects and examples should have been selected randomly or through some other logical and unbiased system.

Evaluate the method of data collection — observation, experiment, or survey conducted by phone, mail, or personal interview. If possible, look at the actual instrument used. Are there leading questions or unrealistic forced choices in the interviews and questionnaires?

Even if you are not an expert, you can spot bias introduced into the research method, for example, through the phrasing of directions or the ways the findings are analyzed and presented.

(2) Avoid misleading statistics.

We know that language is ambiguous, but we tend to believe that numbers make straightforward statements; there is no mystery in $2+2=4$. However, numbers *can* be just as ambiguous, with statistical pitfalls to trap the unwary.

The fallacy of the average

A critic once said, with tongue in cheek, that a person could stand with one foot on a block of ice and one foot in a fire and be *statistically* comfortable. While the average is usually a useful tool for analysis, it sometimes can give a picture absurdly at odds with reality.

Less absurd, but just as misleading, might be the report that the Smurge Company has an average of twelve computer terminals per department. In fact, the Accounting Department has forty terminals, and most other departments have one or none. As this demonstrates, calculating the arithmetic *mean* is not appropriate when one or two extreme cases skew the distribution. The *median* (number or score that falls at the midpoint of the range) or the *mode* (the most frequently occurring score or number) can be more meaningful averages to use in this example, although they too can be abused.

The fallacy of the unknown base

When a speaker uses percentages and proportions, he or she can imply that a large population has been sampled. In fact, data is sometimes reported in this manner to give credence to unscientific or skimpy evidence. "Two out of three mechanics recommend this synthetic oil."

Most listeners would see this as shorthand for "we polled 300 mechanics around the country, and 200 of them recommended this synthetic oil." How valid would this recommendation seem if it came to light that in reality only *three* were polled?

"Eighty percent of the crimes in this county were committed by teenagers," seems to point to a serious problem. It certainly has more impact than "we had five burglaries this year, and four were committed by teenagers." Four instances do not make a crime wave; *80* percent is an epidemic.

The fallacy of the atypical or arbitrary timeframe

Recently an executive of a computer circuitboard company told us that sales in February had doubled over the previous month. This data could be misleading unless you knew that January is always the worst month in the yearly cycle of the small computer industry. If the executive had compared February and November, the month in the cycle where the pre-Christmas home computer and videogame buying frenzy reaches its peak, then the picture would have been quite different. A more valid comparison to demonstrate company growth would have to compare February with February of the previous year.

By choosing longer or shorter timeframes, this executive could give varying impressions of company health. If he chose November – December – January, with its sharply downward trend, he might convince employees this is no time to talk about raises. Or, he might reassure stockholders by reporting a gradual but steadily upward trend revealed by the figures from the last five Novembers.

(3) Make your numbers and statistics clear and meaningful to your listeners.

The stereotypical dry, plodding speech is the one that is overloaded with statistics. After a short while the audience becomes overloaded too and starts to build a dike against the numbers flowing over them. When you do use statistics, round them off. Say "about fifteen hundred" instead of "one thousand four hundred eighty-nine point six." Use comparisons to make the numbers more understandable:

> For the amount of money they propose to spend on this weapons system we could provide educational grants in aid to all the needy students in the eleven western states, or triple

the government funding for cancer research, or upgrade the highway system in this state and its three neighbors.

The immensity of time taxes our ability to perceive it. The universe was created 20 billion years ago; our distant mammal ancestors watched the dinosaurs die out 65 million years ago; our closer ancestors came down from the trees 20 million years ago; recorded history began a scant seven thousand years ago. Think of this in terms of a cosmic calendar: the Big Bang set off the celebration on January first. It wasn't until late on December 30th that mammals began to supplant the giant reptiles, and not until 7 P.M. on December 31st did protohumans start feeling more at home on the ground than in the trees. And recorded history did not begin until three seconds before midnight on that same day.

Avoid overused comparisons. Too many dollar bills have been laid end to end and too many large objects have improbably been dumped onto football fields or placed next to the Empire State Building. Furthermore, audiences are no longer shocked to consider the "five people in this room" who will suffer some fate, or the dire toll of outside events that will be racked up "by the end of this speech" or "by the time I finish this sentence."

☐ **Exercise 4.** What additional information would you need to have before accepting the following statistical evidence?

Studies show that over two-thirds of the total meaning a person communicates is conveyed nonverbally.

Of people who chew gum, four out of five surveyed prefer sugarless gum.

Researchers have found that the average social drinker has eight serious hangovers a year.

Dozens of cases of police harassment have been brought to my attention during my opponent's term of office.

12e. Draw on testimony from authorities.

Often we call on statements from other people to get our point across. Testimony can be looked upon as an outward extension of the speaker's own fact-finding. When we do not have the opportunity to verify something through our own senses, we rely on the observations of others. Even if you have never been arrested or never been a public safety officer, you can be credible giving a speech on the penal system, by making judicious use of testimony.

Testimony can report either experience or opinions. It might be effective to recite the events of a typical day in prison or to deliver the comments of an inmate on the surroundings. You can draw on the authority of experts or eyewitnesses. A prison riot could be described by an inmate or analyzed by a famous criminologist. Testimony may be cited directly or paraphrased. One might use a direct quotation in the following manner:

> According to a report of the Second Circuit Court of Appeals: "Beginning immediately after the state's recapture of Attica on the morning of September 13, and continuing until at least September 16, guards, state troopers, and correctional personnel had engaged in cruel and inhuman abuse of numerous inmates. Injured prisoners, some on stretchers, were struck, prodded, or beaten. Others were forced to strip and run naked through gauntlets of guards armed with clubs ... spat upon or burned with matches ... poked in the genitals or arms with sticks."[2]

Or, one might paraphrase the statement like this:

> A report of the Second Circuit Court of Appeals catalogues the cruel and inhuman abuse following the Attica riots. When the state regained control, guards and prison personnel subjected the prisoners to harsh physical punishments.

(1) Use short quotations to make ideas clear and memorable.

Certain words and phrases you hear or read are so forceful and unforgettable that you exclaim "I wish I'd said that." If they have this effect on you, they will probably affect your audience similarly. Cogent, thought-provoking quotations that summarize or analyze points you wish to present can be put to good use in your speech. However, do not let the conviction that someone has said it better than you induce you to construct a speech that is nothing more than a string of quotations.

Phrases like the following rarely serve to prove a point. Their authors may not be acknowledged experts on the topic at hand. Yet use of

---

[2]Jessica Mitford, *Kind and Usual Punishment: The Prison Business* (New York: Alfred A. Knopf, 1973, 265–66.

such citations can enhance your speech through their inspirational quality, humor, apt metaphor, or stylistic grace:

We have met the enemy, and they is us.

— Pogo Possum

I wouldn't join a club that would have me as a member.

— Groucho Marx

Even if you're on the right track, you'll get run over if you just sit there.

— Will Rogers

Technology, while adding daily to our physical ease, throws daily another loop of fine wire around our souls.

— Adlai Stevenson

(2) When you use testimony as proof, evaluate the credibility of the authorities you cite.

You do not have to research a controversial topic for very long before you find that there are seemingly authoritative quotations to cover every side of an issue. It is easy to find citations that say almost anything, but it is much more difficult to select those that really provide legitimate support for your points. Test the credibility of the authorities you quote by asking these questions:

Does the authority have access to the necessary information?

A person does not have to be famous to be an authority. The eyewitness to an accident can tell you authoritatively what happened in the intersection. Your neighbor does not have to be a China Watcher to report on a trip taken to that country. The farther removed someone is from the source, however, the less trustworthy that person's information. A quotation from the accident eyewitness is preferable to a quotation from an acquaintance telling what the eyewitness said.

Ambiguous descriptions can be misleading. "My brother works for the government and he says there's a massive conspiracy to cover up the cost overruns in the Defense Department" or "It is the opinion of a noted psychologist that the assassin is definitely insane" is testimony that loses its effect when we find that the brother is a postal clerk and the psychologist had only read the newspaper accounts of the assassin's trial. When you use an authority, be sure that the person had firsthand experience, direct observation, or personal access to relevant facts and files.

Is the authority qualified to interpret data?

As stated above, anyone can credibly describe what he or she saw. It is when a person starts making interpretations, forming opinions and conclusions, and proposing recommendations that the standards of credibility become stricter. People earn the right to be considered experts either through holding specific credentials — such as a law degree, Ph.D., Realtor's license — or by having established a record of success and experience.

Is the person acknowledged as an expert on *this* subject?

When the Washington Redskins football team executed a play suggested by then-President Nixon, we saw a peculiar variation of the practice of presenting a sports figure in commercials as an authority on nutrition or automotive engineering. President Nixon's acknowledged expertise in the field of foreign policy does not make him a credible football authority. There are other cases where an expert's opinions have subtly stretched beyond the range of his or her expertise. A tax attorney may be presented as an expert on constitutional law, a social psychologist may express an opinion on the causes of schizophrenia, or a well-known chemist may receive national attention for his views on the efficacy of vitamin C. The opinions they express may or may not be valid, but their expertise in a related field makes them, at best, only slightly more credible than an informed lay person.

Is the authority figure free of bias and self-interest?

It is not very surprising when the Chair of the Democratic National Committee characterizes the party platform as a blueprint for justice and prosperity, or if a network spokesperson describes a new television show as an incisive and intelligent portrayal of the human condition. It is not surprising, nor is it very persuasive. We would give much more credence to the opinion of a political analyst or a television critic who appears to have no personal stake, ideological or monetary, in the response to the opinion. What would be surprising, and highly persuasive as well, is reluctant testimony. If you were able to find testimony from a person speaking *against* his or her interests, presumably because of honesty or as a duty to a larger concept, then it certainly would be an effective addition to your presentation: "Even the National Committee Chair admitted that the platform is fuzzy on foreign policy."

12f. Weave supporting materials smoothly into the speech. Cite your sources.

When you have chosen appropriate definitions, facts, examples, statistics, and testimony, the challenge remains to marshal these supporting materials and present them effectively. You will want to emphasize the quality of your materials, make them clear and understandable, and organize them appropriately in relation to the points they support.

(1) Cite the sources of your supporting materials.

By giving credit for your supporting materials, you build your own credibility, showing the range of your research. You are also providing information your listeners are almost certain to want. Very few audiences will settle for "studies show ..." "one researcher found ..." "a friend once told me ..." In order to evaluate these statements, they need to know more about where the information came from.

This does not mean that you are required to present regulation footnotes in oral form, citing volume and page numbers. Nor need you recite an authority's complete biography or necessarily explain a study's design intricacies. Although you should know the *who*, *why*, *when*, and *how* of every bit of data you use, you will probably mention only a couple of these in introducing the evidence.

How then do you decide which to include? You can follow two basic suggestions. The first one encompasses those questions you predict your audience will have. Put yourself in the listeners' place and adopt a skeptical outlook: what would you question about the data? A hostile audience might want to know whether your expert was objective, a group of social scientists might be questioning whether the opinion poll you cite was scientifically conducted. The second suggestion for selecting details about a source is: stress what is most compelling and impressive. If you have a thirty-year-old quotation from a Supreme Court justice, but you think the sentiment expressed is timeless, stress the who and not the when. What is the best feature of the evidence — its recency, the large size of the sample, the prestige of the journal where it appeared?

(2) Take care, when editing quotations, to retain key points without distorting meaning.

Truncating quotations to highlight the basic thrust of the message is perfectly acceptable. What is unacceptable is editing a person's statements to such a degree that they appear to support positions other than or even opposite the actual quotation. There is the old joke about the movie critic who wrote that "the wretchedness of the acting in this film is nothing short of amazing!" only to find later that an advertisement for the movie quoted him as saying "this film . . . is amazing!"

Do not edit a source so radically that the quotation loses all substance. Virtually content-free quotations are sometimes used as a deliberate tactic to confuse listeners or to overwhelm them with an apparent preponderance of evidence. A common example of this is the recitation of the conclusion reached by an authority without including any of the reasoning that lead to the conclusion. "About the job retraining program, the mayor has said that it 'is a disappointment.' The president of the Chamber of Commerce stated that it 'has not fulfilled our expectations.' The chair of the Council of Unions labeled it 'a failure.' " The people cited may be authorities on the subject, but it is entirely possible that their reservations result from an analysis that is not at all pertinent to the speaker's point. For instance, they may all be complaining of inadequate funding rather than attacking the concept of the program. It is impossible to tell from these cryptic quotations. It is also possible that these experts could be wrong. A listener would need to hear more about *why* they drew the conclusions they did.

(3) Use a variety of lead-ins for stylistic effectiveness.

Do not get into the habit of introducing all your illustrations, or all your statistics, and so on, with the same phrase. "Some figures about this are . . . some figures about that are . . ." Be prepared enough that you can employ a number of different lead-ins for each kind of supporting material. There are many possibilities, such as:

To support this idea . . .
This point is verified by . . .
_____ put it well, I think, when she said . . .
In the words of _____ , . . .
What causes this situation? One answer to that question was offered by _____ when he wrote last year . . .
Let me tell you about a survey taken in the early fifties by a Brandeis psychologist . . .
There are several examples of this. Let me share just two . . .
I was immediately struck by the similarity to an experience I/she/_____ once had . . .

However you decide to introduce a quotation, do not say "quote, unquote," or wiggle pairs of index and middle fingers in the air to approximate quotation marks. A subtle change in your voice or posture is enough to indicate to your listeners the boundaries of a direct quotation.

☐ **Exercise 5.** Compare the use of supporting materials in the four speeches in the **Appendix**. Note the presence of explanation, definition, examples, statistics, and testimony in each.

Does every speech use a variety of methods?
What are the two favored forms of supporting material
    in the Huxtable speech?
    in the Sprague speech?
    in the Cunningham speech?
    in the Postman speech?

13

Visual Aids

Use visual aids appropriately and effectively.

There are places in a speech where a visual aid can help you make a point more clearly and in a shorter time than if you were forced to use words alone. Conversely, visual aids poorly used or overused can make your ideas obscure and slow the pace of your speech. Too heavy a reliance on visual aids will cut into time that should be spent on analysis or development of points and ideas.

A visual aid is best used in two places: when you are attempting to explain a complex or technical idea, and when you want to reinforce a particular message. For example, a geneticist might find it useful to have a model of the DNA double helix when talking how that remarkable molecule duplicates itself. Or, the speaker wishing to impress upon his

> Some speaking situations have protocols that demand a particular visual aid, regardless of subject or speaker. Specifically, a number of companies require that any person giving a report outline that report on posterboard or blackboard. We don't find this practice appealing or especially useful. It vitiates any climactic sequence the speaker's ideas and conclusions may have, while patently insulting the intelligence of the audience.

or her audience the importance of stiffer drunk-driving penalities may choose to reinforce a recitation of traffic fatality percentages with a "pie" graph that demonstrates the overwhelming predominance of drunk-driving over lesser causes of traffic deaths.

13a. Select a visual aid appropriate to the point you wish to illustrate or clarify.

We can put visual aids into three categories.

(1) The object or a physical reproduction of it

While demonstrating the superior simplicity of a new lens-to-camera attachment system, a speaker can put force behind his or her words by using the actual camera and lens to show the ease of coupling. It would take many more words by themselves to convey the same message. With a large audience, however, this sort of demonstration might not work, because of the smallness of the equipment. In this case, the speaker could use larger-than-life-size models to make sure the message was clear. Other objects are obviously too small or large to use, like a microchip or the actual *Queen Mary*, so scaled-up or scaled-down reproductions are necessary.

There are other considerations when deciding between an object and its reproduction. Most audiences (other than groups of medical professionals) would be grateful if the speaker explained valve structures and their functions by using a plastic replica of a human heart rather than the real thing.

(2) Pictorial reproductions

These can include photographs, sketches, plans, pictures, slides, film clips, videotapes, and the like. If the mechanical device that makes the lens-camera coupling so easy is in itself complex, perhaps the speaker would use an "exploded" three-quarter-view schematic drawing to show the interaction of all the pieces. A large photograph of the human heart may be preferred by the speaker wishing to show the musculature. As in **(1)**, size of object and size of audience are important factors in determining which to use.

FIGURE 13-1

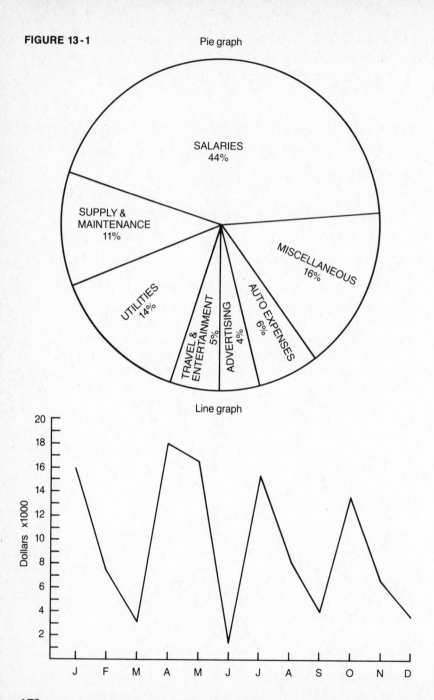

Pie graph

Line graph

Bar graph

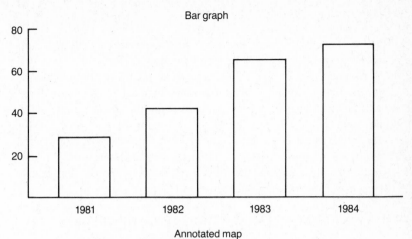

Annotated map

Slogan or memorable phrase

THE "FOUR D's"

Drop it
Delay it
Delegate it
Do it

(3) Pictorial symbols

These are used with more abstract concepts and can include graphs, charts, diagrams, and lists of important words and phrases.

Bringing a derelict in off the street would probably get an audience's attention, but it would not be as useful, when speaking on the declining state of the economy, as a line graph showing the buying power of the dollar through the last two decades. An aerial photograph of San Jose would not be as appropriate to a speech on local politics as would a map showing city council district boundaries. If a speaker wants a motto, inspirational phrase, or name of a product reinforced, then suitably lettered posters can help. (See Figure 13-1.)

13b. Prepare clear and manageable visual aids.

(1) Prepare visual aids large enough to be seen by the entire audience.

The nature of the place in which you will be speaking and, as stated in **13a(1)**, the size of the audience determine to a great extent the type and size of visual aid. It will help to look over the facility in advance, if that is possible. Stand at the back of the room and envision the scene, or, if you already have a rough mock-up or draft of one of your aids, place it where you expect it to be when you speak. Obviously, if the aid is too small you will need to enlarge it. One option is to design transparencies to show on an overhead projector. Reduce any aid that is larger than it need be, considering the size of the room, or is so unwieldy you will have to wrestle with it.

Lines on charts should be thick and bold. Model parts should be large enough to be distinguished. Screens for slides or film strips should be large enough for the size of the room, and projectors should have focal lengths great enough to fill the screen.

(2) Keep your visual aids simple and clear.

Do not construct overelaborate aids. They should contain just enough detail to allow your listeners to distinguish easily one part from another. Look at the two cut-away drawings of an airplane in Figure 13-2. The one on the right would be the better one to use if you wanted to demonstrate the hydraulic system. It provides information on where the hydraulic system is in relation to the rest of the airplane, without subjecting the

FIGURE 13-2

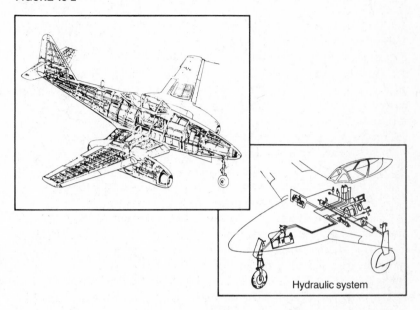

Hydraulic system

audience to the eyestrain of trying to distinguish it from the fuel system, control system, structural members, and so on. Similarly, do not crowd maps, charts, graphs, models, and photographs with so much data that your audience ends up confused about which part you are referring to. For instance, you should have one map showing only city council districts and another only county supervisorial districts in the city. Avoid having so many lines on a line graph that an audience will "take a wrong turn" while following one line across. For photographs, try to find one that shows the object in isolation, or in sharp focus in relation to other objects.

Keep the wording on any visual aid simple and familiar, printed in clear block lettering. Use no more words than strictly necessary to label parts and ideas.

Maintain continuity when you spread your information out. If you have used a pie graph for your first aid, any following aids dealing with similar or related information should also be pie graphs.

Use color to delineate different aspects of the object or symbol. A large model heart with bright blue, red, and yellow parts may not look totally realistic, but the audience will find it a lot easier to keep the parts separate in their minds as they follow the explanation.

(3) Design visual aids for maximum audience impact.

The design and form of your visual aids can sometimes enhance your credibility, add humor, provide information beyond the data presented, or just maintain the interest level of your listeners.

A professional-looking aid can do much to lend a polished tone to an entire speech. You need not hire a professional to prepare one, however. Art supply stores stock transfer letters, stencils, colored plastic in various geometric forms — all sorts of simple graphic materials that even the unartistic can use to produce a neat and attractive visual aid.

Basic, unexotic colors are best to use, unless there is a color that is popularly associated with the object or idea being depicted. And, of course, there are standard uses, like green for forests, blue for water, red for Soviet arms spending, and so on.

Along this line, you can construct your visual aids in a manner that underscores the theme of your speech. Consider, for instance: instead of using bar graphs to indicate yearly differences in logging revenues, substitute tree outlines with the proper relative dimensions. Or, compare rows of objects — houses, missiles, stick figures with dunce caps — where each object represents a certain number of housing starts, strategic warheads, or failing high school students. A particularly subtle way of using visual material to drive home a verbal message was demonstrated by President Reagan when he went on television to present his tax plan to the American public. He displayed a line graph depicting the projected government spending that would result from his plan and the spending that would result from his opponents' plan, explaining it by saying, "Our plan, shown here by the *solid* line . . ." and ". . . the Democrats' proposal, which is the dotted line . . ." Using a solid line on the graph invested his position with the semblance of stability and careful planning, while the insubstantial dotted line represented the lightweight, disjointed thinking of the opposition.

13c. Introduce your visual aids so that they blend smoothly into the speech.

(1) Practice with your visual aids.

Your aids should be prepared early enough that you can practice with them several times. See **21d**. This will alert you to any changes that might be necessary. Become comfortable with them so you do not fumble around during the presentation.

(2) Maintain eye contact.

Be so familiar with your material that you can look at your listeners while explaining the visual aid. Often a speaker will turn his or her back on the audience and talk directly at the visual aid. This deprives the speaker of feedback and will strain the listeners' hearing.

(3) Keep talking.

Avoid long pauses when demonstrating a process. If there is some complexity, or if many steps are needed to produce your desired result, you might be wise to take a hint from television cooking shows and prepare a series of aids to demonstrate various phases. Doing this will eliminate those periods where both you and the audience are waiting for something to happen. For example, a speaker could say: "Then you apply glue to the two blocks, press them together like this, and let the bond dry. Here are some that have already dried, and I'll show you the next step . . ." When you cannot avoid a time lag introduced by some process, have a planned digression — some bit of history related to the process, perhaps — to fill the gap.

(4) Do not let your visual aids become a distraction.

Keep your visual aids covered, out of sight, or turned away from your audience until you are ready to use them. Remove or recover them immediately after they have served their purpose.

Refrain from passing objects through the audience, as that will cause a ripple of inattention over the next few minutes. This rule is flexible, especially when you are dealing with an unusual object and a small audience, but still it is probably best to share the item *after* the speech, say during the discussion period. By the same token, handouts should be distributed after a speech. You want the audience to listen now and read later.

Finally, visual aids are most distracting when you are clumsy with them. Be sure your charts are in the right order, your models are set up, your equipment is in perfect working order. Avoid visual aid fiascoes by practicing carefully, arriving in plenty of time for setup, and being pessimistic enough to carry with you pins, tape, extension cords, extra projector bulbs, and the like to ensure that what you envision will come to pass.

☐ **Exercise 1.**   Suggest three different kinds of visual aids that might be used for speeches on each of these topics:

Herbs and spices
How a check is processed
The workings of a lock
Instituting mandatory national service

☐ **Exercise 2.**   Rank order the four speeches in the **Appendix** by the need for visual aids. Justify your decision in terms of audience, occasion, and topic. If you decide that visual aids would complement some of the speeches, recommend what kinds of aids, and indicate where in the speech they should go.

14

Motivational Appeals

Motivate your listeners toward your speech purpose through appeals to their emotions, needs, and values. Be sure that these appeals supplement, but do not replace, the sound logic and evidence upon which you base your speech.

This book stresses the role of clear analysis in support of ideas, but it also emphasizes making those ideas meaningful to an audience. A good speaker is constantly aware of the humanness of the audience. To be human is to be rational, but it is more than that. Love sometimes over-rules logic, reverence transcends reason, emotion contradicts evidence. Understanding the humanity of your audience means reaching them as total persons—packaging your essentially logical case so that it touches the listeners' feelings, needs, and values.

14a. When developing the content of your speech, be conscious of the emotional impact you want to create or avoid.

Keep in mind that everything you say has the potential to trigger some sort of emotional response in your audience. Generally, you can strengthen your speech by selecting main points, supporting material, and language that can engage your listeners' feelings. Positive emotions—hope, joy, pride, love—are surefire motivators. Negative emotions like fear, envy, disgust, and contempt can also motivate; witness the popularity of roller coasters and horror films. The motivational effects of negative emotions are less predictable, however, and can sometimes boomerang. Research on fear appeals, for example, shows that moderate levels of fear appeal enhance persuasion, but higher levels work against the desired effect. Some presentations feature gory films of traffic accidents, vivid visual aids showing cancerous lung tissue, or detailed description of the plight of a family whose breadwinner had no insurance. These either cause the audience to tune out the unpleasantness or just seem too extreme to be statistically plausible fates for the listener to worry about. When adding emotion to your speech, remember the old adage, "although some is good, more is not always better."

DEVOID OF EMOTION

A dose of 600 rems produces acute radiation illness. Japanese A-bomb victims experienced a variety of physical symptoms and usually died within two weeks of exposure.

MODERATE EMOTION

A dose of 600 rems or more produces acute radiation illness. Thousands of Japanese A-bomb victims died from this sickness within two weeks of the bomb explosions. Such exposure to radiation kills all actively dividing cells in the body: hair falls out, skin is sloughed off in big ulcers, vomiting and diarrhea occur, and then, as the white blood cells and platelets die, victims expire of infection and/or massive hemorrhage.[1]

EXCESSIVE EMOTION

The bomb has fallen, and you're unlucky enough not to have been killed immediately. There's nothing you can do except sit there dumbly, in your own vomit and excrement, while the omnipresent radiation kills off the process of life. With no cell growth, your skin becomes leprous and detaches from your body in great clumps; but you don't notice because your white blood cells have died and dark swelling has overtaken all of your body, immersing you in a pain that will not subside until a weakened artery in your brain bursts in a final geyser of black blood.

On any topic there are these three levels. What you have to do very early is discern where your audience draws the dividing lines. Try to include the optimal amount of emotional appeal — not so little that you fail to touch them, not so much that you turn them off.

---

[1]Helen Caldicott, *Nuclear Madness* (Brookline, Mass.: Autumn Press, 1978), 29.

14b. Relate your speech to the needs of your listeners.

The most well-known way of classifying human needs is the hierarchy devised by Abraham Maslow.[2] See Figure 14-1.

In this hierarchy the lower needs have to be met or satisfied before an individual can become concerned with the needs on the next-higher level. For instance, if speaking on the topic of physical fitness, you could appeal to your audience at any of the following levels:

- The effect of exercise in reducing cardiovascular disease appeals to the survival need.
- Security might be drawn in by mentioning how physically fit people are more likely to be able to resist attackers.
- The need for belonging can be linked to becoming trim and attractive as well as making friends through physical activity.
- Esteem needs can be tied into the current popularity of fitness and the social desirability of an active image.
- Finally, a speaker might relate fitness to the need for self-actualization—the highs of exercise, the mental and physical challenge of reaching one's potential.

The significance of Maslow's hierarchy to the speaker is apparent. You must analyze your audience well enough to determine which need is most salient for them. Listeners whose jobs are in danger and who are

**FIGURE 14-1
MASLOW'S HIERARCHY**

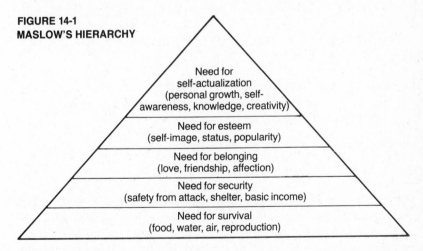

Need for
self-actualization
(personal growth, self-
awareness, knowledge, creativity)

Need for esteem
(self-image, status, popularity)

Need for belonging
(love, friendship, affection)

Need for security
(safety from attack, shelter, basic income)

Need for survival
(food, water, air, reproduction)

---

[2]Abraham Maslow, *Motivation and Personality*, 2nd ed. (New York: Harper & Row, 1970), 35–58.

struggling to feed their families do not want to hear you contrast local economic programs in terms of the implications drawn from Keynesian theory. They want to know which one will create jobs — being absorbed with their security needs, they are not likely to respond at the self-actualization level.

It is ineffective to aim your emotional appeals too high. It is unethical to aim your appeals too low. Take a speaker who wants to convince colleagues to adopt a different software system than the one currently in use in that department. If the company is healthy and the colleagues are satisfactory employees, then it would be inappropriate to use a fear appeal with visions of the organization going out of business and people being tossed into the street if the new system is not adopted. The more ethical approach would be to build a case related to the colleagues' needs for efficiency, productivity, success, and prestige (esteem and self-actualization levels).

To be fair, you should respond to existing needs, not create a new and artificial sense of insecurity in your listeners. Speakers who abuse their influence in this way falsely assume that the most primitive needs are the strongest. We disagree. Altruism is an extremely effective motivator. In fact, we might place another pyramid beside Maslow's, illustrating our belief that every person has a basic need to *protect* others' survival, to *give* security, to *spread* love, to *build* esteem, to *nurture* self-actualization. Appeals to the idealistic, caring sides of human nature can be at least as powerful as self-oriented appeals.

14c. Relate your speech to the values of your listeners.

When, in a presentation, you use the argument "and this procedure will speed up your assembly line," you are actually unveiling only a part of the following syllogism:

Anything that speeds up your assembly line is good.
This procedure will speed up your assembly line.
Therefore, this procedure is good.

You assume that your listeners share increasing production speed as a value, and as a result, you do not feel it is necessary to burden your talk with the other parts of the syllogism. As it turns out, however, these particular listeners are currently satisfied with the speed of production, but are more concerned with the accuracy of assembly. A little audience analysis could have alerted you to the fact and you might have worked from the following syllogism:

Anything that improves accuracy is good.
This procedure improves accuracy.
Therefore, this procedure is good.

Both arguments are logically sound (and, we hope, both are true), but the second is psychologically more effective because its underlying premise reflects the dominant value of the listeners.

We hold a certain value if we believe that a particular thing is either good or bad, in the broadest sense of those terms. Specifically, we *evaluate* concepts, people, objects, events, or ideas every day as we label them just or unjust, wise or foolish, beautiful or ugly, and so on. Whereas emotions and needs are considered to be innate (and therefore consistent across cultures, societies, and individuals), values are judgments or choices made by individuals. Looking at two people in isolation we could predict that they both feel fear and the need for status, just on the basis of their humanness. We could not easily predict if one hated homosexuals or if the other was a passionate supporter of the free enterprise system.

(1) Incorporate appeals to the general values of the culture.

Although values are individually chosen, the choice is not often a totally conscious and rational one. Culture has a strong influence, shaping values through families, schools, media, and peers. Moreover, values are rarely formed in isolation; they are organized and structured into related clusters. By knowing the culture of your listeners, the influences on them, and perhaps some of the other values they hold, you can make an educated guess how much particular values might shape their attitude toward your speech topic.

Look at the results of one study that classifies the positive values held by residents of the United States.[3]

1. Puritan and pioneer morality: tendency to view the world in moral terms as good or bad, ethical or unethical.
2. Value of the individual: primacy of individual welfare in governmental and interpersonal relationships.

---

[3]Edward Steele and W. Charles Redding, "The American Value System: Premises for Persuasion," *Western Speech* 26, 1962: 83–91.

3. Achievement and success: primary desirability of material wealth and success; secondary desirability of success and achievement in vocations, professions, social service, etc.
4. Change and progress: widespread belief that society is progressing and developing toward better things and in change as an index of progress.
5. Ethical equality: ideal of spiritual equality for all in the eyes of God; closely related to equality of opportunity promised in part by free public education.
6. Effort and optimism: obsession with the importance of work; hopeful, optimistic effort will cause all obstacles to yield.
7. Efficiency, practicality, and pragmatism: higher regard for practical thinkers and doers than for artists and intellectuals.
8. Rejection of authority: freedom from restraints by government or society.
9. Science and secular rationality: faith in human reasoning and its power to understand an ordered universe.
10. Sociality: getting along, making contacts, being friendly.
11. Material comfort: desire for personal possessions, consumer goods, pleasure, and entertainment.
12. Quantification: tendency to equate value with size or number.
13. External comformity: desire to be like others, to be accepted as one of the group.
14. Humor: poking fun at oneself and at authority.
15. Generosity and considerateness: humanitarian concern for underprivileged, spontaneous helpfulness in crisis.
16. Patriotism: good citizenship, pride in the U.S., willingness to serve and defend country.

Sometimes identifying values in your own culture can be extremely difficult. With the constant currents of change, predominant values and trends often do not become clarified until a decade later, much too late to do a speaker any good. However, there is always at least one writer or commentator who captures the essence of the changes while they are occurring. Your audience analysis will be enriched by awareness of the changes in mainstream values caused by economic and technical trends, countercultural movements, and liberation movements. In recent decades our understanding of subtle changes in the texture of the American value system has been enhanced by such books as Sloan Wilson's *The Man in the Gray Flannel Suit*, Marshall McLuhan's *The Gutenberg Galaxy*, Betty Friedan's *The Feminine Mystique*, Charles A. Reich's *The Greening of America*, Alvin Toffler's *Future Shock*, Christopher Lash's *The Culture of Narcissism*, or Arnold Mitchell's *The Nine American Lifestyles*.

Read new works by such social philosophers, or at least read detailed reviews of them. Pay attention to the editorial writers and news commentators that help you get a clearer picture of the "national mood." Be aware that many public opinion polls on specific issues like abortion, school prayer, capital punishment, and women's rights contain a few questions specifically addressed to values. One resource for poll information is the Inter-University Consortium for Political and Social Research (ICPSR) databank in Ann Arbor, Michigan. See **4b**.

(2) Identify and relate to the core values of your audience.

If the members of a culture share common values, why do we not see lockstep agreement on every issue? Obviously, not all members of a culture give equal importance to the common values, nor is there a standard ranking of them. Values are very general, and any particular issue can touch on many values, both on the pro side and the con side. An example of this value conflict can be seen in the controversy over prayer in public schools. A person may be drawn toward school prayers as a result of holding the value of *pioneer morality*, but this individual may also have reservations about prayer legislation, because of belief in the *value of the individual* and *rejection of authority*. The resolution of this conflict is a function of how he or she has prioritized these values.

Because nearly every topic stirs up such value conflicts, a list of audience values would not be useful unless it were supplemented by some estimate of the relative ranking. One way to map this prioritizing is to imagine a series of concentric circles, with the deepest-held values at the *core*, the degree of importance of the other values determining their distance from the center. (See Figure 14-2.) The innermost circle contains *core values*, the ones so central to a person that to change one of them would amount to a basic alteration of that person's self-concept. The next band out from the center contains the *authority values*, the values that are influenced by and shared with groups and individuals most significant to the person. *Peripheral values* form the outer band.[4] These are the more-or-less incidental evaluations, easily made or changed.

Say that over the course of several political campaigns Rodney developed a distaste for the kind of content-free commercials that are normally done. This value, though peripheral, can be strong enough to influence Rodney's voting behavior in contests where, other things being equal, he has not taken a position. Other things are rarely equal, though. In a race between a Republican who uses content-free commercials and a non-Republican who does not, Rodney's values would come into conflict.

---

[4]This approach to values is adapted from Milton Rokeach's method of classifying beliefs by their centrality. Milton Rokeach, in collaboration with Richard Bonier and others, *Open and Closed Mind* (New York: Basic Books, 1960).

FIGURE 14-2

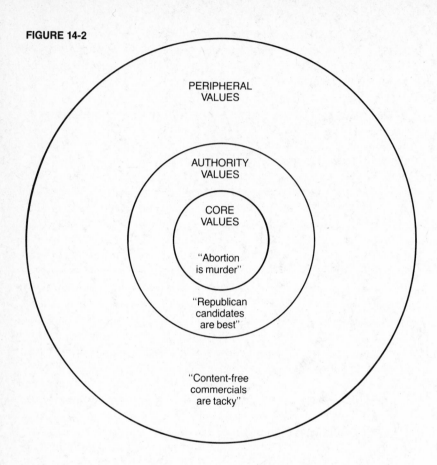

PERIPHERAL
VALUES

AUTHORITY
VALUES

CORE
VALUES

"Abortion
is murder"

"Republican
candidates
are best"

"Content-free
commercials
are tacky"

Since his preference for Republican candidates is tied to an authority value and therefore closer to the core than a peripheral value like esthetic dislike of content-free commercials, he would normally resolve this conflict in favor of the Republican. However, the non-Republican opponent supports a constituional ban on abortion while the Republican views such an amendment as an unwarranted government imposition on the individual. Rodney's opposition to abortion is one of his most deeply held moral principles. Again, he would experience conflict, but would resolve it in favor of the core value over the authority value—to do otherwise would require a thorough rethinking and reevaluation of his ethical system.

Understanding this, you should try to make reasonable inferences about your listeners' core values and stress them in your speech or presentation. For example, suppose you have an educational innovation you would like the local school system to adopt. In speaking to the school board, you might stress the values of practicality, efficiency, and local control of education. In speaking to the teachers, you might stress the more idealistic value of progress in education. While your approach in these two cases is different, this does not mean you assumed teachers are impractical or that school board members care nothing about educational progress. The members of both groups probably hold each of these values. However, as a speaker you made a decision to stress those values that are likely to be closer to the core in each audience.

(3) Forge strong, logical links between the issues of your speech and the values of the audience.

The *issues* of your speech are the questions that must be resolved in your listeners' minds before your speech purpose can be met. See **2b**. Decisions about what is worth knowing, what should be done, or what touches our spirit, often depend on the prior acceptance of certain values. Not only do people differ in what values they hold and how they prioritize them, but people also differ in how they perceive connections between particular values and particular issues. Even when listeners share almost identical values and priorities, it is possible for them to perceive links differently. Take two audience members who value crea-

Issue	Obvious value links	Less-obvious, but probably valid, value links
Equality for women & minorities	Justice, fairness, compassion	Increased productivity, avoiding waste, patriotism (world image)
Buying a word processor	Efficiency, speed, scientific advancement	Creativity, expressiveness, economy (in the long run)
Deregulate small business	Lack of government interference, pioneer spirit of small entrepreneur	Honesty, trust of fellow citizens, dislike of red tape & paperwork
Welcome delegation of foreign businesspersons	International harmony, U.S. hospitality, pooling of information	Efficiency, progress, pragmatism

tive freedom and efficiency, with efficiency being closer to the core. If your issue were the abolition of tenure, one listener might link that issue to creative freedom and be antagonistic to your speech goal, while the other might link it to efficiency and look upon your proposal favorably. It is not enough, then, to know what values your audience holds. You must try to discover which values they see linked to your topic. Often you will need to spell out for them new issue-value links that are logical but perhaps not readily apparent. As you prepare a speech, draw out as many *valid* links to values as you can discover. One of the less-obvious ones may be just the connection that strikes through to a core value.

14d. Avoid excessive and inappropriate use of emotional appeals.

Throughout this section we promote the effective use of appeals to the emotions, needs, and values of your listeners. We must end with a caution about the overuse and misuse of these appeals. A speech with too much emphasis on feelings can embarrass and offend the audience. If these listeners perceive that the speaker is playing on their emotions to the exclusion of sense and logic, they can become infuriated. It is always a mistake to underestimate the intelligence of an audience.

Aside from the issue of effectiveness (advertisers and politicians show us that many times these appeals *can* be effective), there is the question of ethics. For centuries the mainstream rhetorical tradition has been that the speaker's first responsibility is to present a logically sound, well-documented argument. If you agree with this ideal, then you will not be tempted to substitute pseudological emotional appeals for the logical foundation of your speech. Appeals to your listeners' feelings are legitimate ways to support and emphasize your points. But when these appeals cease to be secondary to sound reasoning, you then enter the realm of propoganda. Some years ago a group of journalists offered the following as the seven most common propaganda devices.[5]

(1) Name calling

By attaching a negative label to an idea or person, a speaker can raise fear or hatred in an audience. Highly charged words such as "sexist," "communistic," and "unprofessional" are used to short-circuit a listener's

---

[5]Alfred McClung Lee, and Elizabeth Briant Lee, *The Art of Propaganda* (New York: Harcourt, Brace & Company and Institute for Propaganda Analysis, 1939), 23–24.

critical faculty. The speaker hopes this tide of emotion will gloss over the lack of substance to his or her position. See **11e(1)**.

(2) Glittering generalities

At the other extreme is the creation of a positive response to a concept or statement through the use of words or phrases that represent some abstract virtue. This technique attempts to convert listeners, not on the merits of a position, but because adopting the position would be patriotic, or good for motherhood and such.

(3) Testimonials

Another way to generate positive emotions is to link a popular figure with some cause or product. Here sound argument is replaced by the inappropriate extension of a person's credibility. An actor may become admired in his role as a doctor, but when he is used to endorse a headache remedy, he is way beyond his qualifications and the testimonial is based on a misleading impression.

(4) Plain folks

It is fine to build identification with your audience so that they will be receptive to your ideas. This process goes too far, though, when the speaker implies: "You should believe me, not because of the inherent validity of what I say, but because I'm just like you." Some examples of the we-are-all-plain-folks-here-together technique are the politician whose entire platform is "I'm just a farmboy myself," or the speaker who discounts the theories and findings of educational psychologists on the grounds that "those of us who are parents know how kids really are." This device is often anti-intellectual in that it makes an unwarranted distinction between the "common sense" of the audience and the hare-brained reasoning of experts, academics, and opponents in general.

(5) Card stacking

In this method a speaker carefully uses only facts or examples that bolster his or her position, and the highly biased selection is passed off as representative. An opponent of hiring more police officers might stress accounts of police sexual misconduct and reports of pilferage of confiscated drugs, and ask: "Do we want to spend money to put *more* of that kind of person in positions of responsibility?"

(6) Bandwagon

This technique is useful to a speaker who wishes to discourage independent thinking. The "everyone is doing it" approach appeals to the need for security, and plays on fears of being different or left out. Speakers frequently cite public opinion polls to support their position. The fact that many people are in favor of some proposal does not necessarily make it right. A proposition should be sold on its merits, not its popularity.

(7) Transfer

To make some unfamiliar thing more acceptable (or less acceptable) to an audience, many speakers will ascribe to it characteristics of something familiar. Often there is no true relationship between the two. For example, a local perennial candidate's last name is the same as a famous golf professional, and although this candidate does not play the game, he always files with "Golf" as his nickname on the ballot. Characterizing video game arcades as a "cancer spreading through our society" plays on the knowledge that probably every audience member has had firsthand or secondhand experience with that fearsome disease.

☐ **Exercise 1.** Which needs are appealed to in each of these examples?

a. Following the dress-for-success formula has helped countless people advance in their careers.
b. Unless we develop this weapons system we will no longer have nuclear parity with the Soviet Union.
c. Meditation will enhance your understanding of the universe.
d. Some of the marijuana available on the street is laced with deadly chemicals.
e. This shampoo makes your hair more touchable.

☐ **Exercise 2.** Identify at least three appeals to needs in each speech in the **Appendix**.

☐ **Exercise 3.** It has been a few decades since the list of positive values in **14c(1)** was formulated. How closely does it reflect the value system of the United States as you see it today? Which of the values have remained the most salient? Which would you delete or revise? What new ones, if any, would you add?

☐ **Exercise 4.** Identify at least three appeals to values in each speech in the **Appendix**.

☐ **Exercise 5.** Analyze the audience in your speech class or another audience you speak to regularly in terms of their probable responses to a speech on the problems of mental illness.

What needs could you appeal to?
What core values could you appeal to?
What authority values could you appeal to?
What new value-issue links could you forge?

☐ **Exercise 6.** Do you find examples of propaganda devices in any of the speeches in the **Appendix**? Do you find any examples of motivational appeals that strike you as excessive or in poor taste?

15

Attention and Interest

Adapt your speech material so it will capture your listeners' attention and retain their interest.

Think back to your most recent walk through a department store. Did you notice every single display, each ten feet from the last and all competing for your attention? Or did you pass most without a flicker, being brought to a halt by a few that drew you to them through color, or movement, or contrast, or an unusual juxtaposition of images?

Some attention factors are universal, and some are more idiosyncratic. Such things as sudden movement or bright color would catch almost anyone's eye, but *you* might stop by snow tires while you friend looks at computer games. Or you might linger in the food department on a day you are hungry, but rush by it on another day when your thoughts are on the fact that you have no luggage for the trip you wish to take.

Why is it that some things always catch attention and others will be noticed only by some people or only in some situations? And of the thousands of things that receive momentary notice, what causes a few to be chosen for closer scrutiny? As a public speaker, you can profit from giving some thought to questions like these. After all, when you give a speech or presentation your words are competing for attention with every other sight and sound in the room and with every daydream or concern in the mind of each listener. The better you understand the psychology of attention, the more likely you will receive the compliment most sought for and appreciated by speakers: a sincere and simple "That was an interesting speech!"

15a. Engage your audience's attention by making extensive use of techniques that enliven your speech.

A common misconception is that once you have grabbed your listeners' attention with a snappy introduction, that attention is yours until you relinquish it at the end of the speech. Unfortunately, it takes more than a clever opening to keep an audience listening. Adults are distracted nearly as easily as children. Unless reengaged, their minds may wander off every half minute or so. When composing a speech, take every opportunity to weave in materials and to phrase statements characterized by the factors that have been identified as most likely to gain attention. These are:

1. Activity or movement
2. Reality
3. Proximity
4. Familiarity
5. Novelty
6. Suspense
7. Conflict
8. Humor
9. The Vital[1]

People are intrigued by things that are unusual or spark their curiosity. Paradoxically, they also respond to well-known, everyday references. Most of all, as in the case of the vital, people attend to material they see as connected to their own self-interest. Do not worry about using plenty of these. Think of all the speeches you have heard labeled dull or boring. Did you ever hear a complaint that a lecture was too fascinating? The use of these factors can be made second nature without much effort or time.

NOT: A college athlete might be having trouble in one of his classes.

BUT: Suppose Larry Linebacker can't tell the difference between Bizet and "The Bizarroes" in his Music Appreciation class. (Humor, Reality, Familiarity)

[1]Douglas Ehninger, Alan H. Monroe, and Bruce E. Gronbeck, *Principles and Types of Speech Communication*, 8th ed. (Glenview, Ill,: Scott, Foresman and Company, 1980), 142–158.

NOT: Many oil companies decided to dismantle their credit card systems or provide discounts for cash sales in an attempt to lower costs and attract customers.

BUT: Driving into the gas station just down the street I noticed some bright, new stickers on the pumps. As I pumped fuel into the car, I read them with some curiosity. When I saw that one told of a five-cent discount per gallon for paying with cash rather than a credit card, I immediately dug into my purse to see just how many loose bills I had . . . (Activity, Proximity, The Vital)

NOT: The residents of Fremont, California, many of them unemployed auto workers, followed the negotiations between Toyota and GM with great interest.

BUT: The unemployed auto workers talked about the GM-Toyota negotiations everywhere — at home, at the store, in the corner tavern. Would the negotiations lead to the reopening of the Fremont plant? If it opened, would it be all robots? If the workers were rehired, would they have to sing company songs and attend quality circles? (Conflict, Suspense, The Vital, Reality)

NOT: When time is short, a good executive takes action first and then worries about causes, procedure, and policy.

BUT: If I told you people in the fourth and fifth rows that that chandelier's going to fall in ten seconds, what would you do? Darn right! You'd get out of the way! Later, we'd talk about why it happened, whose fault it was, and how to fix it. (Proximity, Novelty, Suspense, Reality)

Be guided by the following principles as you incorporate attention factors into your speech:

(1) Use materials that are concrete and close to home.

Examples are always more interesting when they are specific and real. Notice how these paragraphs from a speech by Edward Kennedy create pictures in your mind — more tangible and believable than vague references to "the victims of our economic crisis."

> I have listened and learned.
> I have listened to Kenny Dubois, a glassblower in Charleston, West Virginia, who has ten children to support, but has lost his job after 35 years, just three years short of qualifying for his pension.
> I have listened to the Trachta family, who farm in Iowa and wonder whether they can pass the good life and the good earth on to their children.
> I have listened to a grandmother in East Oakland, who no

> longer has a phone to call her grandchildren because she gave
> it up to pay the rent on her small apartment.
>   I have listened to. . . .[2]

Never say "a person" or "one" if you can give a name. Use well-known figures, members of the audience, or hypothetical characters. Use place names, brand names, dates, details.

(2) Keep your audience involved.

A popular lecturer once went blank on an example he frequently used. "What's the name of that Marquette basketball coach?" he mused out loud. Thirty voices called out "Al McGuire!" Noticing how attentive the people in the front row remained after that, he made it a practice always to forget one detail early in a speech. He analyzed the listener response to be "I had better stay awake in case he needs my help again." While we do not recommend always using a technique quite this contrived, it does illustrate the importance of creating an active rather than passive role for your audience. Even though it is your show when you speak, you can still stimulate a sense of interaction in your listeners. Use audience participation techniques. Ask for shows of hands if pertinent, have them provide examples, ask questions of them.

> How many people here had breakfast this morning? Ah, I see
> about half of you raised your hands. What did you have, sir?
> Bacon and eggs? Over there? Coffee and a donut. I hear juice
> and toast, yeast shake, Cheerios, and yogurt. Would anyone
> care to hazard an answer to this question? What percentage
> of elementary school students go to school with no breakfast
> at all?

When you do not want to relinquish control or when overt audience participation is impractical for some other reason, you can still keep your audience mentally involved and active. Ask rhetorical questions. Have your listeners visualize examples. Ask them for nonverbal feedback and respond to it.

Are there any Monty Python freaks here? Great, I can see there are. Well, do you remember the sketch about the cheese shop?

---

[2]Edward M. Kennedy, "Principles of the Democratic Party," *Vital Speeches of the Day* 46, no. 23 (Sept. 15, 1980): 716.

There is yet another problem with home repairs. I'll bet this has happened to everyone here . . .

I have one colleague who always gives me feedback at the wrong time and place. Do you know people like that? Several of you are nodding. Isn't it frustrating?

We can learn from our mistakes. Think of the last mistake you made. Take a minute to recall a big one. Do you have it in mind? OK. Now I want you to think about how you felt.

An even less-complicated technique to maintain attention is the liberal use of the word *you*:

You've probably seen . . .

Do you sometimes wonder . . .

In your morning paper . . .

Now, I'll bet you're saying to yourself . . .

You could undoubtedly give me a dozen more examples.

In your city here . . .

(3) Keep the energy level of your speech up through variety and movement.

Change attracts attention. Sameness is dull. One visual aid may add interest to your speech, but a succession of visual aids can drag a speech down if they are not used judiciously. If your content or delivery becomes totally predictable, minds in the audience will start to wander.

Vary forms of support—do not rely on just statistics on just testimony. Draw examples from many domains. Three political illustrations of one point are less interesting than a single political illustration combined with a sports example and an example drawn from a popular film. Similarly, repetition of the same sentence constructions and overuse of a word or phrase should be avoided. See **18d**.

Whenever possible give the speech a sense of movement. Create images of activity. Use verbs with vivid connotations and stay in the active voice as much as possible. For instance, instead of saying "Five new businesses can be seen downtown," say "Drive down First Street and you will see five new businesses." If you need to point out the features of a piece of equipment, describe it in use, with fingers flying over the keyboard or gears turning or shutters clicking or even electrons crackling.

In your delivery, too, remember the importance of variety and movement. A deadpan speaker monotonously delivering a presentation while standing on a particularly adhesive spot on the floor certainly would benefit from reading sections **23c** and **24**.

15b. Convert attention to interest.

Prehistoric people quickly discovered that keeping a campfire burning continuously was easier than laboriously rubbing two sticks together to light a new fire for each individual task. You will be working altogether too hard as a speaker if you must constantly light new fires under your audience with a succession of attention getters. If, however, you can kindle a sustained *interest* in your topic, your job becomes easier. When an audience member becomes more than merely attentive, but actualy interested, then he or she starts to take a more active role. The listener puts forth effort to stay with you even through complicated lines of thought or technical material — focusing concentration and pushing distractions aside.

When you have gained attention, through the methods recommended in **15a**, you need to use those moments to demonstrate how and why your topic is worthy of your listeners' interest.

(1) Emphasize the link between your topic and the listeners' self-interest.

Most times when people say. "So what?" they are really saying, "What's it to me?" Do not assume that the benefits of your particular approach are obvious; motivate your audience to listen by spelling out the rewards. Do careful audience analysis and tie into as many of your listeners' needs and values as possible. See **14**.

If you take the time to learn the basics of car maintenance, you'll no longer be at the mercy of a mechanic. You can shop around for the most economical and reliable car care and have the added peace of mind of knowing that you'll be able to spot potentially dangerous conditions.

I know that many of you work in the helping professions — as teachers, social workers, counselors, and nurses. Learning to read the subtle cues of body language will help you interpret messages your clients may be unable to transmit in words.

You don't have to be a vegetarian or a gourmet cook to benefit from these menu ideas. By serving just a few meatless meals a week, you can save $30 to $100 on your monthly grocery bill and also provide a healthier diet for your family.

(2) Incorporate some of the techniques of effective storytelling.

A reader will innocently open a book at bedtime to read a few pages before turning out the light. Dawn comes and the bleary-eyed reader is still engrossed, even if the subject is not one that normally produces any interest or relates to a part of the reader's life. A well-constructed story, whether it deals with elves and hobbits or secret agents in the world of international financial intrigue, commands the interest of nearly everyone. The raconteur who can take the chaos of everyday experience and produce a compelling narration will never have trouble attracting an audience.

People are fascinated by human interest stories, as well as hard news of matters that concern them directly. Notice how excellent feature articles and documentary films share many of the qualities of good fiction or drama. A speech, even if it is an annual report, can capture an audience it if unfolds in a narrative fashion with suspense, conflict, intriguing characterizations, lively bits of dialogue, and a moment of climax leading to the denouement. Your speech need not promise to make your listeners rich or famous it if takes them outside their experience in an engaging way.

☐ **Exercise 1.**   Identify the attention factor or factors in each example:

A good accountant can help you avoid paying extra taxes.
You've all heard the phrase, "the bottom line."
Our own accounting department has developed some new techniques.
I was trembling when I went into the tax auditor's office. Could Melvin's ledgers save me or was I . . . ?

☐ **Exercise 2.**   Describe how you could use at least five of the attention factors from **15a** in a speech on each of these topics:

Computers
Art frauds and forgeries
Federal regulatory agencies

☐ **Exercise 3.**   Identify at least four attention factors in each speech in the **Appendix**.

☐ **Exercise 4.**   Select one speech from the **Appendix** and discuss how the speaker transforms attention to interest.

16

Humor

Integrate humor into your speech. Make sure it is appropriate to your personality and to the situation.

Of the many factors of attention, humor is so powerful and at the same time so tricky that it deserves a section of its own. An infusion of humor into any speech can break tension, deflate opponents, enhance the speaker's image, and make points memorable. You need not consider yourself a humorous speaker or your speech a humorous talk to benefit from this unique attention factor.

Developing your use of humor is not a matter of collecting jokes and gags which have limited usefulness. What is important is the ability to spot a potentially humorous idea in your speech and to develop it into a genuinely funny moment. To do this you must know the essentials of all humor and decide which ones work for you.

16a. Become familiar with the devices of humor.

Why do people laugh? An answer to this question would help us learn how to make people laugh. Researchers have posited a number of intriguing answers under such labels as theories of superiority, or incongruity, or surprise, or release. No concensus has been reached, but two themes run through these. One is the necessity of creating a playful context. Making scary faces at an infant or watching a person make a pratfall is funny only when it is clearly understood that it is in play. In a speech one must signal a change in mood that gives listeners permission to respond with amusement to material that might otherwise be serious. A casualty list is certainly not funny, but it can produce a rueful smile when used with understatement or irony as a speaker attacks a policy that created the casualties.

The other pervasive theme in humor is the impact of the unexpected. Gelett Burgess describes it this way:

> Our minds have associated ideas connected by thought-tracks much like the network of a railroad system. Procedure along these tracks gives ideas that are logical, or at least natural and normal. In the comic, however, there is a frustration of this logical process, much as if a train jumped the track, arriving at an unexpected terminus. ... [T]here is always a gap which must be filled by reasoning and the difficulty, or shock, we feel as comic. Why it should be pleasant, amusing, or funny, is hard to say.[1]

Do not be reluctant to set the audience up for a track-jumping twist.

Here are some of the devices a speaker can use to inject humor into a speech.

(1) Exaggeration

Taking an idea one or more steps beyond the limits of logic can be funny. (Such exaggeration into the absurd should retain a link to the original premise, though. If you get so carried away that you lose sight of the point you are lampooning, then it follows that the audience will also.)

> Mr. Howard, the department head in charge of hygiene at the facility, has a reputation for being the best in the business. In fact, when he walks into a room you can hear the cockroaches in the cabinets keeling over in cardiac arrest.

(2) Understatement

Just as "too much" can be funny, so can "not enough." An obviously impoverished description or a painfully inadequate response to a situation startles and amuses.

> When a power outage darkened all the stoplights at rush hour, there was a noticeable decrease in the efficient movement of traffic.

---

[1]Max Eastman, *Enjoyment of Laughter* (New York: Halcyon House, 1936), 339.

The rains had turned the road into an estuary, so I left my car at the foot of the hill and walked up. John's house was still standing, but the mudslide had filled it as if it were a jello mold. The front door was jammed shut. I squeezed through the broken picture window and found John trying to dig his way to a closet door. When he saw me he put down his shovel and shook my hand, saying "some weather we're having."

(3) Irony

When we encounter opposites in an unexpected way, the effect can be humorous. This opposition takes a number of forms. One is *sarcasm*, where words of praise or approval are said in a way that indicates the speaker believes just the reverse. Perhaps the most famous example of this in literature is Marc Antony's avowal that "Brutus is an honorable man." Another example:

> In the early 1970s Detroit produced an automobile that required removal of the engine to change the spark plugs. This car, certainly, is a glorious tribute to the sagacity of automobile designers in general.

A second form is the *irony of fate*, the improbable juxtaposition of incongruous events.

> The chief of police addressed the United Concerned Parents last Thursday on the topic, "The Decrease of Juvenile Crime in Our City." He had to take a cab home. After the meeting he went to the parking lot and found his car on blocks, its tires and wheels missing.

NOTE: Notwithstanding the constant misuse of the word by sportscasters, *irony* is not mere coincidence. There must be a bitter or tragicomic twist for an event to be ironic.

Socratic irony is a third form, where a speaker feigns ignorance in order to point out the weakness of an opposing position.

> Proponents of grading on the curve tell me that it serves the students' best interests. "But why is it in the students' best interest to fail a certain percentage of them?" I ask.
> "So everyone won't get high grades," they say.
> "But, if we teach them all to perform at a high level and they all meet our standards, why shouldn't they get high grades?" I ask.

"In that case, we need to raise our standards," they say.

I don't get it. If I accidentally teach too well and too many of my students succeed, then I have to find a way to fail them. Of course, if I fail as a teacher lot of them will fail. So then I'm a success.

(4) Anticlimax

This device consists of compiling a series of events, qualities, or accomplishments. The humor is produced by the sudden letdown when the last item of the series is out of place.

> When I looked over your program, I felt very much alone. Among your speakers are the mayor of New Orleans, a dean of law school, the speaker of the Louisiana House of Representatives. ... What is a speech professor doing in this company?
>
> As I studied the program I was reminded of a story that Sol M. Linowitz, a prominent lawyer, told about William Howard Taft's great-granddaughter.
>
> When she was asked to write her autobiography in the third grade, the young lady responded: "My great-grandfather was President of the United States, my grandfather was a United States senator, my father is an ambassador, and I am a brownie."
>
> On this morning at this elegant hotel here in the French Quarter in this distinguished company, I feel like a brownie.[2]

(5) Word Play

The ambiguity and richness of language delights as well as confuses us. The harmless commission of the semantic fallacy — see **11e(5)** — brings a smile when a word used in one sense is taken in another sense.

Interviewer: Regarding the missing merchandise, do you think thieves are responsible?

Police
Inspector: Oh no. I think thieves are very irresponsible.

You can also entertain an audience by a playful combination of words, as can be found in alliteration, rhyming, coined words, and funny names.

---

[2]Waldo W. Braden, "In the Heads of Listeners: Principles of Communication," *Vital Speeches of the Day* 44, no. 2 (Nov. 1, 1977): 42.

Last week, Innocent Irv met Jaded Jennifer in the *Backward Bagel*, the scene of many a role reversal. Sipping her sloe gin fizz, she locked her eyes on his and quizzed, "Can I buy you a drink?" He discovered that the new morality, or the new moronity if you prefer, was more than a mere myth.

16b. Analyze your own humor.

Everyone is funny. There are differences in terms of frequency, intensity, subtlety, and point of view. Do not devalue your style of humor and what it might add, just because you have not thought of yourself as the class clown or the life of the party. Guffaws are not the only measure of humor; a smile indicates pleasure as much as a laugh. An ironic turn of phrase or a slightly skewed perspective that adds nothing more to your speech than a surge of enjoyment is still worth the trouble to refine or develop.

Make it a project to examine your own humor. This is not the same as your sense of humor — what you laugh at may be quite different from how you amuse other people.

First, think back and remember when you evoked amusement. Did you convulse your family by imitating Aunt Evelyn? Were your friends in stitches over your vivid account of the aftermath of your car stalling in the intersection? Have you entertained your co-workers at breaks by extending to absurdity scenarios of company policies? Have your plays on words forced groans from your spouse? Continue this analysis by noticing in the next few days those times when you cause people to smile or chuckle. Look for patterns in your past and present interactions. From this you can become conscious of the essence of your unique humor.

The most effective humorists have focused their humor into a coherent point of view. One may be the befuddled victim, another the bemused social critic, a third the innocent outsider. Even comedians who merely string jokes together do not try to do everything. They select only those jokes that center on the common theme or persona they use as a trademark. Following this example, you should build on your primary strength, develop some of the secondary ones you have identified, and do not try to become the embodiment of the total spectrum of humor.

Here is how three different speakers could inject their own, specialized humor into a speech on restaurant dining. One might tell a story:

Two men went into a rather seedy restaurant. A gum-chewing waitress came over wearing a stained dingy-gray uniform and a frayed red cardigan. One man said, "I'll just have coffee." The second man said, "I'll have coffee too, and be sure the cup is clean." The waitress came back in a few minutes with two steaming mugs and asked "Which of you guys wanted the clean cup?"

Another might create a scenario combining exaggeration and under-statement.

After I waited a half an hour to be shown to a table near the kitchen, after another half hour during which I memorized the menu, and following a third half hour I spent mapping the routes the waiters took that allowed them to avoid eye contact, I was beginning to have my doubts about the guidebook recommendation.

A third might settle for the paradoxical one-liner:

Nobody goes to that restaurant anymore, it's too crowded.

16c. Avoid these humor pitfalls:

(1) Steer clear of humor that may offend your audience.

As important as humor is, a laugh should always be secondary to keeping the good will of your listeners. It is a safe bet that ethnic jokes, sick humor, and coarse vulgarities will offend someone in every audience. Sensitive audience analysis should cause you to revise or eliminate stereotypical treatments of women, homosexuals, mothers-in-law, and senior citizens. Knowledge of your listeners will also help you make a judgment about the inclusion of a slightly risque remark or politically loaded story. Insults or ridicule — unless stylized as in a "roast" — should be avoided except if you are very sure the object of your putdown genuinely enjoys public teasing.

(2) Avoid irrelevant humor.

A speech has a different purpose than a comic monologue. Every bit of supporting material in a speech has to make a direct contribution to the thesis. Humorous material is not exempt from this rule. Being funny is not enough; a string of unrelated jokes and stories or aimless clowning pulls the focus away from your topic. Constructing a transition that huffs and puffs with exertion to tie in an unrelated joke is a waste of time.

Some stories can be adapted to fit various situations by changing the occupations of the people involved or shifting the setting to one more familiar to your listeners.

(3) Do not tell jokes unless you have mastered the techniques of joke telling.

Everyone is funny, but not everyone can and should tell jokes. Telling a joke takes skill, and telling a long, complex joke with accents, intricate timing, dialogue, and physical movement takes consummate skill.

An excellent public speaker should not impair his or her image of competence by bungling a joke in these all-too-familiar ways:

- Inadequate lead-in or setup
- Omitting a crucial detail
- Forgetting the punch line
- Telegraphing the punch line
- Fizzling midseries in a climactic joke ("So anyway this same thing happens four or five more times.")
- Rambling, repetitious word choice ("he sez . . . she sez . . . he sez . . .")
- Apologizing ("Well, it was funny when I heard it" or "I guess you had to be there.")
- Laughing hysterically at one's own joke
- Not committing oneself actually to telling the joke. Describing the nature of the joke and delivering the punch line, but never getting into the storytelling aspect

(4) Do not overintroduce your humorous material.

Speakers should forecast the change to a humorous tone with subtle but unmistakable verbal and nonverbal signals. When they fail to do that they lose the laugh or smile they could have gotten had they not thrown the line away. However, many, many more speakers make the mistake of belaboring the transition.

When you come to a humorous moment, do not oversell it with tedious and empty lead-ins like:

Now here's a real funny story my cousin told me. It really points out what I'm talking about and you're going to love it.

OR

A funny thing happened to me the other day along these lines. I couldn't believe it. This was really bizarre. Things like this are strange.

OR

And if you want to remember this, just think of the word GOOSE. I made up this acronym; it's cute and funny and people always like it because goose is sort of a silly word. "G" is for the . . .

(5) Avoid overused material.

The best way to keep your humorous material fresh is to create your own. But this would be an unrealistic assignment to set oneself and, in fact, we all draw on and adapt the humor of others. When you do decide to borrow a story, joke, or turn of phrase, do not assume that if it is new to you it is new to everyone else. While preparing and practicing for your speech, ask your friends and critics if your humor works. Look for feedback from your audience as another originality check. You can make some judgments about the material if quite a number of heads start to nod halfway through the story, or if, conversely, there is a sharp crack of surprised laughter as you finish the story.

There is a lot more risk in a long story than a one-liner. A two-minute joke that everyone recognizes after the opening sentence will make you work harder at its completion as you try to reengage the audience's interest. You have less to lose, though, if a short piece of humor is familiar to many. Phrases like "deep inside he's a very shallow person" or "on a scale of one to ten it's about a C−" only take a moment to inject; presumably they make a point; and they may evoke a smile from the half of your listeners who have not heard them before. Even one-liners should be cut, however, when they become clichés, "With friends like that, who needs enemies?" or "an oral agreement isn't worth the paper it's written on" were funny at first, but today might sound hackneyed.

16d. Draw humorous material from a variety of sources.

(1) Look for the humor in your everyday experience.

Most of us have days when one disaster follows on the heels of another, and there comes a point where we have to take an objective look at the humor of the situation — or crack. "This will make a good story . . . someday" is an utterance that bears witness to the fine line between tragedy and humor. The boring, frustrating, and mundane aspects of life all have their humorous elements.

Take note of the everyday things that make you laugh: on your job, in your relationships, on television, in the paper. Decide which of these humorous items have any bearing on potential speech topics. Some are just amusing; some are both amusing and instructive. Jot them down, clip them out, and establish some sort of filing system so that you do not say to yourself six months later, "Now, what was the funny phrase that the judge used?"

(2) Be selective when you draw on collected humor.

A speaker can definitely benefit from reading books *on* humor,[3] but care should be taken when using books *of* humor. Timeliness and original twists are so important to humor that the lag time involved in publishing renders stale much of the content of such books. Nevertheless, topically organized books of humor can sometimes yield just the gem you need. Better than jokebooks or magazine joke pages, though, are the works of genuine humorists. Read Mark Twain, Will Rogers, Robert Benchley, and contemporary columnists like Art Buchwald and Erma Bombeck. They introduce you to comic points of view that are more useful than jokes.

☐ **Exercise 1.**   In a sentence or so characterize the comic style or persona of each of the following people with whom you are familiar. Which one or two are you most like when you are at your funniest? Are these the same ones you find most amusing?

Woody Allen
Carol Burnett
George Carlin
Rodney Dangerfield
Richard Pryor
Don Rickles
Andy Rooney
Lily Tomlin
Dick Van Dyke

☐ **Exercise 2.**   Think over the spontaneous laughs you have had in the last few days in unstructured interpersonal interactions. Can you describe what your friends or acquaintances did that amused you? Do these people have uniquely funny approaches to life, or ways of responding to events?

---

[3] Particularly Bob Bassingdale, *How Speakers Make People Laugh* (West Nyack, N.Y.: Parker Publishing Co., 1976) and Max Eastman, *Enjoyment of Laughter* (New York: Halcyon House, 1936).

17

Credibility

Establish your credibility, both before and during your speech, by projecting the qualities of *competence*, *concern*, *trustworthiness*, and *dynamism*.

Your content and delivery determine to a great extent whether or not your listeners believe what you say. However, there is a force at work independently that can doom even the most exquisitely wrought speech to failure. Beyond what you say and how you say it, your audience is influenced by who you are — or, more accurately, who they think you are. Your *credibility* is that combination of perceived qualities that makes listeners predisposed to believe you. For centuries scholars have been fascinated by credibility — from classical discussions of *ethos* to contemporary investigations of concepts labeled *image*, *personality*, and *charisma*. What is it about some speakers that makes you want to accept what they say, while others make you want to reject what may be an identical message? Aristotle observed that audiences are most inclined to believe a person they see as having good sense, good will, and good character. Modern social scientists have tried to isolate the characteristics that distinguish the most credible speakers from others. Their lists include: competence, dynamism, intention, personality, intelligence, authoritativeness, extroversion, trustworthiness, composure, and sociability.

You can enhance your credibility and thus the chances of meeting your speech objective by projecting these qualities. You may build up your prior image or reputation going into the speech, and you can take steps to improve your credibility as you are speaking. The first step, though, is to assess your present image.

17a. Conduct an honest assessment of your speaking image.

While the perfect speaker would be seen as competent, concerned, trustworthy, and dynamic in discussing all topics with all audiences, most of us fall short of this ideal. One speaker might seem warm, charming, likable—but somehow have trouble being taken seriously on weighty issues. Another may have a demeanor that immediately inspires confidence—but suffers from seeming dull or distant, not human enough.

Before you can work on improving your credibility, you need to see where you stand now. Is your overall credibility high or low? Do people agree with you because of, or in spite of, the personality you put forth? Which components of credibility are strongest for you? Which need to be developed? If possible, have some friends or acquaintances help you with this appraisal. It is very hard to estimate how others see us.

As you answer the following diagnostic questions, you will see that they fall into three areas: your image *prior* to the speech, your *content*, and your *delivery*. Suggestions for improving your credibility in each of these areas are provided in **17b**, **c**, and **d**.

(1) Are you perceived as *competent*?

PRIOR: Do you have education, experience, or credentials to make you an expert on this topic? Does your audience know that?

CONTENT: Have you researched broadly and deeply? Does your speech reflect this with well-documented, factual information?

DELIVERY: Does your delivery connote competence? Do you seem to be "on top of your information," well organized and composed?

(2) Are you perceived as *concerned* about your audience's welfare?

PRIOR: If you have a prior history of generosity or selflessness on relevant issues, is it known? (For example, have you sponsored a scholarship, or volunteered your time, or made a sacrifice of some sort?)

CONTENT: Do you stress the audience's needs and goals throughout the speech?

DELIVERY: Is your delivery warm, unaffected, friendly, and responsive to the audience?

(3) Are you perceived as *trustworthy*?

PRIOR: Is your past record one of honesty and integrity?

CONTENT: Do you make a special effort to be fair in presenting evidence, acknowledging limitations of your data and opinions, and conceding those parts of your opponent's case that have validity?

DELIVERY: Is your style of presentation sincere and honest — not too slick or manipulative?

(4) Are you perceived as *dynamic*?

PRIOR: Is your image one of an active, fairly aggressive person — a leader rather than a follower, a doer rather than an observer?

CONTENT: Does your speech have a sense of movement? Do the ideas build to a climax rather than dropping into a static heap? Is your language lively and colorful?

DELIVERY: Is your delivery animated, energetic, and enthusiastic?

☐ **Exercise 1.**   Complete your image inventory. In a few sentences describe your prior image as a speaker in your speech class or in a social or professional group you relate to reguarly. Which is your strongest area: competence, concern, trustworthiness, dynamism? Which is your weakest?

☐ **Exercise 2.**   Consider how your credibility varies from topic to topic. Name three topics where you have high credibility and three on which you would have to work very hard to establish credibility.

☐ **Exercise 3.**   Rate the last four United States Presidents' credibility as high, medium, or low on competence, concern, trustworthiness, and dynamism. Discuss your choices and reasons.

☐ **Exercise 4.**   Name a public figure who you believe is competent, concerned, and trustworthy but whose image suffers due to lack of dynamism. Can you think of a public figure where the opposite is true?

17b. Build your credibility prior to the speech.

(1) Provide the contact person with adequate information about your qualifications.

Do not be overly modest when asked for information for advance publicity. Send a résumé that lists your background and achievements. Include clippings, testimonials about your speaking, books or articles, and a photograph if appropriate.

(2) Help the person introducing you to set a favorable tone.

In addition to providing written information, be available to consult by phone or in person with whoever will introduce you. If there are aspects of your background you would like to have stressed for a particular speech, be sure to say so.

(3) Be aware of your image in all dealings with the group prior to the speech.

In a speech class you know that you have a certain image. You can tell if you are considered serious, funny, prompt, lazy, cheerful, argumentative, intelligent, informed, and so on just from daily classroom interactions. These perceptions will affect the way your first speech is received. A similar situation exists if you are to speak in front of the service group you belong to, or your professional association.

Speaking before an unfamiliar audience is different. Since these people have little to go on to form an impression, recognize that just about all of your interactions with them will affect your credibility. Your friendliness, professionalism, and confidence in negotiating arrangements and even in making social small talk prior to the speech will be very influential.

17c. Bolster your credibility through your speech content.

As you prepare your speech outline and select your supporting evidence and examples, think about ways to communicate your competence, concern, trustworthiness, and dynamism. The following suggestions are especially relevant to the opening minutes of the speech, while first impressions are being formed (see **9a**), but many credibility boosters can be woven in throughout the entire speech.

(1) Present your credentials.

The majority of inexperienced speakers find it difficult to "blow my own horn" and do not do as much credibility building as they should. Do not be reluctant to provide information about your qualifications to speak.

In my fifteen years as a kindergarten teacher . . .

The most common error I see in the twenty to thirty loan applications I look at each week is . . .

I've had a special awareness of the barriers the physically handicapped face since 1969, when my brother Dave returned from Viet Nam . . .

Judgment and tact are important in deciding which qualifications to mention and how to work them into the speech. Our culture frowns on bragging and name-dropping, yet false humility is out of place. The too-humble speaker insults the audience by implying that if they knew anything at all, they never would have invited the person to speak. However, you can include many statements of your qualifications without seeming boastful, if you play it straight and present them matter-of-factly. Include only relevant qualifications. Do not talk about how many celebrities you know unless it relates to the topic. Do not expound on financial success unless the speech is specifically about making money. Acknowledge those things which may be thought unusual. A senator may casually state, "At breakfast with the President the other day, I said . . ." If you are a local businessperson, though, a breakfast conversation with the President would be more credible if introduced by, "As a representative of a Small Business Task Force, I was fortunate enough to have been invited to breakfast with the President. During the conversation . . ." Most people prefer a straightforward statement to a thinly disguised effort to slip the information in sideways. Meeting a friend you had not seen in a while, which would your prefer to hear?

The parking is bad here, but it's nothing like Boston. Last week, when I was there to receive the Freedom Foundation Award, I spent over an hour trying to find a place.

OR

A wonderful thing happened since I saw you last! I won the Freedom Foundation Award!

Most people would react better to the second example, because the first implies that to common folk like the listener the Freedom Foundation Award may be important, but to superior folk like the speaker it is no more important than parking spaces.

(2) Show that you have a thorough understanding of your topic.

To communicate a sense of expertise you must let the listeners know that you have done your homework. Mention the nature of your research when appropriate:

The seven judges I interviewed all agreed on one major weakness in our court system.

I read the minutes of all the committee hearings on this bill, and not one expert mentioned . . .

There is considerable disagreement on this point in the books and articles I read. Several scholars say . . .

Use concrete examples, statistics, testimony. Be sure you have your details straight. One obvious error early in the speech can ruin your credibility.

Just imagine what it would have been like for the Union soldier crouching in the trenches around Richmond, his jacket zipped up tight in a futile battle against the cold and the wet.

The people listening to this would probably think, "If this speaker doesn't know that the zipper wasn't invented until long after the Civil War, I wonder what other information is all wrong?

(3) Be sure your material is clearly organized.

A sense of competence depends on being in command of the material and seeming to know where you are headed. Listeners will label you as uninformed rather than unorganized if you wander from topic to topic, or must apologetically insert "Oh, one thing I forgot to mention when I was discussing . . ."

(4) Make a special effort to present a balanced and objective analysis.

To seem fair, trustworthy, of good character, go out of your way to acknowledge the limitations of your evidence and argument, if appropriate:

Now, I know there are some problems with relying on surveys, but this one was carefully conducted. It seems safe to conclude that at least *many*, if not *most* working mothers are disatisfied with the quality of child care available to them.

I'm not saying television is the only cause of these problems. I realize that's an oversimplification. But I do think that TV has had a pronounced effect on the imaginative thinking of the last two generations.

Also be sure to acknowledge the existence of opposing evidence and opinions:

There are some studies that indicate an alcoholic can return to social drinking, but . . .

I recognize the contributions the administration has made to social welfare programs, but it has failed in so many other areas that I still maintain it is time for a change.

Acknowledge self-interest when it exists, to prevent the audience from thinking you are trying to hide something from them. If they discover later that you are more partisan than you made it sound, then your credibility would be dealt some powerful blows.

It's true I'm a Realtor and I stand to profit by having folks invest in real estate. But that's not my main reason for urging you to invest.

(5) Explicitly express your concern and good will toward the audience.

Let them know that your speech is offered to serve their interests.

I'd do anything to save your families the headaches and heartaches that go along with having a relative die without a will.

Taking up tennis has added so much to my life I'd love to see some of you share in that fun.

17d. Use your speech delivery to increase your credibility.

Too many expert and well-prepared speakers lose effectiveness because they cannot *transmit* these qualities to their audience. Dropping cards, reading in a shaky voice, fumbling with whatever is at hand all suggest lack of competence. An unexpressive face and voice might be interpreted as disdainful and detract from perceived good will. Hesitancy and uncertainty is sometimes falsely seen as shiftiness or dishonesty. Listless, monotonous, colorless speaking is the very opposite of dynamism. To be seen as a believable source of information and opinion, continue to work on all aspects of delivery covered in sections **23** and **24**.

☐ **Exercise 5.** How does each speaker in the **Appendix** directly establish his or her credentials to speak? Which example do you find effective? Are there any that strike you as heavy-handed or arrogant?

☐ **Exercise 6.** What special problems of prior credibility do you think Mary Cunningham faced in addressing the Commonwealth Club? What steps did she take to confront those problems?

☐ **Exercise 7.** Find an example of how each speaker in the **Appendix** explicitly established concern for the welfare of the audience.

☐ **Exercise 8.** What sections of the speeches in the **Appendix** seem to present the speakers as fair, objective, honest people?

18 Style

Choose words and constructions that make your ideas clear and memorable.

Style is a word of many shadings. A "stylish" person is one who conforms to the latest fads and fashions. A "stylized" drawing is one in which the artist includes the least amount of detail needed for comprehension. Style is decorator colors — whatever that means. Style is tight jeans or loose jeans, depending on the year. Style is none of these things to a speaker.

In the context of speaking, style is simply your choice of words and the way you string them together. "Good" style is choosing and combining those words so that your audience can easily understand and assimilate your content. Good style is clear, appropriate, vivid, and varied language.

18a. Understand how oral style is different from written style.

Speech is very much a slave to the fourth dimension, time. Words are uttered, and immediately the resonances and overtones start to fade. Listeners have just one contact with each word; memory is the only instant replay. On the other hand, a written essay exists as a time machine: it allows a reader to return to a place where the eye had been a few seconds or many years before. This quality of the written word has obvious implications regarding comprehension, and while oral style and written style use the same components, a speaker should not think the styles are interchangeable.

Naturalness is a theme that runs through this handbook. The natural-sounding speaker understands how oral style is different and uses that understanding to talk to an audience rather than deliver what appears to be a ten-page quotation. Listeners expect to hear patterns that reflect the norms of conversation, if more refined.

There are some important ways in which oral style differs from written style. Even with the redundancy built into the language, a speaker is more likely to use repetition to insure comprehension. In oral style there is a greater frequency of signposting, internal summaries, and internal previews to make the organization clear. See **8**.

Shorter sentences and words of fewer syllables are characteristic of oral style. Sentence fragments are acceptable, as are contractions. Even in a formal setting, a speech will still be more colloquial than an essay on the same topic.

Written Style	*Oral Style*
As mentioned above . . .	As I said a few minutes ago . . .
One cannot avoid individuals with this characteristic.	We can't avoid people like that.
A hypothetical case in point might be a situation where government . . .	Imagine this. Suppose Uncle Sam . . .
It is unlikely that such will result.	Well. Maybe.
Subjects were randomly assigned to either a control group or one of three experimental treatment groups, pretested for initial attitudes toward the topic, then post-tested after each experimental group had received a persuasive message containing one of three levels of fear appeals.	Here's how we did our research. First we randomly assigned the subjects to four groups. Next we gave all four groups a pretest to see what attitudes they held toward the topic. Then three of the groups heard persuasive messages. One had a high level of fear appeals, one a medium level, one a low level. Last, we post-tested the attitudes of all four groups, including the control group that received no message.

☐ **Exercise 1.**   Rewrite these segments in a style more appropriate to oral communication.

> After having removed the air filter, one can begin to investigate origins of the problem.

> All clerical and administrative personnel will undergo
> semiannual performance appraisals designed to evalu-
> ate their competence and clarify objectives for the next
> appraisal period.

18b. Strive for clarity in your language.

Although we prize elegant and graceful language, we cannot forget that the primary reason for the invention of words was clear transmission of information. "Bear come. We go. Now!" may not be subtle or poetic, but it certainly conveyed an important image from one prehistoric human to another. Some modern speakers in love with their own verbiage should do so well! If you understand the priorities of communication, the first question you will ask yourself is "Did my listeners get the picture?" When the speaker and the listeners end up with totally different mental images, something has gone awry. Perhaps the speaker has used words in nonstandard, ideosyncratic ways; or chosen words so general that they evoke many different responses; or buried the significant words in an avalanche of extraneous phrases.

To construct clear messages you must do two things. First, invest some effort in clarifying your own thoughts. Know exactly, not approximately, what picture you want to get across. Second, consider the receivers of the message and what the words are likely to mean to them.

(1) Be precise.

To combat fuzzy and ambiguous communication, you need to seek out the word that means precisely what you wish to convey and use it in a structure that illuminates, not obscures, its meaning.

Use the proper word.

Many words can denote the same object or idea; however, each may have a slightly different focus. Do not say a person was "indicted" for robbery if in fact you mean "arrested" (much less serious) or "convicted" (much more serious). Learn important distinctions and honor them.

Be careful around words that sound similar but have no similarity of meaning. "Allusion" means *a passing mention*, "illusion" means *a false perception*. Some other troublesome near-homophones are affect/effect, imminent/eminent, casual/causal, and asthetic/ascetic.

Remember that oral language is simpler than written language. Avoid using a precise word when it may seem pretentious.

Pretentious	Better
I was appalled at the feculence that oozed from the typewriter of this so-called greatest living American novelist.	I was appalled at the filth that oozed from the typewriter of this so-called greatest living American novelist.
Then I butted heads with the misoneists of the planning commission.	Then I butted heads with the planning commission, which seems to have a pathological hatred of change.
Hear my obsecration!	Hear my supplication!

Be quite sure you know what an unfamiliar word means before rushing into using it. Malaprops are funny for the audience, but devastating for the speaker. Imagine the response to a speaker who means to say "The answer I've reached is inescapable" but actually states "The answer I've reached is inexplicable."

Keep your figurative language unmuddled.

See **18d(2)**. In attempting to convey your picture vividly, do not confuse the issue by throwing discordant images together.

The wife of an official charged with taking a bribe accused the government of entrapment in this manner:

> The FBI has created the *illusion* of a crime. It's like raping
> Alice in Wonderland.

No doubt the speaker knew what she meant, but the rest of us were not so lucky. Wonderland is a crazy, illogical world where the powers-that-be are capricious — and that is a good picture to accompany an accusation of entrapment. But used as it was, it only left her listeners deaf to the rest of her words while they tried to pick out the real meaning of the image.

(2) Use specific and concrete language.

The more specific and concrete your words, the less is left to your listeners' imaginations. When a speaker says "NCAA academic standards for college athletes are ineffective," one listener may think "Yes, they are racist," while another may think "Yes, they are too low," or another, "Yes, they should be set by the faculty at each college." Yet all of these may be at odds with the intentions of the speaker, who perhaps feels that the standards are too high.

Do not have your words name a broader category than they need to.

Do not say	If you really mean	Or even
We need to attract individuals.	We need to attract customers.	We need to attract grocery shoppers.
This will cause problems.	This will be too expensive.	This will cost us $2,500 we don't have.
Our committee has studied it.	Our committee researched and discussed it.	Our committee read documents, heard testimony, and deliberated for several hours.

Minimize the use of abstract words such as love, freedom, justice, beauty — words that have no tangible, physical referent. When you have no option but to use abstract words, supplement them with concrete examples to make them less cerebral and ethereal:

> What is more important to me than peace? Freedom is more important to me than peace.
> If I weren't able to travel where I wish, if I weren't able to worship as I please, meet to discuss grievances, read and write what I want, then I would struggle to regain all these things.

(3) Be economical in your language.

The bloated language of the bureaucracy, both civil and military, is a common target of ridicule in the schools and media. Unfortunately, all this attention has done little to slow the general acceptance, or at least tolerance, of wordy, euphemistic language. In the interest of clarity, you should express yourself with the fewest, most straightforward words that still effectively convey your meaning.

Sometimes speakers use long words, extra words, and convoluted constructions for the following untenable reasons:

TO HIDE MEANING—AS WITH DOUBLESPEAK.

Uneconomical	Economical
We sustained losses through death by misadventure.	We shelled our own troops.

TO AVOID RESPONSIBILITY—AS WITH THE PASSIVE VOICE.

Uneconomical	Economical
It has been determined that your services are no longer needed.	I have decided to fire you.

TO SOFTEN UNPLEASANT MESSAGES—AS WITH EUPHEMISM.

Uneconomical	Economical
Jesse has gone on to his reward.	Jesse died.

Most often, though, wordiness results from lack of discipline. Editing is not a simple process, and many people shy away from it. These speakers prefer a machine-gun style of word choice, spewing out redundancies while bracketing the target with approximate synonyms. The clear speaker is more like the sharpshooter who takes careful aim and makes every word count.

WORDY

Some individuals express their feeling that it is objectionable to eliminate and remove laws which serve to protect female members of the labor force. No one could really be in favor of doing away with protective laws for workers if the elimination of these laws would lead to the exploitation of the people no longer covered. The question I want to raise, however, is whether there is really any relevance to the sex of those workers who should be protected from exploitation, since wages and working conditions ought to be equitable for all employees?

ECONOMICAL

There are objections to wiping out laws protecting women workers. No one would condone exploitation. But what does sex have to do with it? Working conditions and hours that are harmful to women are harmful to men; wages that are unfair for women are unfair for men.

— Shirley Chisholm

18c. Use appropriate language.

There is no standard style to use in speaking. Different audiences and topics require different approaches. You must, in the light of audience analysis, make decisions about the degree of formality, which part of your personality to project linguistically, and how deeply you descend into specialized language. Your age, status, and personality also determine what language is appropriate for you. Listeners have expectations about the vocabulary and stylistic level suitable for a senior executive, for instance, that differ from those for a teenager or a poet-in-residence.

(1) Suit the formality of your language to the occasion.

Just as you dress differently for formal and casual events, so should you tailor vocabulary and usage to fit the situation. Might it not be a little startling if the organizer of a PTA bake sale finished an announcement in the following fashion:

> This, then, is my plea to you: for the sake of our children, for the sake of our school, for the sake of our PTA, give of yourself for this culinary endeavor.

Equally inappropriate would be a presidential address at a moment of national crisis that began:

> Well, folks, things look kinda grim, but don't get bummed out, we'll be OK if we just hang in there.

In general, the more formal the occasion,

> the more serious the tone,
> the more subtle the humor used,
> the more elaborate the sentences,
> the greater the number of figures of speech,
> the greater the departure from everyday word choice.

More-formal occasions would be policy statements, debates, ceremonial speeches. Less-formal occasions would be business conferences, roasts, rallies, and after dinner speaking.

(2) Be judicious in your use of jargon or slang.

Both jargon and slang can be used to create a bond with a specialized audience. At times jargon can also allow you to get a point across more quickly. Slang, when called into play at opportune moments, can enrich the texture of your language. But the perils they introduce are substantial. You may confuse your audience with technical terms or sacrifice your credibility by using slang expressions that are offensive or are already out of date.

Notice how this excerpt from a talk on "Preventive Maintenance" is made understandable to a larger audience by substituting plain English in the second version:

SLANG AND JARGON VERSION

Let's look at how Jack could have benefited from a little PM. He burned a lot more #2 than he needed to before he got around to running the rack on his Slam-bang. A maintenance schedule would have pointed out any problems long before the engine started smoking. Same thing with the front SQ drop-in. He wouldn't have cooked it if he periodically checked and renewed the oil.

PLAIN ENGLISH VERSION

Let's look at how Jack could have benefited from a little preventive maintenance. He burned a lot more diesel fuel than he needed before he got around to adjusting the fuel injection system on his dump truck. A maintenance schedule would have pointed out any problems long before the engine started smoking. Same thing with the drive axle gears. They wouldn't have overheated and failed if he periodically checked and renewed the oil.

(3) Avoid substandard usage.

Remember that the competence of the speaker as perceived by the audience has a great bearing on the credibility they ascribe to him or her. While acceptable usage varies from place to place, there are many words and constructions that are rated substandard by consensus. The speaker who consistently uses ain't for isn't or who gets sloppy with noun-verb agreement will find that a large percentage of the audience will not give serious consideration to his or her points. Of course, you can sometimes break the rules for dramatic effect, like capping your opposition to a proposal with "Ain't *no* way!"

Where will you find a guide for what is standard? Some of us do not remember all that went on in high school English. Expose yourself to models of literate and graceful usage by reading quality magazines and good literature, and by listening to respected public speakers and commentators. This exposure often leads to an intuitive recognition of correct usage. If you have never heard one of your language models say,

"This here's the nexus of the problem," then you would be wise not to say "this here" yourself.

Substandard	Standard
Ten items or less.	Ten items or fewer.
. . . said to my friend and I . . .	. . . said to my friend and me . . .
I could care less!	I couldn't care less!
There was a large amount of people at the rally.	There were a large number of people at the rally.
Where'd you put it at?	Where'd you put it?
He hits the ball good.	He hits the ball well.
They couldn't hardly see what happened.	They could hardly see what happened.
I would have went there myself.	I would have gone there myself.

(4) Use language that is respectful and inclusive.

Referring to a group or individuals by the name they prefer is a sign of respect. When changes are made, those changes are often symbolic of a new status or image. For those used to the word "Negro," the transition to "black" in the 1960s caused some problems, yet it now seems natural. Today many adult females want to be called women, not girls or ladies. It is not possible to please everyone or to be on top of every trend. (Is it Mexican-American, Chicano, Hispanic, Latino? Is it Minority, Third World, People of Color? There are definite differences in the meanings of these words and preferences as to their use.) What you can do is make a reasonable effort to learn which reference people prefer. You can make a commitment to flexibility. Acknowledge that it is worth the temporary inconvenience of changing a language habit if that change is highly symbolic to the person involved.

A more complex stylistic issue is the use of the generic *he*, *man*, *mankind*. Now that attention has been focused on these images, no speaker or writer can feign innocence of their impact. One may not mean to exclude females from their language, but one should be aware that many male and female listeners now find the generic terms jarring. If you want to avoid distracting, possibly offending, many listeners, consider using "he or she" and replacing "man" with "humanity," "people," or "humankind." If you are worried about distracting the dwindling segment of an audience offended by the current trend, you can avoid the issue altogether by using plural and collective nouns instead of pronouns and by replacing words like chairperson with presiding officer and mail person with letter carrier.

☐ **Exercise 2.** Rewrite the following sentences so they are clearer. Make them more concrete, economical, correct, and inclusive.

> It's a very unique sort of thing how Karen just makes everybody feel sort of good. She's real notorious as the most respected girl on our whole staff of salesmen.

> At this time I'd like to say that one point to consider is the fact that we were totally surrounded by smokers who caused us considerable irritation and distress and aggravation.

> Plus, I personally feel that we also face a serious crisis of psychological morale. We need to get off our duffs and sit down and talk about this epidemic that has us running on only three cylinders.

18d. Use vivid, varied language.

Keep your listeners attentive and interested by avoiding dull, stale, and predictable language. Your message may never get past their short-term memory if you do not infuse it with vigor and a sense of newness. Why settle for the common and trite? Energize your language by effective use of the following:

(1) Employ imagery.

When you describe something, put the senses and the imaginative capacities of your listeners to work.

NOT: The life of the long-haul trucker is rough. Aside from being worn down by the effort of driving, the trucker can get discouraged by the tedium.

BUT: The long-haul trucker pulls to the side of the road. Throughout the day the road has fought back through the springs and steering wheel. Even though the truck is stopped, his arms up to his elbows still throb to the rhythm of hitting 400 miles of highway expansion joints. The harsh roar of the engine and the cacophonous flexing of the cab rivets leave him with an unfuriating ringing of the ears. After a boring, wholesome dinner the trucker slips into the cramped womb of the sleeper cab, hoping to sleep. In the morning the cycle of noise, sweat, and stress starts anew.

(2) Use stylistic devices.

Enliven your language through the planned use of figures of speech and certain arrangements of words and phrases.

Simile and metaphor

You can add vigor to your speaking by using language that connects objects or ideas to vivid images. A simile makes a comparison between two things ordinarily dissimilar. "When she came in from shoveling off the walk, her hands were as cold as ice." No one would mistake a hand for some ice, but in this case they share the characteristic of extremely low temperature. A metaphor creates a figurative equation which implies two unlike things are the same. "Her hands were ice cubes." Or: "We stand in horror as our money disappears down the gluttonous maw of the federal government." Making the government a shark forms a more compelling image than "We stand in horror as the federal government operates with fiscal irresponsibility."

Personification

One way to bring objects or ideas to life is to imbue them with qualities of human beings. We know that no room is really "cheerful," that winds do not actually "whisper," and that, being legless, the economy cannot possibly "limp" — but all of these images are potent because we find it easier to identify with reflections of our own behavior.

> Israel now faced the choice of either to be choked to death in her southern maritime approaches or to await the death blow from northern Sinai.
>
> — Abba Eban

Hyperbole

To emphasize a point, you may deliberately overstate it in a way that is clearly fanciful rather than misleading.

This paperwork will be the death of me.

227

I thought about nothing else for the next three days.

The 49er victory in the Super Bowl has been San Francisco's most glorious moment.

The governor has repeated this same promise to you a million times.

Repetitive language or structure

Repeat key words or phrases to make your listeners feel that your points are snowballing to a certain conclusion. Use parallel structure to emphasize relationships.

Sometimes a syntactic construction is repeated:

> How serious is the morale crisis? We have lost several key employees. What has caused the problem? Lack of clear upward and downward communication. How can we change things? By hiring an interpersonal and organizational communication trainer for a series of workshops.

Notice no phrases are repeated, but the question-answer, question-answer format gives a sense of momentum to this paragraph.

You can use repetition to introduce consecutive paragraphs. For instance, a speaker can build a sense of urgency or dedication by repeating the phrase "We must act now to . . ." as each problem is presented.

Within a paragraph you can achieve a similar effect by starting a series of sentences with the same words.

> We know that if we lose this fight, all fruits will wither and fall from the tree of liberty. But we shall not lose it. We shall not lose it because the people of Britain stand and will stand in undaunted fortitude and magnificent resistance. We shall not lose it because, although some nations may lie crushed today, their souls can never be destroyed. We shall not lose it because we, on this continent of North America, who have been the pioneers of the frontiers of freedom, have already begun to stamp out the prairie fire of tyranny, anarchy and barbarism which every day draws close to our homes.
>
> —W. L. Mackenzie King

Or, you may end several sentences with the same words.

> What remains? Treaties have gone. The honor of nations has gone. Liberty has gone.
>
> —David Lloyd George

Finally, for emphasis you can repeat key words or phrases within a sentence.

> But, in a larger sense, we can not dedicate — we can not consecrate — we can not hallow this ground.
>
> —Abraham Lincoln

> I see new generations of concerned and courageous Americans — but the same kind of Americans; the children and grandchildren of those Americans who met the challenge of December 7 — just thirty-two years ago.
>
> —Gerald Ford

Alliteration and assonance

These consist of saying the same sound in a sustained sequence. [Sorry about that silly sentence.] Whether it is with consonants (alliteration) or vowels (assonance), this repetition can make an idea more memorable, or at least charge it with a sense of poetry.

At his brother's grave, Robert Green Ingersoll said the following:

> He who sleeps here, when dying . . . whispered with his latest breath: "I am better now." Let us believe, in spite of doubts and dogmas, and tears and fears, that these dear words are true of all the countless dead.

Antithesis

When you want to contrast two ideas, certain sentence structures serve to dramatize the differences. Antithesis uses forms like:

Not . . ., but . . .
Not only . . ., but . . .
Never . . ., unless . . .

> We live in a society that emphasizes military expenditures over education. We spend millions teaching young people how to kill and be killed, but we won't spend money teaching them how to live and make a living.
>
> —Harry Edwards

> It was we, the people; not we, the white male citizens; nor yet we, the male citizens; but we, the whole people who formed the Union. And we formed it, not to give the blessings of

liberty, but to secure them; not to the half of ourselves and the half of our posterity, but to the whole people — women as well as men.

— Susan B. Anthony

(3) Use fresh language.

The power of figurative language lies in the image stimulated in the listener's mind. After too many repetitions the original psychological impact is lost. "Fresh as a daisy" at first summoned a picture of a clean, bright, dew-studded blossom. At the first turn of the phrase "it went in one ear and out the other," its aptness produced pleasant surprise. Now both expressions are likely to be processed as just extra, empty words.

Certain fad words attract a cult following. "Bottom line," "prioritize," and "networking" become overnight sensations and are used to the exclusion of many good (and fresher) synonyms. Purge your language of such flatulent phrasing. Invest the time to select original combinations of words and phrases that capture the image, mood, or thought you want to get across.

(4) Vary the rhythm of your sentences.

Although oral style is characterized by simpler, shorter phrases with fewer different words, you are not compelled to homogenize your sentences into dullness. The singsonginess associated with doggerel can creep into a speech if you fail to pay attention to how you are stringing your sentences and phrases together. Be sparing in your use of parallelisms and repetition.

> The Association's annual convention should be user supported. The convention is attended by a core of regulars. The average Association member doesn't benefit from the convention. These average members shouldn't have to bear more than their fair share.

The choppiness of this tedious passage results from the sameness of sentence length and structure. Recasting the sentences will create a more fluid and graceful paragraph.

> The Association's annual convention should be user supported. Who attends the convention? A core of regulars. The average Association members, who don't benefit from the convention, shouldn't have to bear more than their fair share.

☐ **Exercise 3.** Use at least two different stylistic devices to enliven each of these phrases.

A cold, rainy day
An unworkable policy
A delicate, intricate procedure
A very stern leader
A huge crowd

☐ **Exercise 4.** Identify at least three different examples of imagery or stylistic devices in each speech in the **Appendix**.

☐ **Exercise 5.** Think of fresh ways to replace these overused phrases:

Like comparing apples and oranges
Caught between a rock and a hard place
Two steps forward and one step back
Always darkest before the dawn

19

Persuasive Strategies

Plan a strategy based on analysis of audience attitudes. Select and arrange your content for maximum persuasive impact.

When you choose to use a statistic or include a humorous anecdote or make any of the other content decisions discussed in **11–18**, you will find that the choice is never independent of the factors covered in the other sections of this book. What you say will depend on your analysis of the audience, the organizational pattern you select, and the way you phrase and deliver your speech. All the specific tactical decisions you make must be woven into a strategic tapestry. "Strategy" may bring to mind calculated moves by generals or gridiron game plans, but in speech it carries none of the combative or manipulative and tricky connotations of these images. A speech strategy is this only: a master plan for combining your content with other elements of speaking to meet a certain goal.

While every speech should have a strategy, the generally more complex nature of persuasion, with its layers of interacting components, makes it imperative that the strategy be well thought-out and integrated. The following section offers some guidelines for the persuasive speaker.

19a. Adjust your speech content in light of your audience's attitude toward your topic and you.

Section **3c** asks you to analyze your listeners' possible reactions to the thesis of your presentation. Based on surveys, observations, or inference, you can make some discrimination of their predisposition toward your topic. The following continuum classifies audiences according to that predisposition:

Types of Audiences

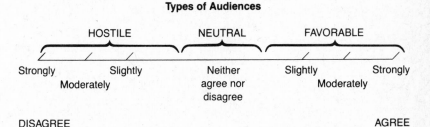

Here are some suggestions on how to deal with such favorable, neutral, or hostile audiences.

(1) Favorable audience

A speaker facing a favorable audience is relieved of a number of burdens. In this situation as a speaker, you will rarely need to establish credibility: your listeners, perceiving your position as identical to theirs, approve of you and your good taste already. Furthermore, you will find that a favorable audience will not be raising internal counterarguments for you to deflect or defuse.

Being relieved of a few burdens, however, does not release you from all responsibility as an effective champion of your position. A poorly prepared speech can actually erode audience support. On the other hand, if you realize and accept the challenge of speaking to a favorable audience, you can solidify or strengthen their attitudes, or cause them to move from theoretical argument to positive action.

Make use of emotional appeals to intensify your listeners' support.

The difference between intellectual agreement and commitment to some purpose, and the difference between commitment and action, is usually a function of emotional arousal. Out of the vast number of positions you would say you agree with, there is a much shorter list of issues that you really *care* about. This list contains topics that appeal to your most basic needs, touch on your core values, or have a personal effect on your life.

To get your speech on your listeners' list, make extensive use of appeals to basic values such as patriotism, humanitarianism, and progress; appeals to basic needs such as survival, security, and status; and appeals to basic emotions such as fear, pity, and love.

Here is one example of how a position can be intensified. Look also at the examples in the appropriate sections of **14**.

Logical Stem	Emotional Intensifier
It is only fair to allow groups with which we disagree to exercise their legal constitutional rights.	Where will it stop if we allow *selective* enforcement of the protection provided by the Bill of Rights? Today the Nazis in Skokie may be denied their rights as Americans; tomorrow it may be any of *us*. (Appeal to fear, appeal to core value of civil liberties.)

When an audience agrees with you but is not taking action, they probably do not feel personally involved with the subject. A major task in speaking to a favorable audience is the creation of that personal involvement in two ways: First, be very specific about how their lives are affected; second, show them that their actions can make a difference.

Your ten-dollar check can feed a Cambodian family for a week.

If you can take that extra second to switch off the lights as you leave the room, you can save yourself 50 dollars a year.

For most audiences emotional appeals should be handled sparingly and cautiously, but for the favorable audience you can hardly be too vivid or personalized as long as you avoid bad taste and redundancy.

Get your audience to make a public commitment.

Invite your listeners to offer suggestions, sign a petition, raise their hands in agreement, lend their names to a letterhead, or talk to others. People who have made a public commitment, either oral, written, or physical, are less likely to change their minds.

Provide several specific alternatives for action.

The following audience reaction is not enough: "Yes, somebody really should do something about that situation. I should get involved myself one of these days." Make it easy for them to take action by offering several very specific choices. Do not say to people who have shown up at a rally for a candidate: "Stop by campaign headquarters sometime." Instead say: "I'd like everyone here either to walk a precinct or to spend an evening making phone calls. Sign-up sheets are being passed around now. If you can't help out in either of these ways, Judy will be standing at the door and can tell you about other things that need to be done to insure our success." With a favorable audience do not settle for urging them to do "something." Tell them what you want them to do, and make the execution easy and attractive: If you want them to write letters, give them addresses; if you want them to reduce their sodium intake, give them low-sodium recipes.

Prepare your audience to carry your message to others.

You can tap the potential of audience members as persuaders in their own right. Each of them may find themselves discussing your topic with co-workers, neighbors or friends who are neutral or hostile toward it. Give the less-facile listeners ammunition for these interactions, and make that material as memorable and quotable as possible. When, in front of a favorable group, you offer examples, arguments, and statistics that support your position, your goal is not the persuading of your immediate audience. Rather, you are aiming at the second generation of listeners.

A part of this preparation is providing your audience with ready answers to refute standard counterarguments. See **19d**. This also serves to inoculate your listeners against the persuasiveness of those counterarguments.

> You may meet people who tell you that the Administration's economic policy is designed to help the average worker. Just ask those people why the greatest tax relief goes to the rich. Have them explain to you why a person who earns $300,000 a year will have a 50% reduction in taxes, but a person making $18,000 a year will see a reduction of only 6%. They may say, "Ah, but we are creating new jobs." Ask them this . . .

(2) Neutral audience

An audience could be neutral toward your position for one of three reasons: They are *uninterested*; they are *uninformed*; or they are genuinely *undecided*.

Stress attention factors with an uninterested neutral audience.

An audience is uninterested in a topic or position because they do not see how it affects them directly. With this sort of audience draw on all the attention factors described in **15**, but give special emphasis to the *vital*. Their interest and attention can only be gained through concrete illustrations of the impact of your subject on their lives.

> A lot of you are probably saying "So what? So what if somebody across the room lights up a cigarette? It's a free country, and *he's* inhaling the smoke, not me." Would you say "So what?" if I told you "secondhand" smoke can blacken your lungs just as badly as if you smoked two to twenty-seven cigarettes a day?

Be sure the facts and statistics you use are relevant to your listeners' experience. Sprinkle your speech with humor and human interest. Make a special effort to have a lively and animated delivery and style to stimulate them.

With an uninformed neutral audience, emphasize material that clarifies and illuminates your position.

Before you can expect people to agree with you, they must have some comprehension of the topic. When they lack that essential background, you must spend a significant portion of your speech filling them in, even if it means sacrificing time you would have spent making points to support your position.

The main concern is clarity: use explanation, definitions, examples, restatement. See **12**. Visual aids can be helpful. Keep your language simple and your organization straightforward.

A direct persuasive appeal should be saved until the very end of the speech.

For an undecided neutral audience, establish your credibility by presenting new arguments that blend logical and emotional appeals.

The undecided neutral audience is both interested in and informed about your topic, but they find the arguments for each side equally compelling. Let them know that you understand their ambivalence. Grant the complexity of the issue and admit that there is truth on both sides.

Most audiences are uncomfortable with such uncertainty and seek to be rid of it. They would like to make a decision and are looking for a legitimate basis for one. Offer yourself as the vehicle for reducing their discomfort. Establish your credibility by communicating expertise and integrity. As you present the arguments for your side, stress any recent evidence or new interpretations which could justify a decision. By definition, this audience finds sense in some aspects of the opposing arguments. You must not ignore this fact. Acknowledge and respond to the major arguments against your position, using the techniques in **19d**. Similarly, you need to inoculate your audience against arguments they may encounter later. When unanticipated, these arguments may tip the scales back to the balance point of indecision, or worse. When anticipated, these arguments can be dismissed by your listeners as having been dealt with already.

In short, a well-documented, logical presentation works best for the undecided neutral audience. Appeals to emotions, needs, and values can be effective only if used sparingly and if clearly interwoven with the logical argument of the speech.

(3) Hostile audience

Murphy's Law: Anything that can go wrong, will. A corollary of this law, especially true for speakers with a hostile audience is: Anything that *can* be interpreted wrong, *will* be interpreted wrong.

A hostile audience is by no means a belligerent one—remember that hostile is defined to encompass anything on the *disagree* side of neutral, starting with *slightly disagree*. However, the more intensely the audience disagrees with you, the more they will be predisposed to reject both you and your message. Any idiosyncracies of appearance and style of delivery will allow them to dismiss you as the lunatic fringe. One joke that falls flat labels you a buffoon. Express yourself with conviction and you will be branded a fanatic.

At the same time, your audience realizes the disadvantage you are working under. If you are able to handle the situation with grace and aplomb, you can earn their grudging respect. The results can be gratifying when you approach the speech to a hostile audience as a challenge to your skill.

Set realistic goals for a single speech.

Do not try to do too much with a hostile audience. Attitude change takes place slowly. If most of your audience falls at the *strongly disagree* end of the continuum, do not expect your ten-minute speech to change them to strong agreement. Sometimes the measure of success is that they threw eggs and not bricks. Even if it means modifying your thesis sentence, set a goal you have a reasonable chance of achieving, such as easing the *strongly disagree* over to *moderately disagree*, or *moderately disagree* over to neutrality. Trying to do too much can alienate your audience and lead to a boomerang effect where the attitude change that occurs is in the opposite direction of that which you were seeking. Do not make an express call for action when such action is highly unlikely. It would be self-defeating to ask a pro-choice group to contribute money to the campaign coffers of a right-to-life candidate. Better to ask them to think about the issues you have raised, or to ask them to work together to find a compromise.

Stress common ground.

However great the difference between you and your audience on any particular issue, there are bound to be many places where your opinions and experiences overlap. When you think about the hostile audience you face, ask yourself what goals and values you share, what enemies you have in common. Even the intensity of the disagreement between you and your audience over school busing reveals a common concern for your children's education. Or, if your opponents think unemployment can best be combated through government programs and you feel that private enterprise can deal with the problem successfully, it is still true that both agree that unemployment is "bad."

Common ground is important to every speech, but certainly crucial to the speech to the hostile audience. Stress it in your introduction and at several points throughout the speech. When you minimize the differences between you and your audience, you create the basis for communication to occur.

Base your speech on sound logic and extensive evidence.

The hostile audience is skeptical of your position and will reject most emotional appeals as manipulative. Your only chance to persuade them is to build an irresistible case supported by impeccable, unbiased evidence. With this audience you must clearly indicate every step of your reasoning—nothing can be taken for granted. Discuss and defend even those assumptions that seem obvious to you. Spell out the logical links and connections that hold your argument together. Do not overstate your points; be careful not to claim more than the data allow. Say: "These examples suggest" rather than "These examples prove"; "Smoking contributes to cancer" rather than "Smoking causes cancer."

Use factual and statistical evidence and always cite your sources completely. If you mention the results of a survey, for example, tell when, where, and how it was conducted, and where it was presented or published. When supporting your points with testimony, quote reluctant experts if possible or highly respected unaffiliated authorities. Quotations from your own partisans are hardly worth giving. See **12e**.

Confront directly the arguments that are foremost in your listeners' minds. Do not be afraid to concede minor points that do not damage your basic case. State the remaining counterarguments fairly and answer them forcefully, but never stoop to ridicule. In fact, it has been shown to be advantageous to state your opponents' view *even more elegantly than they have*, before proceeding to refute it.

Pay particular attention to establishing a credible image.

Nowhere is the careful establishment of good character, good sense, and good will more important than in a speech to a hostile audience. See **17b**. Plan every detail of your speech content and delivery to project an image of a calm, reasonable, fair, well-informed, and congenial person. The judicious use of humor can aid this image while releasing tension and putting the issue in perspective. Direct the humor at yourself, your position, a common enemy, or the ironic aspects of the confrontation. Never direct it at your audience and their beliefs.

Although you do not want to seem combative, do remain firm in your position. It is fine to build rapport by stressing common ground and granting minor points, but do not waffle or be overly conciliatory.

Resist the temptation to be snide, shrill, defensive, paranoid, outraged, arrogant, sarcastic, facetious, or patronizing.

Do not become frustrated by heckling or other indications that you are not getting through to them. See **25d**. Remember attitude change is a slow process and that by maintaining your dignity and rationality you will not hurt and may help your cause in the long run,

☐ **Exercise 1.** Examine the speech by Mary Cunningham in the **Appendix**. Do you think she perceived her audience as hostile, neutral, or favorable? What strategic decisions reflected in the speech content justify your conclusion? Name two specific adjustments she should make if presenting this speech to each of the other possible types of audiences.

19b. Consider using an audience-centered organization pattern.

The speech organization patterns discussed in section **7** — topical, spatial, and chronological — grow out of analysis of the speech content. However, another way to divide a complex topic into segments is to select points that reflect the mental stages through which the audience progresses as they listen to the speech. When your primary objective is to persuade your listeners, this sort of echoing or anticipation of their mental set can be very effective indeed. Several such psychological patterns have been studied.

(1) The motivated sequence is perhaps the most widely used organizer for persuasive speeches.[1] *(Note that it includes the speech introduction and conclusion, unlike the sample outlines in* **ORGANIZATION***.)*

ATTENTION	The speaker must first motivate the audience to listen to the speech.
NEED	Auditors must become aware of a compelling, personalized problem.
SATISFACTION	The course of action advocated must be shown to alleviate the problem.
VISUALIZATION	Psychologically, it is important that the audience have a vivid picture of the benefits of agreeing with the speaker, or the evils of alternatives.
ACTION	The speech should end with an overt call for the listeners to act.

Here is an example of a speech that follows the motivated sequence:

Thesis: Reduced salt consumption is vital to your health.

ATTENTION	INTRODUCTION: You may be one of sixteen million Americans who suffer from a serious disease and don't even know it!
NEED	I. The American high-sodium diet is responsible for millions of cases of hypertension.

---

[1] Douglas Ehninger, Alan H. Monroe, and Bruce E. Gronbeck, *Principles and Types of Speech Communication*, 8th ed. (Glenview, Ill.: Scott, Foresman & Company, 1980), 142–58.

SATISFACTION	II. To combat this problem, most Americans should reduce their salt intake drastically.
VISUALIZATION	III. Herbs and spices can be substituted to provide a delicious low-sodium or salt-free diet.
ACTION	CONCLUSION: Push away that salt-shaker. Begin now to experiment with some of these flavorful recipes.

(2) **It is even possible to imagine your audience making specific demands and comments around which you structure your points.**[2]

HO HUM	The audience must be stirred from lethargy or complacency.
WHY BRING THAT UP?	A gripping attention getter is suspect unless quickly tied into some legitimate area of concern. You need to explore the range of the problem and introduce your solution.
FOR INSTANCE?	Elaboration and documentation must be provided.
SO WHAT?	In closing, you should call for a behavioral commitment. Tell the listener what to *do*.

Here is how the reduced-salt thesis could be developed using this pattern:

Thesis: Reduced salt consumption is vital to your health.

HO HUM.	INTRODUCTION: Most Americans consume twenty to thirty times the amount of salt their bodies actually need.

---

[2]Richard C. Borden, *Public Speaking As Listeners Like It* (New York: Harper & Row, 1935), 3–18.

241

WHY BRING THAT UP?	I. Excessive salt consumption leads to serious, often symptomless, health problems, so Americans must change this eating habit.
FOR INSTANCE?	II. Hypertension and atherosclerosis affect over thirty-four million Americans.
SO WHAT?	CONCLUSION: It is possible to drastically reduce your salt consumption and still enjoy delicious meals. Start pushing away that saltshaker today!

(3) **Another psychological pattern is based on steps that go into planning long-range persuasive campaigns.[3] Occasionally these same three phases can be adapted to the shorter time frame of a single speech.**

UNFREEZING ATTITUDES	Do not introduce your new perspectives until you have weakened your audience's preconceptions by probing inconsistencies and challenging underlying premises.
CHANGING ATTITUDES	Only when your listeners are receptive should you present your major arguments for change.
REFREEZING ATTITUDES	Gaining intellectual agreement is not sufficient. You will need to solidify and reinforce the new attitudes by tying them into other firmly held beliefs. The chances of erosion are then reduced.

For example:

Thesis: Reduced salt consumption is vital to your health.

UNFREEZE	I. Dietary preferences are largely a matter of custom and culture. A. A delicacy in one part of the world is considered disgusting in another.

---

[3]E. H. Schein, I. Scheier, and C. H. Barker, *Coercive Persuasion* (New York: W. W. Norton & Company, 1961), 119–120.

               B. Foods that are your favorites now may have tasted bad to you as a child.

               C. You can learn to appreciate new tastes and flavors in a short time.

CHANGE   II. Most Americans should reduce their salt intake drastically.

               A. A high-sodium diet causes hypertension in millions.

               B. Alternative seasonings can make food palatable.

REFREEZE   III. In a short while you will wonder why you ever used salt in the first place.

               A. You will feel healthier.

               B. You will appreciate subtle natural flavorings.

               C. You will start to find food with salt in it horribly overseasoned.

19c. On the basis of audience predisposition, select either a climax or anticlimax order of persuasive points.

Ideally, all of the arguments supporting your thesis statement should be strong. In reality, you will find you must use arguments of varying strength. These should not be arranged randomly. Be aware that people will remember the first and last points more than the others. In light of this, the most effective patterns for you to use are the climax (strongest last) and the anticlimax (strongest first). To choose between the two of these, draw on your knowledge of the audience.

    In general,

(1) Use the anticlimax format with an audience that is uninterested in your topic.

(2) Use the anticlimax format with an audience that is hostile toward your position.

(3) Use the anticlimax format for an audience with which you have low credibility.

Beginning your speech with a powerful argument can overcome indifference, deflect hostility, and enhance your credibility. The probability of these kinds of audiences listening to the rest of your points is greatly increased.

(4) Use the climax format when your strongest argument has high emotional content.

Sometimes your best and strongest argument will be one with which you hope to evoke intense emotion. It takes time to establish a receptive frame of mind in your listeners. You will rob your argument of its power by introducing it too soon. Even if you could arouse your audience early in the speech, you do not want them too agitated to pay attention. This can be important enough for you to disregard **(1)**, **(2)**, and **(3)** above.

(5) Use the climax format in all other cases.

When you have no special information about your audience's predisposition toward you or your topic, you should lead up to your strongest point. Other things being equal, the argument heard last is most likely to be recalled and accepted.

☐ **Exercise 2.**   Which of the speeches in the **Appendix** follow a climax order? An anticlimax order? Can you justify choices made by each speaker in terms of the information you have about the intended audience?

19d. In addition to presenting your own viewpoints in a persuasive speech, you may often find it advisable to deal with opposing arguments.

When time is limited it is hard to decide whether to present just your own side of an issue or to bring up opposing arguments and answer them. In the first instance you run the risk of appearing to have a weak position. In the second instance you take time away from developing your own arguments and there is always the chance that you might introduce a point against your case that would not have occurred to your audience otherwise.

(1) Use audience analysis to decide whether to answer counterarguments.

In general, you should discuss and respond to counterarguments when one or more of these conditions exist:

You have an initially hostile audience.

When a Democrat speaks to Republicans or a pro-choice advocate addresses a right-to-life convention, it is only reasonable to confront directly the points that are foremost in the listeners' minds. Ignoring the arguments will not make them disappear.

There is a high probability that your audience will be exposed to counterarguments.

At the end of a straightforward pro speech your audience may agree with you, but if a few hours or a few days later they become aware of powerful opposing arguments, they may discredit your entire position. Speakers often inoculate their audience by presenting a few counterarguments and answering them. Then, when these points are brought up later, the listener will say, "Oh, yes, I was warned about this." Inoculation has created "antibodies" to resist the opposing position.

The audience is well educated.

Presumably, education develops critical thinking. Well-educated listeners will raise counterarguments in their own minds and want to hear your answers. Also, a balanced presentation is more intellectually appealing than a highly-one-sided approach.

Conversely, answering counterarguments is less important or unnecessary with favorable audiences, audiences who are not likely to be

> If you know that there are serious objections to your thesis, which you are unable to answer or concede, you have some ethical concerns to ponder. Is it right to thrust your admittedly flawed position on others? Should you take advantage of the absence of counterarguments to manipulate favorably disposed, poorly educated persons? Salespersons, politicians, and teachers are just a few of the persuaders who must confront these issues.

exposed to counterpersuasion, and less-educated audiences. However, just because you do not address opposing views as a main point of your speech, it does not follow that you can ignore them in your preparation and analysis. You should be able to answer these points if they are raised after the speech.

(2) Address the opposing arguments directly, using refutation techniques.

If you choose to respond to a point, you may follow these steps of refutation:

1. State the opposing view fairly and concisely.
2. State your position on that argument.
3. Document and develop your own position.
4. Summarize the impact of your argument and show how the two positions compare.

Here is a distilled example:

1. Many people argue that flexible work schedules lead to reduced productivity.
2. I challenge the underlying assumption that most people work only for money and will do as little as possible. Employees who are treated like responsible partners take pride in their work and are dependable and productive.
3. There are several research studies which support my point of view: [Speaker introduces and explains the studies.]
4. So, these examples refute the position that flextime will lead to decreased productivity. I have shown you how that argument is based on a false assumption about why people work.

Effective refutation can take various forms. In a speech against capital punishment a speaker might follow the points supporting the thesis with this main point:

IV. Arguments in favor of capital punishment do not justify its continuation.
   A. It is argued that capital punishment deters crime: The facts do not support this.
   B. It is argued that it is very costly to provide life sentences for serious offenders: This is true, but expenditure of money is not a justification for collective murder.
   C. It is argued that dangerous criminals are released on parole and endanger lives: This may be a problem, but we can respond with stricter parole policies rather than execution.

Note that counterarguments may be handled in different ways. Point A is denied directly. Point B is conceded but labeled unimportant. Point C is partly conceded, then analyzed in a different light. Responding to a counterargument does not mean utterly obliterating it. You may concede it, minimize it, dismiss it as irrelevant, attack the evidence supporting it, or the premise underlying it.

(3) In most cases, answer counterarguments after developing your own position.

Pro-to-con order is almost always more effective than con-to-pro. The only exception to this rule applies to when you know the audience is so preoccupied with an opposing position that they may not listen to you. In that case, respond to the point immediately.

☐ **Exercise 3.** Do any of the speeches in the **Appendix** address opposing viewpoints directly? Identify the paragraphs that serve this function. In terms of what you know about the audiences of all four speakers, evaluate the decision of each speaker to answer or not to answer counterarguments.

☐ **Exercise 4.** Select a position you believe in strongly. Consider one widely used argument against that position. Write out your refutation of that point exactly as you would present it in a speech, following the four steps in **19d(2)** and including evidence and support.

PRESENTATION

INTRODUCTION

There are more efficient ways of transmitting information than speech. Certainly the redundancy of spoken language relative to the written word demonstrates this. However, Keynote Handouts have not replaced Keynote Speeches at conventions, nor have memos usurped the role of conferences. The combination of voice, body, and personality — as well as on-the-spot chemistry — makes speech a form of communication with compelling vitality. It is exciting to listen to a good speaker.

By good speaker we mean someone who has something to say and says it well. Too often, when people describe a speaker as good or poor, the reference is to the speaker's delivery only. "He didn't have anything to say, but he was a very good speaker" is a contradiction that points up how necessary it is for speakers to have strong presentation skills if they expect to have their message heard. An audience will listen avidly to a well-delivered speech, even if at the end they discover there was little of substance in it. They will not afford the same consideration to a poorly delivered speech, no matter how exciting or important the content.

Recognizing the importance of the performance aspects of a speech, some speakers prepare as actors do: blocking out each movement, planning every vocal change. Carried to its extreme in a movement known as elocution, this approach led to the detailed marking of a manuscript or outline so that a typical sentence might look like this:

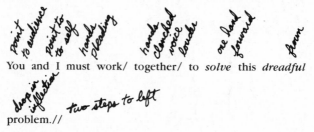

It is almost impossible to find the words among all the stage directions! When voice and bodily action are consciously orchestrated to this degree — whether or not they are written down — the ideas of the speech are lost to both the speaker and the listeners.

Preparing for a speech as an actor prepares for a play is inappropriate because the two situations are so different. As an actor you assume the role of someone else, speak words written by another person, and strive to perform each line exactly as rehearsed. As a speaker you present your own personality, speak your own words, and try to adapt to the response you receive. Thus public speaking is far more like conversation than like acting.

We advocate an approach to speech delivery called the *natural theory of delivery*, which emphasizes speech as an interaction of ideas as opposed to speech as a performance. However, this does not deny the performance aspects of a public speech. It *does* claim that the performance will be most effective when conceptualized as amplified conversation (rather than as a whole new kind of speaking.)

Paradoxically, the less you think about your speech delivery the more effective it becomes. Perhaps you have heard a speaker go through a speech presentation stiffly and mechanically, then heave a sigh of relief and ask for questions. Suddenly a great transformation occurred! In the question-and-answer period the speaker had more facial expression, more variety of tone, more body language while clarifying points. It was as if the speaker had thought "I'm through with 'my speech.' Now I can really talk to these people." The delivery became much better as the speaker's attitude toward the situation shifted from a performance orientation to an interaction orientation. There is an explanation, if oversimplified, for this change. We have all had more practice communicating than performing. The natural theory of delivery is based on the assumption that you communicate well many hours of every day without consciously thinking about speech mechanics. When you are intensely involved in conversation you do not stop and think, "Now I'll furrow by brow and point my finger." Changes in your voice and action just happen naturally when you are wrapped up in communcating your message. If you are similarly wrapped up in the content of your speech, your delivery should take care of itself. The single most important delivery goal for any speaker is to internalize this conception of speech as conversation. Once you feel the sense of interaction with an audience — the sort of give-and-take contact you experience in other conversations — your enjoyment of speaking will increase along with your confidence and skill.

Now, are we saying that a successful speech will result from talking just as you do every day? Certainly not, if your everyday speech is listless, ungrammatical, and marred by distracting habits. What we are saying is that this natural theory of delivery ought to ensure that your public style is *no worse* than your private style, but ideally your speech delivery should be lively and unobtrusive. This can be difficult: a conversation with fifty people is very different from a conversation with three. Projecting your voice and personality in this setting may seem and sound strange at first. But you can amplify and exaggerate your conversational style without acting like a different person. Be yourself. There are many sides to a person's self, of course, and different ways of speaking associated with each. Neither the intimate shorthand of lovers nor the lazy, rambling style of a telephone conversation between best friends would be appropriate models for public speaking. We suggest you picture the way you describe an exciting event to friends, or picture yourself as you talk about a strongly held opinion. That is, imitate yourself as you are in your liveliest and most animated conversation. Disregard for now the more reserved and introspective aspects of yourself. You have chosen to be (or have been thrust into) the center of several people's attention, so call on that side of you that is most outgoing and expansive.

This may not be easy, since the fears surrounding public speaking can put you in touch with the facets of yourself that are shy, apologetic, and self-protective. Thus a lively delivery may not feel really "natural" — hiding under the podium could feel more in character. Nevertheless, learn to play a role as you speak, and the role you will play will be yourself: the most confident, poised, and expressive side of yourself. Quite literally, call up past triumphs of lively and effective speech. "I want to communicate as I did at lunch the other day telling about my trip. I don't really feel comfortable here, but that's the sort of speech personality I want to try to project."

Effective, natural delivery is also unobtrusive. Your audience should neither be thinking "what an awkward gesture," nor "what a beautiful voice." They should attend to *what* you are saying. If you do have problems of a vocal, verbal, or physical nature, work on them, by all means. But only up until your speech begins. At that juncture, devote your attention to your message. If your habits have not changed by the time you start speaking, another ten minutes is not going to make any difference.

Sections **20-27** deal with the diverse aspects of speech presentation. Depending on the situation, you will find yourself using one of four standard *modes of delivery*. Whatever the mode, careful planning and execution of your *practice sessions* is necessary. Even with practice, though, you may find that you must *overcome fear of speaking* before you can present your speech. To transmit your message effectively you must understand the dynamics of *vocal delivery* and *physical delivery*. Another skill in this effective transmission is being able to *adapt to the speech situation* and modify your presentation to account for differences between how you envision a given speaking event and how it really turns out. Finally, if you go about *answering questions* properly in the question-and-answer period, you can have more chances to reinforce your message. When these skills are mastered, you can apply them not only to routine speaking assignments, but to the requirements of *special speaking occasions* as well.

20

Modes of Delivery

Select a mode of delivery that is appropriate to your topic, audience, and occasion.

Decide early if your speech will be: off the cuff—*impromptu*; given from notes—*extemporaneous*; written out and read—*manuscript*; or *memorized* word for word. Settle on the predominant mode you will use, but be aware that no speech is purely *one* mode. Even in an extemporaneous speech, for example, it is often advisable to write out the introduction and conclusion and partially memorize them. And any speaker who encounters hecklers must expect to engage in some impromptu retorts.

20a. For most speaking situations use the extemporaneous mode.

Extemporaneous speaking is the most common mode of delivery, and is the one you should use in all but a few special cases. This mode is sometimes confused with impromptu. Although it shares some aspects of spontaneity with impromptu, the extemporaneous mode is considerably more structured. In this mode you prepare extensively: constructing the progression of ideas with the aid of an outline, planning your content thoroughly, practicing until you are comfortable and conversational, but never committing yourself to a rigid, exact sequence of words. Preparing a set of ideas rather than a set of verbatim paragraphs is the only practical and realistic method for most teachers, trial lawyers, salespersons, and others engaged in speaking for hours at a time or for large portions of the day. But even for the occasional public speaker, the extemporaneous mode, once mastered, gives a sense of power and confidence. You will sound more natural and conversational if you phrase your sentences as you go along. Your mind will be on your ideas and on your audience's reaction to them—so you are less likely to go blank than if your were focusing on recalling certain words. Finally, you will find that speaking extemporaneously is flexible. You can adjust to audience response. If you find your listeners nodding knowledgeably at points you thought would be confusing and in need of clarification, you can drop your extensive examples and move on. Conversely, you can spend more time on points where you have hit unexpected resistance or do not get the response you anticipated.

Prepare an extemporaneous speech in three steps.

1. *Begin with a full-sentence outline*. Follow the recommendations in **5**, **6**, and **7** to arrange your material in a logical and effective manner.

2. *Convert your outline to speech notes*. See **21a** for directions on how to transfer your content to key words and short phrases in a format that provides easy visual cues to which you can refer.

3. *Word the speech*. Speaking from your notes, practice putting your ideas into words. Listen to yourself carefully to hear what sounds clumsy or to remember an exciting turn of phrase. The second time through, some of the clumsy phrases will have disappeared (and some of the exciting ones, maybe) as you play with sentence structure, rhythms, and so forth. Third time, fourth time, fifth time through—your topic is becoming more and more familiar, giving you the freedom to relax and to allow yourself to really experiment with construction. You will also discover that no one way of expressing a set of thoughts is necessarily better than another: you have said the same thing five times, differently each time, but all of the last three ways work equally well.

20b. Avoid impromptu speaking. But learn to cope with the situation if it is thrust on you.

No one should set out to give an important speech in the impromptu mode. Those good speakers who seem to be able to speak fluently on the spur of the moment are usually speaking extemporaneously, stringing together practiced "bits" to fit the subject that has been dropped into their laps. Do not let this illusion of spontaneity mislead you into under-preparing.

There are three sets of circumstances that can result in impromptu speaking.

No excuse

A lazy or overconfident speaker may decide to "wing it" even though there has been plenty of time to prepare. The resulting shoddy word choice, lack of organization, repetition, generalities, and unsupported assertions will be a monumental waste of the audience's time.

Should have seen it coming

Many impromptu speeches could have been extemporaneous if the speaker had analyzed the requirements and potentials of the situation. An expert caught flat-footed by a question at a press conference probably could have seen it coming by visualizing the event and anticipating the varied perspectives of the questioners. The Best Man who has not prepared a toast is guilty of failing to investigate his responsibilities.

Legitimately unexpected

There are some instances where no realistic amount of preparation or anticipation would lead one to think that he or she would need to speak. The executive who finds fifty demonstrators in his boardroom could be excused for not having a prepared statement. Similarly, it would be a bit conspicuous if the recipient of a surprise award proceeded to give a two-hour speech of acceptance. In a meeting you innocently agree to a whispered request to nominate a colleague, and to your dismay the chair then announces: "Now we will have the nominators make statements about their candidate's qualifications."

If you too often find yourself speaking in the *no excuse* or *should have seen it coming* scenarios, the solutions lie in other sections of this book, especially **4**, **5**, and **21**. The suggestions that follow pertain to the third, *legitimately unexpected*, case.

(1) Keep your composure.

Do not apologize. Knowing the situation is truly a surprise, the audience will have realistic expectations of you. You should have realistic expectations yourself and not fall apart if what comes out is not your most polished performance. Speak slowly and confidently. Remind yourself that you speak all the time without extensive preparation. In any casual conversation not only are you speaking, but you are planning what to say next. You do mental composition *all the time*. Do not let the stress of a speaking situation make you forget that!

One important benefit of maintaining your composure is that you can take full advantage of the time between the surprise announcement of your speaking and the actual beginning of that speech. Whether you have the thirty seconds that it takes to walk to the podium, or the ten minutes after hearing that the featured speaker is caught in a snowbank in the next county, use the time to go through an accelerated speech preparation. However short the period, the steps should be the same: pick a theme, an organizational pattern, and a beginning and ending sentence.

(2) Select a theme.

Very quickly list several possible approaches to the topic. Do it mentally, but if time permits, with pencil and paper. By thinking beyond the most obvious approach, you may discover a way to link your topic to a subject you are conversant with.

(3) Select an organizational framework.

You will not have time to make an extensive outline, obviously, but that does not mean you are justified in bouncing erratically from point to point. You can hook your topic to a simple framework like one of the following:

Past-Present-Future
Pros and Cons
Problems and Prospects
Concentric rings (Main points progress from immediate concerns to universal concerns, for example: In the Home, In the School, In the Community; Locally, Regionally, Nationally, Internationally)
Domains (Develop the different spheres touched by the topic, for example: Politically, Socially, Economically; or Practical Implications, Theoretical Implications, Moral Implications)

After you have divided your topic along the lines of one of these frameworks, find one means of support or development for each idea, such as an explanation, an example, a story, a fact, or a statistic.

If time permits, make a rudimentary outline. Even a few key words on a napkin can reassure you and keep you on the path once you have started to speak.

(4) Whenever possible, plan your first and last sentences.

The beginning and ending are the most difficult parts of any speech, and this is especially true in impromptu speaking. Even the simplest attention getter can propel you through that awkward first moment. When you know there is a concluding sentence ready to slap on, you will avoid the panicky feeling that comes with looking for an ending when you run out of steam. Having introductory and concluding sentences averts the aimless rambling so characteristic of impromptu speaking. When you know your task is to start with sentence A and work your way to sentence B, you will have a ready reference against which to judge ideas that occur to you as you are speaking.

Look at what you might do and think — along the lines of **(2)**, **(3)**, and **(4)** — if you unexpectedly find that a speech is expected of you:

You are attending a professional meeting and the moderator looks at you and two colleagues and suddenly says, "I see we have representatives here from three other universities in the area. I'd like to call on each of you to tell us about your department. How are things looking on your campus? What are the developments and trends?

You now have two or three minutes available before you are expected to speak. You know the topic well, but what should you select to say and how should you arrange it? Your thoughts go like this.

> Why didn't I have some warning?
> Help!
> They could have given me thirty minutes notice, or something!
> Oh, well.
> [You take out your pen and start to jot things down as you think:]
> Things are pretty awful in the department right now. Morale is down because we haven't been able to hire a new person in so long. Of course I don't want to seem to knock our part-time faculty. Our travel money is being cut back, we have less secretarial help. But our students are great — though our numbers of majors is down a little from last year. I don't want to sound like things are that desperate, though: actually our enrollment is up thanks to the new speech requirement. I'll bet they'd like to hear about that. Of course, our new graduate emphasis in organizational communication is one of the most exciting developments and I feel comfortable talking about that.
> [Up to this point you have been jotting notes and they look like Figure 20-1.]

FIGURE 20-1

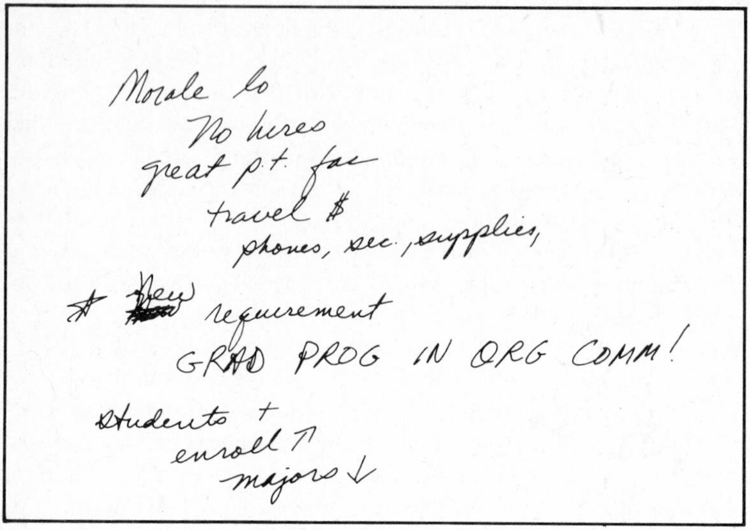

[You look at your notes and ask:]

Let's see, how shall I organize this? Curricular Issues and Personnel Issues? But what's my main theme? Do I want to say things are great in our department, or terrible? In some ways they've never been better; in other ways they've never been worse. Say, that sounds familiar. What's that quotation on best of times, worst of times? Hmm. Why don't I use that to pull this together? I can start out by saying, "When Kevin asked me to tell you about the state of our department I found myself thinking of the opening lines of Charles Dickens's *Tale of Two Cities*: 'It was the best of times, it was the worst of times. It was our summer of hope, it was the winter of our discontent.' That pretty well sums up our department. In some ways things have never been better, in other ways they've never been worse." Then I can talk about enrollments in the required course and our new graduate program and the part-time faculty as good things. Then I can discuss the loss of majors, budget cuts, and no hiring as bad things. I'll end it with something like, "So that is how things look on our campus. It's both the best and worst of times. Being an optimistic person, I think we can build on our strong curricular plans the enthusiasm of our students and faculty to overcome all the practical constraints. I believe the winter of discontent can be edged out by the summer of hope."

[You quickly copy over your notes, arranging then as in Figure 20-2.]

FIGURE 20-2

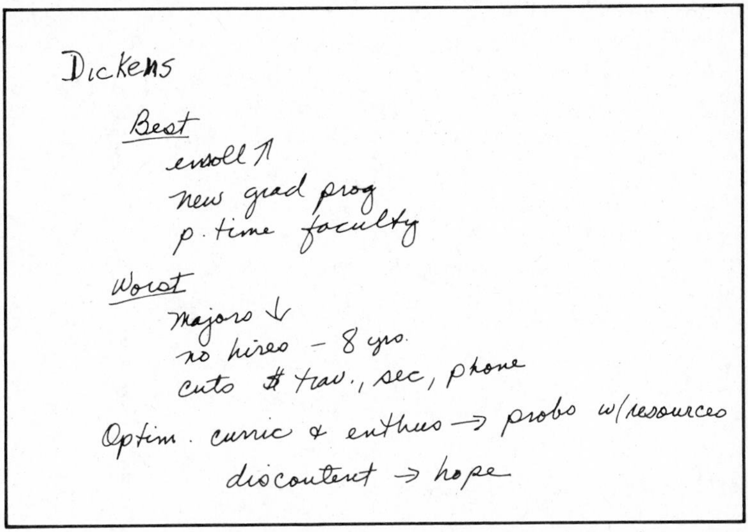

Dickens

Best
enroll ↑
new grad prog
p. time faculty

Worst
majors ↓
no hires – 8 yrs.
cuts # trav., sec, phone

Optim. curric & enthus → probs w/resources
discontent → hope

[The three minutes have passed, and you walk up to the podium.]

20c. Speak from a manuscript when precise wording and exact timing are essential to the situation. Maintain oral style and conversational delivery.

There is a widespread misconception that speaking from a manuscript is the easiest and safest mode of delivery. "I'm not an experienced speaker so I'd better write it out." This is no excuse for avoiding the extemporaneous mode. A bad manuscript speech is much worse than a bad extemporaneous speech. Stilted phrasing, monotonous vocal delivery, and lack of eye contact are all perils facing a novice speaking from a manuscript.

Limit your use of manuscripts to the following situations.

The time allotted is specific and inflexible.

This is mostly the case in the broadcast media. Short Free Speech replies to editorials need to be precise and compact with only a few seconds leeway in the scheduling.

259

The wording is extremely critical.

The section on extemporaneous speaking makes the point that many ways of phrasing a thought are acceptable. But, there are occasions where slight differences in phrasing are *not* acceptable. Exact word choice, or lack of it, can have severe consequences. The most visible examples of this are the public statements made by world leaders during a crisis. As the crisis deepens, the wording of these statements becomes more and more precise to forestall the misinterpretation that could trigger holocaust. Closer to ordinary experience, there are times where the lack of precision in speaking can lead to lawsuits. On some sensitive and emotionally charged topics the consequences of an ill-chosen word can be hostility, hurt feelings, and loss of business. A speaker would also be best advised to use a manuscript for technical or research reports where there is a lot of complex data and specialized denotations for many words.

The style is extremely important.

There are occasions where, although World War III is not a possible result, precision is required all the same. The necessity of precision springs not so much from matters of content but of style. It is expected that your language should be more compact, elevated, witty, or elegant than your everyday speech. For instance, though you still want to sound conversational in a major speech of tribute, the desire for the best possible word choice, sentence rhythm, and polished tone might lead you to use a manuscript.

(1) Prepare an easily readable manuscript in the oral style.

Do not let the fact that you are writing out a manuscript lure you away from the tenets of good organization and composition. Work from a full-sentence outline as described in **5**. Remember that the sentences of the outline are meant to be logical guides and not the actual wording of the speech. To get from the outline form to the manuscript, talk the speech out and onto the paper. You need to check your composition against your ear more than your eye. As you write, and rewrite, keep saying it aloud, listening for the rhythms of oral style. See **18**.

A tape recorder would be a good aid here. Listen to yourself and find the stiff, unwieldy phrases that need revision. To get a second opinion, have a friend listen.

When you have settled on the final version of your speech, produce the copy you will read from, following these guidelines:

- Definitely *type* it. Triple space with wide margins. some speakers prefer to use all capitals or oversized type.
- Type it on heavy paper. Avoid crinkly and transparent onionskin.
- Have everything you are going to say written out. Do not carry fourteen books with bookmarks up with you. All the quotations and examples should have been copied onto the manuscript.
- Number the pages unmistakably. This will prevent frantic searching if somehow a page is out of order.
- Never staple the pages together. Loose pages can be slid quietly to one side, revealing the next one. Attached pages need to be noisily and conspicuously folded over, sometimes pulling the rest of the manuscript off the lectern when the read pages outweigh the remaining ones.
- Use a lot of visual cues on the manuscript pages. Underline. Use different color ink. Write key words in the margins.

Figure 20-3 gives an example of a manuscript page prepared along these lines.

In some speaking situations you will not have your manuscript in your hands, but will be reading it from a Teleprompter or similar machine. See **27e**.

(2) Be familiar enough with your manuscript to look and sound as though you were speaking extemporaneously.

The two biggest problems in delivering a manuscript speech are

lack of conversational inflection, and
lack of eye contact.

Even though every word is written out for you, you should not be sight-reading. Practice your manuscript out loud often enough so that you are comfortable with it. Do not memorize — but be familiar with the flow and rhythm of the words. If you have followed the hints for composing in oral style, you should not find yourself slipping into a singsongy cadence or gasping for breath between overlong sentences.

The typed, easy-to-follow page mentioned in **20c(1)** is essential to maintaining good eye contact in a manuscript speech. The spaces and visual cuing make you less likely to lose your place while looking out at the audience regularly. Only through sustained eye contact will you reap its benefit: feedback. An occasional neck-snapping glance up from the

FIGURE 20-3

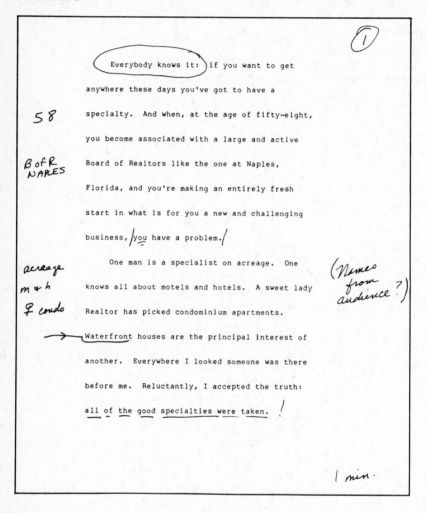

①

Everybody knows it: if you want to get

anywhere these days you've got to have a

5 8   specialty. And when, at the age of fifty-eight,

you become associated with a large and active

B of R
NAPLES   Board of Realtors like the one at Naples,

Florida, and you're making an entirely fresh

start in what is for you a new and challenging

business, /you have a problem./

One man is a specialist on acreage. One

acreage   knows all about motels and hotels. A sweet lady

m & h   Realtor has picked condominium apartments.

& condo

→ Waterfront houses are the principal interest of

another. Everywhere I looked someone was there

before me. Reluctantly, I accepted the truth:

all of the good specialties were taken. /

*(Names
from
audience ?)*

1 min.

page will not provide you with much information about what is going on
in your audience, and that jerky movement can be just another distraction. If you have practiced your speech enough, you will have time to
raise your head and engage the audience with unhurried and unchoppy
motion.

Never read your first or last few sentences. Have them memorized so that you can start your speech holding eye contact with your audience. Never read your punch lines.

20d. Memorize a short, important speech only on those occasions where holding a manuscript would be out of place.

By definition, giving a memorized speech would entail the delivery of a manuscript speech — without the manuscript. The only times you should give a memorized speech, therefore, are the same as put forth in **20c**, with the added limitations that the speech should be a short one and the situation inappropriate for reading. These occasions are most often ceremonial: giving a toast, presenting a plaque, or accepting an honor.

(1) Memorize the structure of the speech before memorizing the speech word for word.

Learn a few key words that will help you internalize the main sequence of ideas. For example, if you were presenting an award to your company's Salesperson of the Year, you might learn this outline for your brief speech.

   I. Selection process for the award
  II. Chris Welch's sales record for this year
 III. Chris' qualities as a successful salesperson

Or even more simply:

Process.
Record.
Qualities.

(2) Read the speech aloud several times and then work on learning it paragraph by paragraph.

Always keep your mind on the meaning. Do not try to learn sentences in isolation, but rather work on whole paragraphs at a time, reinforcing their logical and conceptual unity.

(3) As you practice, visualize giving the speech.

Avoid thinking of your speech as lines of text in a social vacuum. You do not want to be startled and lose your concentration when you realize that you are actually facing a roomful of people.

(4) Do not go into a trance when delivering the speech.

Once again, be comfortably familiar with your material so that you can maintain eye contact and rapport with your audience, instead of having your eyes glaze over and your voice and body tighten with concentration.

(5) If you go blank, switch to the extemporaneous mode and recall the structure of the speech rather than groping for the next word.

Speaking along the general lines of the point you know you were trying to make, you can collect your thoughts and soon click back into that which you have memorized.

21

Practice Sessions

Plan your practice sessions. Use them to convert your outlined ideas into the actual speech you will deliver.

Since a speech is delivered orally, it should be composed orally. The practice sessions wherein you actually talk through your ideas should not be viewed as last minute polishing but as an essential step in creating the speech. Leave plenty of time for composition as well as for receiving feedback, preparing notes, and timing the speech.

21a. Make a timetable for your practice sessions.

It is not necessarily true that more is better. In the case of practicing your speech or report, too much practice may make your delivery stale and you run the risk of becoming bored with your topic. Most speakers err in the opposite direction, however, and the result is even more disastrous. To avoid falling into either of these traps, you should plan your practice sessions, write down a timetable of steps and phases, and adhere to it.

Your speech is not going to be static during these sessions. The creative process, as outlined in the introduction to **PREPARATION**, will continue, and the timetable should not be so rushed that the periods of incubation between sessions are squeezed out. Doing a stand-up, full-dress practice once in the morning and once in the evening for three days is immeasurably better than running through the speech six times in a row. With your practice sessions spread out, you are more likely to benefit from the illumination and refinement that follows incubation.

There is no one, arbitrary timetable to adopt. The variations in type of speech and lead time given for preparation make it impossible to prescribe an exact number of practice sessions. The following example shows possible timetables for three speeches where the advance notice is different for each. This can be used as a guide to help you make a schedule unique to your circumstances.

POSSIBLE PRACTICE SCHEDULES

Type of speech	Major policy address	Classroom speech	Routine oral report in a business setting
Assignment was made	Several weeks before	Ten days before	Twenty-four hours before
Research and outline completed	One week before	Four days before	Evening before
Early practice sessions	Two–one week before: discuss ideas with colleagues. Six, five days before: talk through speech once a day	Ten–four days before: talk about speech with friends. Four days before: read outline several times. Practice aloud twice	Afternoon or evening before: talk through basic ideas with friends or colleagues. Evening before: practice aloud one to three times
Middle practice sessions	Four days before: give speech on videotape, review with advisers, repeat	Three days before: give speech to friendly critic, receive feedback, practice aloud one other time	Morning of speech: give speech to colleague, if possible
Final practice sessions	Three, two, one day before: practice aloud once a day. Read notes or outline about once a day. Day of speech: practice aloud once. Review notes just before speaking	Two, one day before: practice aloud one to three times a day. Read over outline and notes several times. Day of speech: practice aloud once just before speaking. Review notes	Day of speech: practice aloud once. Review notes just before leaving for speech

A practice timetable can also be influenced by personal differences in speaking ability. For instance, an experienced speaker giving a classroom speech may not need three final practices a day — one may suffice. Adapt the timetable to an honest evaluation of your speaking skill.

21b. Use early practice sessions to flesh out your outline.

During these early sessions you will be transforming your set of ideas into your speech by adding the elements of language and delivery to the logical framework erected by your outline.

Begin by internalizing your outline. Read it over a number of times, becoming familiar with the flow of the logic. Sit at your desk or a table and mumble through the outline. Try to explain the ideas to yourself— half thinking, half talking it out.

Besides talking to yourself, it is helpful to talk to other people. Try out your ideas and words, seeing if they make sense. You are not, however, practicing your speech in front of them. Work your ideas into conversations over lunch and chats with colleagues and friends. You do not need a reaction to every idea from each individual you talk to. After talking to a number of people, you will find that you have begun to word the speech.

At this point pick a quiet spot and start to put together the speech as it will actually be given. Stand up and give the speech out loud in your speaking voice. Include everything. Do not say to yourself, after making a point, "and then I'll give you a few examples." Give them. Awkward phrases, construction, and word choice should be discovered sooner rather than later. Visualize the speech situation and mentally put yourself there. Do not think "this is a practice session." Make it real—see the faces out there and talk to them. Do not consciously worry about your hands and voice.

Sometime during this stage you will have made the first draft of your speech notes. Do not carve them in stone. They are mutable according to how things shape up as you play with the wording. Remember that you do not want to lock yourself irreversibly into one exact sequence of words.

21c. Use one or more middle practice sessions for receiving feedback.

After you have become comfortable with your material but before the final polishing, there is a point where you should seek feedback on your speech. This is usually sometime in the middle of your timetable. If you start looking for feedback on content, style, and delivery too soon, when you have not finished shaping your basic speech, you will miss getting help on those parts that have not yet been crystallized. If the feedback comes too late in the schedule, you will not have the time to incorporate comfortably the useful information you have received.

(1) Practice your speech in front of others, and ask for their feedback.

People are the best source of feedback: a group of friends, colleagues, family members — seek a variety of responses. Take what you can get; but if you can, find critics as close to being representative of your potential audience as possible. If you are going to speak to a high school audience, for instance, ask your teenage cousin, niece, or friend to listen to a practice session. Give your speech exactly as if you were in front of your actual audience, no nervous clowning around. Do not make it more informal just because they are friends. Do not leave things out and say, "You've heard this story." Tell it. Do not talk about your speech. Give your speech.

Ask for honest feedback on content and delivery, but do not necessarily take any single person's comments as the last word. He or she has quirks and prejudices just like everyone else. This is why a group of people would be better, giving you a sampling of responses.

You should not ask, "How'd you like my speech?" Answers like "It was nice," "I thought it was OK," certainly do not help you much. Lead your critics with a few questions and seek clarification of their answers. You might not like what you hear, but friendly criticism beats ridicule from a roomful of strangers later. Here are some specific questions you can ask.

"What did you see as the single most important thing I was trying to say?" If they do not come up with your thesis sentence, then you must look at your structure again.

"What were the main ideas I was trying to get across?" They should answer with your main points.

It is important to get answers to these first two questions before moving on to finer points of development and delivery. You are speaking for a specific purpose, and everything else is insignificant if your whole reason for speaking is not being understood. If you are satisfied that your purpose is clear, then you can ask questions along these lines:

"Did you think ideas flowed in a logical sequence?"

"Did the speech hold your attention? What parts were boring? Confusing?"

"Did I prove my points?"

"Did my introduction show you where I was going?"
"Did the conclusion tie the speech together?"
"Did I sound natural?"
"Did I have any distracting mannerisms?"

(2) Record your practice session on audiotape or videotape and analyze your performance.

A videotape is the next best thing to a human critic. A video cassette recorder with a camera is not yet as common a household appliance as a stereo or TV, but there are sources for the casual user. Video clubs usually have rental equipment available. If you are taking classes, the school may own a machine to which you can have access. Some speech consultants offer a videotape service. Your company may have videotape equipment for training.

When you view your performance on playback, try to get outside yourself and see the image as that of a stranger. Become the audience and ask yourself the same questions that are raised above in **(1)**. You might not believe it when a friend tells you your "I means" follow every other sentence and you are always picking at your sweater. The evidence is inescapable when you watch yourself do it on tape. A hazard to avoid here is being too self-critical. Seeing yourself on tape can be devastating if you notice only the apsects that need improvement. Look also for things you are doing right. Do not get caught up examining physical attributes, worrying about the shape of your nose or the fact that your ears stick out or that your taped voice sounds different from the way you normally perceive it. This is where it can be helpful to watch the tape with a friend or coach who can give you a more balanced perspective.

If a video cassette recorder is not available, your next best help is, of course, the tape recorder. You will not receive the visual information, but you certainly will be able to get feedback on content, pacing, voice, and so on.

Occasionally you may want to use a tape recorder earlier in the timetable, especially if you are blocked creatively. This is a different use of the machine: it helps you remember good ideas and possible wordings, and complements talking your ideas out with friends.

---

(3) **Practicing in front of a mirror should be limited to a single session, if done at all.**

It is our opinion that practicing in front of a mirror does more harm than good. Concentrating on your image as a speaker while you speak is antithetical to the philosophy of presentation as laid out in the introduction to this section. The picture to hold in your mind as you practice should be of your audience—their faces, their responses. The worst picture to hold as you visualize a speech is one of you standing isolated in front of an unseen group. Practicing before a mirror will make you more self-conscious and more likely to think of the event as a performance rather than an interaction. The methods described in **(1)** and **(2)** above allow the feedback to be *delayed*: after speaking you can shift your focus away from ideas to a more detached assessment of the details of your presentation. With a mirror you are compelled to divide your attention between what you are saying and how you are saying it.

If you have no other way to get a general check on the visual impact of your posture, gestures, and facial expressions, it may be worthwhile to practice before a mirror just once. More than that will lead to a narcissistic obsession with your reflection.

Avoid the mirror and, if you cannot talk to a live person, talk to a blank wall and visualize your listeners. The difference in mental set is crucial to your success.

21d. Use the last few practice sessions for refinements of style and delivery. Be sure you feel ready psychologically as well.

By this time you should be committed to a basic version of your speech, while maintaining the looseness of the extemporaneous mode. You should not be making radical changes right up to the deadline.

(1) Make the final practice sessions as realistic as possible.

If you are going to use visual aids, they should be ready early enough so that you can include them in your final practice sessions. The same holds true for the final draft of the notecards. Check yourself against your time limit. Practice your speech, standing up, at the rate and volume you will be using. Speaking with rudimentary mechanical amplification to a large audience, for example, will use more breath than the conversational volume used in early practice. You need to unabashedly boom out in the final practice sessions, if booming out is going to be what it takes to be heard when you actually give the speech.

Continue reading through your notes and outline, but do not think of these activities as a substitute for the formal practice sessions.

(2) Save the hours just before the speech for one final run-through and for getting into the proper, relaxed frame of mind.

Imagine that you are giving an important speech one afternoon or evening. You should have planned your practice sessions so that, by the night before, your speech is polished and you are comfortable with it. Remember that it is never a good idea to compress your practice into a few frantic hours. On the morning of the event, allow for one unpressured practice session. As you go about the day's activities, you may want to look over your outline or notes one time. If you feel yourself becoming anxious, try some of the relaxation or visualization techniques recommended in **22c** and **d**.

The last quiet, private moment before the speech is the time to go through your notes and outline once again.

This could be done just as you leave your home or office, or sitting on a bench outside the building. In the final minutes before your presentation, go through your introduction and conclusion. Visualize the gross structure of the speech, a macroview of the ideas.

Throughout the constructing of your speech, you should keep in mind what preparation it would take to get yourself to the podium in a relaxed frame of mind. Take time well before the speech to think about those possible situations that could throw you off your pace, and set up strategies to avoid or dilute them. Try to arrange your day so that you are not rushing around picking up dry cleaning or cashing a check. Get the logistics of your life in order early. If you have a meeting just before the speech, one you know is usually tense and upsetting, do not go. Be conscious of your idiosyncratic responses to a number of stimuli. If you know you do not function well on a full stomach, do not eat the rich banquet—just have the salad. Or, if half a glass of wine is the perfect amount for you to be relaxed but alert, drink half and leave the rest. In short, be a little selfish and take care of yourself in the ways you have learned work best. You owe it to your audience and yourself to be feeling comfortable, confident, and composed when you present the speech you have worked so hard to prepare.

21e. Prepare speech notes to act as a guide and a safety net.

You should not confuse speech notes with your outline, as they serve different functions. An outline is used to assure that the speech is prepared in accordance with a logical organization. Speech notes, on the other hand, are used as an aid while you are actually speaking.

Like your outline and wording, your notes can go through several drafts. Work on them, doodle on them, then copy them over. Do not feel committed to the first thing you write. Just the kinesthetic act of copying over your notes is an excellent way to firm up your speech in your mind.

(1) Speech notes should consist of key words and phrases and material that is to be cited directly.

Unlike your outline—in which your points must be parallel, mutually exclusive, and in full sentences, with no "A without a B"—your speech notes do not have a rigid, regulation form. A point can be represented by a word, a sentence fragment, or an actual sentence or two. What goes into your notes depends on what you find you need during practice.

For example, perhaps one point of your speech, which in your outline was developed to the second level of subordination with all its accompanying A's and B's, and 1's and 2's, is one with which you are so familiar that is can be represented in speech notes resembling those in Figure 21–1.

While practicing you may also find that you want more than just a key-word reminder to get through an important but tongue-twisting sentence or to insure that you remember an especially eloquent turn of phrase that has a delicate rhythm. Your notes may also contain material that you will be citing exactly as written out: quotations that are too long to commit to memory or complicated statistics, for instance.

Keep in mind, however, that your notes should remain *notes*. If you make them too extensive and detailed you risk moving out of the extemporaneous mode and into delivering a manuscript speech. Your notes should be referred to, not read from.

(2) Prepare your notecards in a format that aids your delivery.

Generally, most speakers prefer to put their notes on 4″ × 6″ or 5″ × 8″ cards. The 8½″ × 11″ sheet of paper has the disadvantage of being large

FIGURE 21-1

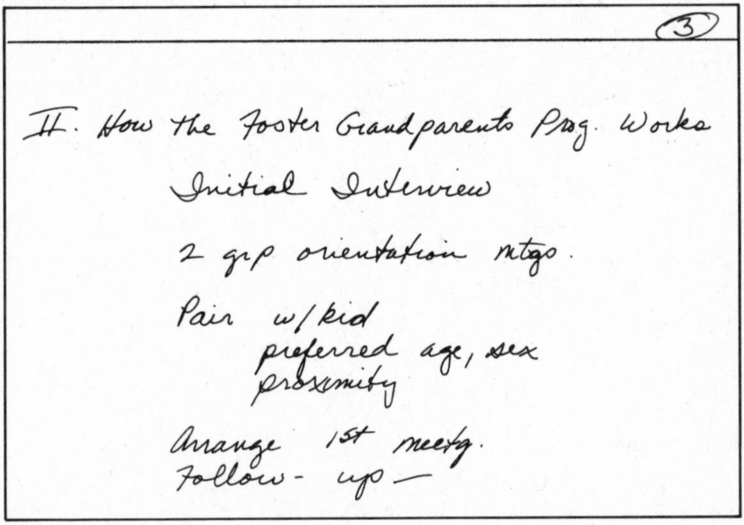

and floppy, inhibiting your gestures and limiting your movement by effectively tying you to the lectern or table. While the 8½″ × 11″ sheet is too large, the 3″ × 5″ card is too small. If you make your notes on them properly, large enough to be read, you will end up with a huge stack of cards through which you are constantly flipping.

A few medium-sized cards can easily become an extension of your hand as you gesture and move about. They will not be distracting to your listeners if you seem comfortable with them. Do not be coy about using your notecards — refer to them honestly. A surreptitious peek at protectively cupped hands will not fool your listeners into believing that you are speaking without aids.

Do not go to the other extreme and get lost in your notes. You should be able to look down, see what is next, then talk about it. If you find yourself burying your nose in your cards, you have not prepared them correctly. The words and phrases should be large, well-spaced, and uncluttered. There should be a lot of visual cues — large card numbers, underlining, indenting, stars, highlighting, different colors — all for the purpose of making it easy for you to find what you want at a glance. Speech notes should also be cued to choices you will make during the speech. Time notations are essential. You might write at one point "if more than 8 minutes, skip to card 6." You might use a special color to mark optional sections of the speech. Examples highlighted in yellow could mean: *include this if the audience seems uncertain about my point. Otherwise omit it*.

Figure 21-2 shows some notes that might have been used for the speech by VerLynn Sprague in the **Appendix**.

21f. Fit your speech into the time limit.

The section on preparation admonishes you to limit your topic according to the time allowed. Often you cannot tell for sure how much time your speech will take until you have gotten well into the practice sessions. In extemporaneous practice you will experience variations in length as you work with the form of your ideas and the style and rhythms of your speaking. This, again, is where envisioning audience response is helpful. Most first-time speakers practice at a rate faster than the one they find necessary for clarity during the speech itself. The more realistic your practice the less likely you are to misestimate your time.

To clock your speech do not glue your eyes to the sweep hand of your watch. Merely note the time when you begin and again when you finish. A sweep hand can induce unnatural behavior like speaking twice

FIGURE 21-2

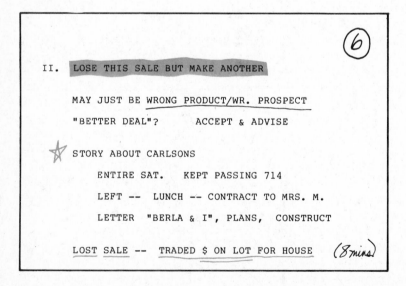

II.   LOSE THIS SALE BUT MAKE ANOTHER   ⑥

       MAY JUST BE WRONG PRODUCT/WR. PROSPECT

       "BETTER DEAL"?   ACCEPT & ADVISE

☆ STORY ABOUT CARLSONS

            ENTIRE SAT.   KEPT PASSING 714

            LEFT -- LUNCH -- CONTRACT TO MRS. M.

            LETTER "BERLA & I", PLANS, CONSTRUCT

       LOST SALE -- TRADED $ ON LOT FOR HOUSE   (8 mins.)

your normal rate for the last minute if you think you are going too long, or, in the opposite case, slowing your delivery to a tired shuffle. There are more sensible ways to address problems of length. The first step is to time the parts of your speech. Two possible ways of doing this are to have a helper jot down the times of your main points on your outline as you practice or to do it yourself with a tape recorder.

Look at the relative proportions of the parts of speech: introduction, body, conclusion. Generally, the body should comprise 75 percent of your speech. Does an extended story make the introduction too long? Look too at the relative proportions of your main points. Are you spending half your time on just the first main point? Is it worth it?

If your speech is too long:

1. Consider cutting out an entire main point. (Adjust your thesis accordingly.)
2. Look at your supporting evidence and examples and cut those that duplicate effort. (But save the ones cut as they may be needed for the question-and-answer or discussion period.)
3. Turn some of your illustrations into examples. (Instead of telling the whole story, toss off a one-liner that capsulizes it.)
4. Eliminate any long stories, jokes, narrations, unless they are absolutely essential to the theme of the speech.
5. Consider using means other than speech to transmit technical or detailed information. Handouts and visual aids are two examples.
6. Polish and tighten your language and phrasing. Speak simply.

If your speech is too short:

1. Find if there are important ideas that are not getting enough development relative to the other points.
2. See if you are too concise for your own good. As is explained in many other places, the spoken word is fleeting and needs repetition and embellishment and illustration to bring home to each and every member of the audience the emphasis that you want to deliver.
3. Make sure you have proved all your points. Double-check your evidence to make sure that you have not assumed too much or made some logical leaps that are not justified.
4. You may have given up too soon at the library. Have you really researched enough?

In a speech class there may be penalties for not reaching a minimum time limit. In most other settings no one is going to be awfully upset if you take only fifteen out of the twenty minutes you have been given. However, taking forty minutes when you have been allotted twenty can disrupt the schedules of countless other people.

The experienced speaker always knows the duration of each element of the speech. Even if the first clocking run-throughs show that the speaker meets the time requirement satisfactorily, she or he still wants to have a point-by-point time breakdown. This knowledge aids adaptation to changes that might crop up in the speech situation itself. See **25**.

When you reach that point in your practicing where the speech consistently comes out the same length, mark the cumulative times of the parts of your notes. For example, you might print "2 mins" at the bottom right of your notes on the introduction, "5 mins" after the first main point, "8 mins" after the second, and so on. See Figure 21-2.

Here, as examples, are two situations where knowing the timing of the elements of your speech will help you adapt without panic.

> You planned to spend five minutes on your first main point. Feedback from the audience convinced you to use eight minutes to make certain they were getting it clear. You decide to drop anecdotes from your second and third points to make up the three minutes.

> You are on a program which is running late but can't go overtime because of scheduling conflicts. The moderator asks you if you can trim your presentation from thirty minutes to ten. You begin doing mental arithmetic, subtracting combinations of points until you arrive at a plausible shortened version of the speech.

Some people have internal clocks that are accurate enough that these speakers do not need external cues. If yours is not that well developed (and most of ours are not), feel free to take off your watch and lay it where you can see it, or have a colleague in the audience give you arranged signals. Avoid excessive reliance on the clock, though. Become comfortable with your presentation by practicing your speech and timing it in practice.

22

Overcoming Fear of Speaking

Understand, analyze, and accept your fear of speaking. Combine thorough preparation with relaxation and visualization techniques to increase your confidence.

22a. Put your fear of speaking into perspective.

(1) Accept some fear as normal.

Many speakers try to be completely calm in every speech situation. This is unrealistic. Whether they call it stage fright, shyness, or speech anxiety, all speakers feel some fear. One out of five people experiences rather serious fear, enough to adversely affect performance. One out of twenty people suffers such serious fear of speaking that he or she is essentially unable to get through a public speech. For most of us, though, the fear can be managed and sometimes even turned to positive effect. People who perform in the public eye — actors, athletes, musicians ... and speakers — have learned to function while concealing their fear. Despite their discomfort, they can use the rush of emotion to energize their performance.

The more speeches you give the more confident you will become. You will recognize that fear is usually worst just before the speech and through the introduction. Once your speech is under way and the audience responds to you, negative emotions are often replaced by exhilaration.

(2) Analyze your fear as specifically as possible.

"I'm scared to death" is a common statement and it describes the emotional intensity of stage fright. Although one survey found that people list the fear of public speaking ahead of the fear of death, few people really expect the experience to be fatal. Just what are we afraid of? An amorphous, ill-defined fear cannot be dealt with. Dealing logically with the fear requires examining its components so you can isolate a number of specific problems to be solved.

It is helpful to list your fears on paper. Be as specific as possible. If you write statements like "I'm afraid I'll make a fool of myself," ask yourself these follow-up questions: How will I do that? (I'll forget my speech"); What will happen next? ("The audience will think I'm dumb"). Use this format for your list:

I am afraid that [specific event] will occur and then that [specific result] will follow.

When you have generated your list, you can classify the fears you have.

For items like: "I'm afraid my visual aids won't be clear," the solution is simple. Check out the clarity of your visual aids with a few people and, if there is any problem, redesign them. As **22b** points out, many fears result from inadequate preparation. The mere act of writing the fears down makes them manageable and often points immediately to a solution.

Other fears on your list may relate to physical responses. "I'm afraid my hands will shake and my voice will crack." If many of your concerns fall in this category, pay special attention to the suggestions in **22c**.

Probably a number of items on your list deal with your failure to meet your own high standards. Recognize this fear as a positive motivation to do the best you can. Realize too, though, that the power of suggestion is great and that dwelling on failure can cause it to happen. Use some of the visualization and verbalization techniques recommended in **22d** to create positive self-expectations.

If your fears are so pervasive you could not even verbalize them, or if you could list literally dozens, or if the consequences you dread are extreme ("I might collapse in the middle of the speech"), consider some of the more formal options mentioned in **22e**.

Finally, look at your list and decide which consequence is the one you are most afraid of. For most of us, like the college teacher who regularly lectures to a large student audience but quails at the thought of presenting a paper to twelve colleagues, the greatest fear is the fear of negative evaluation, particularly by peers or authority figures.

This fear of negative evaluation will translate into fear of your audience. As a group they seem threatening and critical. Remind yourself that an audience is merely a group of individuals and that a speech is just an enlarged conversation. If it would not be frightening to speak to any three or four of them, then it should not be frightening to speak to all of them together.

Of course, there are a few harsh, critical people in the world, but we have found that most listeners are charitable and supportive. They would just as soon hear a good speech; so they will, in effect, be rooting for you. Particularly, they want you to be confident. Recall how you felt when listening to very nervous speakers: your discomfort and embarrassment were almost as great as theirs. This is testimony to the basic empathy of most audiences. Listeners will pick up the speaker's emotional tone, so that, for instance, a tense speaker will create a tense audience. On the other hand, you can actually feel an audience relax when a speaker who gets off to a shaky start hits his or her stride and the speech begins to roll.

If there is one technique that has helped people cope with stage fright, it is reconceptualizing the role of the audience, from "critic" to "recipient." A speaker must break out of the self-absorption of speech fright: "How do I look? Will they like me? Is my speech good enough?" Remind yourself that you are not there to perform, but to share. Center your thoughts on hypothetical audience members who are sincere and responsive. What do you have to give these people? How will the ideas and information you offer enrich their lives?

22b. Build your confidence through thorough preparation and practice.

Why do sky divers think they can reach the ground in one piece? Preparation and practice allay their fears. Why do investors risk large sums of money? Preparation and practice have given them a clear view of the consequences. As we note elsewhere, the fact that good speakers make speechmaking look effortless does not mean that it is easy or uncomplicated. Their seeming lack of effort is based on extensive preparation over a period of time. The confidence they exude is also a result of preparation — not genes or fate or dumb luck. Nearly anyone can be poised and confident giving a speech. The speaker who has prepared thoroughly can be as confident as the sky diver who has exhaustively checked all his gear or the investor who has studied innumerable projections.

If you feel uncertain about getting your speech started, perhaps your introduction needs more work. If you are fearful of losing the continuity of the speech, you may need to practice it aloud several more times to internalize the flow of ideas. If you find yourself becoming generally anxious, use this as a stimulus to go over your preparation yet again. Drill yourself on the particulars of your supporting material. Go over your outline a number of times. Whatever else you do, remember that time wasted fretting about the outcome could better be used in positive action to insure a positive outcome.

As you prepare, follow the suggestions on practice sessions in **21**. Avoid making last-minute changes in the speech and avoid memorizing your speech and practicing it so much that the ideas become stale and your delivery mechanical.

22c. Cope with the physical effects of fear by using techniques of relaxation and tension release.

When we are fearful or anxious, our bodies react by tensing the muscles to brace for attack and by releasing extra adrenalin to prepare us to fight or flee. These "fight or flight" responses, which are helpful confronting a bear in the woods and were adaptive for our prehistoric ancestors, are not appropriate when the threat is psychological. When fear of speaking triggers our primitive sense of danger, we experience such symptoms as rapid heart rate, dizziness, butterflies in the stomach, trembling, perspiring, and dryness of the mouth. Muscular tension in the throat can cause a voice to quaver, sound strained, or even produce the unpredictable squawks of distant adolescence.

These physical symptoms will probably diminish with time as your successful experiences as a speaker make disaster appear less probable. But some degree of physical discomfort is likely to persist. You can master techniques to help you feel more comfortable.

When too much adrenalin makes you jumpy, physical activity usually helps to mitigate the effect. Of course, heavy exercise before a speech is impractical and overstimulating. A brisk walk around the block or a little pacing in the hall can be enough to bring your body back to normal. If you have a few moments of privacy, light exercise will feel good—just a few knee bends, arm swings, and neck rolls. If you remain in sight of your audience before the speech, you may be able unobtrusively to clench and unclench your hands, but do not risk your credibility by going through any bizarre preparatory rituals. Once the speech begins, take advantage of the extra energy the adrenalin provides to make your delivery more vigorous. Appropriate, dynamic gestures will help you discharge the nervous residue.

You can also handle symptoms of nervousness by learning to use relaxation techniques. Relaxation, like any other skill, is achieved through practice. Using any of a number of books or tapes on stress, tension, and relaxation, you can learn first to isolate the areas of your body that are tense and then to relax them. Try meditation, biofeedback, or self-hypnosis. Explore such methods as tightening, then relaxing, certain muscle groups; visualizing serene settings; or imagining sensations such as warmth or heaviness in parts of your body. There are great individual differences in people's responses to these techniques. Continue to experiment until you find one or more that are effective for you. After learning and practicing such techniques, you should be able to achieve relaxation, even lower your pulse and blood pressure, while taking a few deep breaths before you speak.

Chemical aids to relaxation — alcohol, drugs, tranquilizers — are not advisable. Most have side effects that impair your mental and physical performance during a speech, not to mention fabricating a false sense of security.

22d. Use positive self-suggestion to combat your anxiety.

(1) Visualize success.

Psychologists have discovered the tremendous power of visualization in influencing performance. When you experience fear, you are visualizing the most negative outcome for your speech. The more powerful your imagination the more horrible and graphic are the disasters you can dream up. It is possible, however, to turn these fantasies around. For example, tennis players, field goal kickers, and concert pianists, among others, have found it helpful to visualize what they are striving for.

When preparing a speech, do not let yourself think about failure. When you detect those thoughts in your mind, replace them with a positive scenario: "I will approach the lectern calmly, smile at the audience, and begin. My voice will sound strong and confident." Do not set unrealistic standards of perfection. Build some contingencies into your fantasy. "If I forget a point I'll look down at my notecard and concentrate on the main idea I am conveying." Run through these positive visualizations a few times a day before you speak. As you practice, picture the audience responding favorably to the speech. Just before you get up to speak, tell yourself about the general tone and image you wish to project. "As I go up there I am going to communicate my sincerity and concern in a warm, natural, confident manner."

(2) Replace negative internal statements with positive ones.

One approach to reducing fears is based on a therapeutic technique called cognitive restructuring. In essence, it probes our mental commentaries and identifies the unrealistic or irrational statements that cause fear, replacing them with more positive, logical, and realistic beliefs. Each of us has constant narrations running through our minds, voices chattering in the background. These commentaries are so familiar that we are barely conscious of them. With some introspection you can bring them to the front of your mind and examine the effect they have on your behavior. It is helpful to remember that these are not statements of fact, but are statements we ourselves have created and that we can choose to replace if they interfere with our efficient functioning. Once you become fully aware of the commentaries that govern your response to public speaking, you can work on replacing the unproductive beliefs with more positive ones.

False Belief	Positive Replacement
My speech will be a failure unless everyone in the audiences likes it.	I will be successful if most people present respond favorably.
A good speaker never says, "uh," "er."	A few nonfluencies aren't even noticed unless attention is called to them.
I'm going to go blank.	I've practiced several times. I know the basic structure of this speech.
I can't handle this tension!	Even though I feel uncomfortable, I'm able to cope with tense situations.
Someone will ask me a question that exposes my ignorance.	I'm not ignorant. I've researched this topic and I'm prepared for any reasonable question.

Your unproductive responses are habitual and will not change easily. At first you will have to repeat the replacement sentences over mechanically, over and over, as you might learn a new formula or equation. Because the replacement sentences are so reasonable and logical, a large part of your mind will want to accept them. The reassuring nature of the words often helps you to become physically calmer, and this more-comfortable sensation acts to reinforce the new beliefs.

22e. If none of the preceding suggestions work, seek outside help.

Some fear of speaking is too deeply rooted to be remedied by the methods suggested here. If your fear of speaking is almost paralyzing, you may need help in coping with it. Research shows that even severe fear of speaking can usually be reduced to a manageable level when treated by a qualified professional. It is not necessary to commit yourself to a long-range course of therapy that fully explores all the causes of your anxiety. Many training programs for speech fright deal directly with the symptoms by adapting techniques used for overcoming phobias such as fear of snakes, spiders, flying, and so on.

Many colleges and universities offer special sections of speech classes for fearful students. Others offer ungraded workshops to supplement regular classes. These programs use systematic desensitization (a method that combines relaxation exercises and visualization), cognitive restructuring, skills training, or a combination of these and other methods. Psychologists and speech consultants also offer programs to help reduce fear of speaking. Such programs may be publicized under the names of stage fright, communication apprehension, speech anxiety, reticence, or shyness.

23

Vocal Delivery

Speak clearly, correctly, and conversationally. Vary your vocal delivery for interest and emphasis.

As important as preparation, organization, content, and style are, the essence of speech is still your utterings. What a waste of time and brainpower if that which you have to say cannot be heard or understood at the critical moment of speaking. You must pay conscious attention to the mechanics of transmitting sound: articulation, breath control, projection, and so on. At the same time, your most important goal is to develop a style of vocal delivery that sounds natural and conversational. The "orator," with trilling r's and shuddering pauses, can really set one's teeth on edge. Except for the stylized chants of the auctioneer and revival minister, most public speech should sound like private speech, only exaggerated to fit the size of the room.

23a. Identify and eliminate distracting characteristics of your vocal delivery.

Your reason for speaking is defeated when your listeners begin to pay less attention to what you are saying and more to how you are saying it. "That's the fifteenth time she's said 'y'know'." "Why doesn't he clear his throat?" "That repetitious inflection is really irritating." Your voice and speech style should be unobtrusive vehicles for your ideas.

Distracting speech habits are difficult to identify and even more difficult to change. Vocal mannerisms become so familiar to you and your closest associates that they are overlooked and cease to distract, but to a new audience they are blatant. Follow the suggestions in **21c** for receiving feedback. Use videotape, audiotape, and critics to get some objective distance on your performance. When you isolate a problem, do not view it as just a public speaking problem. An overused phrase, a harsh raspy voice reduce your effectiveness in daily conversation as well. Resolve to correct it gradually and permanently by modifying your *everyday speaking habits*.

(1) Identify problems of voice quality.

The resonant, musical voice you view as an ideal may be beyond your reach, but there is, of course, no one perfect voice for effective speaking. There is a range of pleasing voices, and although the quality and timbre of your voice are determined to a great extent by your larynx, and the size and shape of your nasal cavities, you can find yourself within that range unless you are hampered by one or more of the following problems:

Harshness, Hoarseness, or Stridency

These qualities are caused by constriction of the throat or by tension or damage to the vocal folds. The voice may sound husky, rough, or shrill and often gives an impression of anger or gruffness.

Breathiness, Thinness, or Weakness

These qualities are caused by an inadequate airstream, by releasing excessive air, or by speaking in an unnaturally high falsetto. The effect is a soft, often childish-sounding voice that lacks authority and power.

Nasality and Denasality

Incorrect flow of air through the nasal passages creates these problems. Too much air escapes through the nose in the former case, too little in the latter. These problems primarily affect m, n, and ng sounds, and produce either whiny or stuffed-up qualities.

(2) Identify problems of articulation.

Many people have speech problems that are not severe enough to be considered disabling, but are still sufficiently distracting to impede good communication. A stutterer will certainly be aware of his or her condition, whereas the people with lesser problems are usually not conscious of the particular misarticulations that occur in their speech.

285

Listen closely to your own speech for irregularities in the way you produce consonant sounds or blends of consonants. Many articulation errors take the form of *substitutions*, such as "*th*olution, for "*s*olution," or "*d*ese" for "*th*ese." Also common are sound *distortions*: the slushing, hissing, or whistling *s*, or the lazy *l* or *r*. Less frequently encountered articulation errors are *additions* (ath*a*lete for athlete, real*a*tor for realtor), and *omissions* (doin' for doing, reglar for reg*u*lar). If you discover any of these errors, notice if they occur every time you make the sound or if they happen at the initial, middle, or final positions in a word. For instance, a lazy *r* may show up in the middle position but not in the initial position: you can say *r*abbit, but tu*r*key comes out as "tuw-key." Also, consonant sounds you produce well in isolation you may tend to distort in consonant blends: that same *r* sound may give you trouble only in cr, gr, or dr combinations.

The real distraction caused by these misarticulations is not the minor aural irritation it may arouse in your listeners. Rather, these speech problems can create a contradictory message that works against the credibility that you want to project. Sound substitutions are a part of a child's language development and disappear after the child learns to discriminate more precisely among sounds. An audience listening to a speaker who says "wange of pothibilities" will experience conflict between the image of competence and intelligence conveyed by the words and the image of incomplete development triggered by the sounds. Similarly, sound distortions can produce an image of sloppiness that conflicts with an otherwise crisp and concise presentation. Consider the image discord created by the accountant who presents precise facts while slushing his *s*'s in phrases like "the projections for the next fishcal year sheem to shupport our prediction of sholid growth potential." It may be illogical and unfair to associate certain articulation errors with baby talk and drunkenness, but you had best be aware of the unconscious tendency of listeners to do so.

(3) Identify vocalized pauses and other irrelevant sounds and phrases.

Do not be afraid to pause between sentences or thoughts when you speak. But avoid filling those pauses with distracting and meaningless sounds and phrases. When a speaker is nervous, a one-second pause can seem like a ten-second stretch of dead air, and the temptation to fill it with something can be great.

Do you use vocalized pauses: uh, um, err?

Do you fill pauses with other nonspeech sounds: lip smacking, tongue clicking, throat clearing, snuffling? Some speakers unconsciously insert a giggle after every sentence.

Do you repeat to excess certain words or phrases in nonsensical places? Some may have originated as requests for feedback. The coherent question "Do you know what I mean?" following a complicated idea turns into "y'know" tossed in whenever the speaker feels uncertain. From there it is a short step to using it as just another pause filler. In the following example of the phrase "y'know" has no more meaning than "uh."

One of the y'know, advantages of joining a credit union, y'know, is the low-interest auto loans, y'know.

Other irrelevant repetitions may have grown out of an unconscious need to apologize for inadequacies of expression. Tacking on "or whatever" on the end of every sentence is an example.

Here is a list of words and phrases that lose their original meanings when allowed to spread cancerlike through a speech:

OK?
Y'know
See
Like
I mean
or whatever
and so on and so forth
et cetera
in other words
so to speak
you might say
Right?

(4) Identify repetitious patterns of inflection.

While growing up and listening to other people, you learn very early that there are logical and natural places in sentences to vary the pitch of your voice. For instance, in English it is usual to have your voice go higher in pitch at the end of a question or to have it deepen for an emphatic statement. In normal conversation we use a variety of inflection without having to think about it. In public speaking, however, there can be a tendency to deliver every sentence with the same inflectional pattern regardless of the sentence's meaning or grammatical structure. This happens when the speaker is not thinking about the content of the speech, but is nervous, or is reading from a manuscript or recalling a memorized text. A singsong, hypnotic pattern of inflection can easily lead to drooping eyelids in the audience.

(5) Eliminate your distracting habits through a systematic self-improvement program, or by seeking professional help.

Self-Improvement

When you identify a problem and your motivation to correct it is strong, you may devise a simple plan of action, as Demosthenes did when he was troubled by problems of articulation and enunciation. His solution was to practice being understood while speaking over the roar of the ocean with his mouth full of pebbles. This may not suit many modern speakers, especially if they live in Kansas on sandy soil, but there are other sources to tap. Books and recordings are available which provide exercises in breathing and projection. These also have exercises, like tongue twisters, that make apparent the muscle groups used to produce certain sounds properly. You can start with such books as:

King, Robert, and Eleanor DiMichael. *Articulation and Voice: Improving Oral Communication*. New York: Macmillan, 1978.

Anderson, Virgil A. *Training the Speaking Voice*. New York: Oxford University Press, 1961.

Gwyn, Jack, Robert J. Gwyn, and Betty R. Sander. *The Business of Oral Communication: Fundamentals Module 1*. Cincinnati: South-Western Publishing Co., 1980.

For a deeply ingrained habit you may choose to map out a program of behavior modification. This approach, which has been quite successful in helping people to lose weight or quit smoking, is based on the premise that habits that develop gradually are best eliminated gradually. New behaviors are substituted for old ones and the new behaviors are rewarded. The steps are simple:

1. Assess your present behavior. Quantify the exact frequency of the distracting habit.

2. Set a specific, realistic goal. If you say "OK?" after nearly every sentence, perhaps twenty times in a ten-minute speech, resolve to cut down to ten times in a ten-minute speech.
3. Monitor your behavior. Do not just estimate your progress. Have a friend tally the occurrences, or tape each speech yourself. Keep a written chart of your progress.

For most motivated adults knowledge of results is an adequate reward. Just seeing the progress in quanitfied form keeps you working toward the goal. Feel free, though, to use more tangible rewards. You can promise yourself a special treat of some sort when you reach your goal, if you think that such an added incentive would be useful in helping to keep you on track.

For minor problems of articulation you may be able to set up your own course of speech therapy by following the four-step program professionals use:

1. DISCRIMINATION. Often people who mispronounce sounds cannot hear the difference between correct and incorrect pronunciations. "The word is 'with'." *"That's what I said: 'wif'."* "No. 'With'." *"I said that. 'Wif'."* And so on. Training the ear to discriminate between *th* and *f* can take some time.

2. PRODUCTION OF THE SOUND IN ISOLATION. Analyze the mechanics of creating the sound. Where is the tongue placed? How do the lips move? Practice saying the sound over and over again, receiving feedback from a friend or tape recorder.

3. PRODUCTION OF THE SOUND IN COMBINATIONS. Being able to say *th* several times does not guarantee that you can say "the thief withheld the thirty thistles Thursday." Spend a long time practicing the sound in different words, in the initial, middle, and final positions.

4. TRANSFERAL INTO EVERYDAY SPEECH. The most difficult step in speech training is the transfer of new sounds from the practice setting to an actual communication setting. Eventually, if you repeat steps 1, 2, and 3 enough, the new pronunication will become habitual and you will use it even when your thoughts are on other things.

Professional Help

Some problems of vocal delivery are difficult to diagnose or solve without professional help. In seeking help, consider the nature and seriousness of your vocal problem, as well as the time and money you are able to commit. Then consult the appropriate professional person from the following list:

Speech therapists are the best source of help for fairly serious or persistent articulation and voice problems.

Voice coaches may be affiliated with theater, radio, or television. They can help you improve voice quality, diction, and pronunciation. If you also want to work on regionalisms or accents and want to develop greater variety and expressiveness, consider a course in voice and diction or oral interpretation. An acting course will help in these areas and also improve your physical movement.

Public speaking teachers and *consultants* can provide help with voice, articulation, emphasis, and expressiveness within the context of public speaking. Usually work on speech delivery is integrated with the development of speech content.

23b.   Speak so that you can be heard and understood.

(1)   Speak loud enough to be heard by the entire audience.

For the inexperienced speaker just about *any* volume level will sound too loud. This is understandable. There are few occasions for speaking above a conversational level, and even on such occasions, as when we scream our heads off at a football game, we rarely care if we are being understood. For the most part, being loud and conspicuous is, in Western cultures, considered boorish behavior. This adds another dimension of difficulty to being able to use your voice properly when you speak before an audience.

The only thing that will make loud speaking more comfortable and natural is, of course, practice. In the early stages you will have to ignore the feedback on volume that you receive from your own ears and rely on a friend, or perhaps a tape recorder set some distance away. What you are aiming for is a louder voice that retains the rhythms and inflections of your normal conversation. You want to be loud, but not yell like a drill instructor. As you practice you will discover that this takes more wind for each phrase and that you will need to develop breath control to permit you to keep your breathing pauses in normal patterns.

Maintain a mental image of broadcasting or propelling your voice to the far corners of the room. You will then find yourself doing those things which naturally aid projection, such as keeping your head up and opening your mouth wide.

Know how large an audience you can address without sounding strained. Can you speak for an hour at an outdoor political rally, or do you reach your limit speaking to twelve people in a boardroom for ten minutes? (Insist on a microphone if you know that the audience or room will be too big for your voice.) Continue to practice increasing your speech volume. A good goal for the average person would be to be able to speak conversationally, without amplification, to fifty or sixty people in a room with average acoustics.

(2) Speak at a rate your audience can follow.

While there are speaking-circuit veterans who have a 250-words-per-minute rate as one of their gimmicks, most people lose intelligibility at 150 words per minute. An average rate of speaking is around 125 words per minute. To check your rate, select a fairly easy newspaper or magazine article. Then time yourself for three or four minutes of reading aloud. Next, count the number of words in the passage and divide by the number of minutes you read. Be sure to read in as natural and conversational a manner as possible. If you speak faster than 150 words per minute or slower than 100 words per minute, you may be endangering your comprehensibility by overworking your audience. The extremely fast speaker asks his or her listeners to decode and process information more rapidly than they are accustomed. The plodding speaker, who seems to avoid phrases and slowly lays out each word as it if were unrelated to any other, keeps the audience in bored suspension as they wait for the words to gel into some sort of context.

Generally, when giving a speech, plan to speak a little slower than you do in daily conversation. The need to speak a little louder and a little more distinctly will require extra breath. It will be more natural to pause to breathe between phrases than to rush through the last few words of a sentence and gasp noisily for air. To be sure you have timed the speech realistically, practice at the rate and volume you will actually use.

(3) Enunciate words distinctly and naturally.

Even people who have no chronic articulation problems of the sort discussed in **23a(2)** rarely enunciate *every* sound in *every* word. The phrase "jeetyet?" can be deciphered as "did you eat yet?" by a friend who is standing by the person speaking and who has a context for the remark. In public speaking settings much information can be lost due to distance from the speaker and distracting noise. Thus it is important to work on crisp, precise articulation. Use your tongue, teeth, and lips to pronounce every sound. Be sure you say "govern*n*ment" rather than "goverment" and "hundred" rather than "hunnerd." Do not mumble, slur words together, or swallow whole phrases.

You can enunciate properly and still sound natural. It just takes the practice that comes from incorporating precision into your normal conversation instead of creating a separate "speaking persona." Some people, in a misguided attempt to sound more formal or "literate" during a speech, will overarticulate words or take on affected mannerisms or

If you have a regional accent or if you are not a native speaker of the language you are using, you may be concerned about being understood. Do not try to eliminate or hide your accent. Your manner of speaking is part of your unique personality. The differentness can add interest and charm to your presentation. To insure comprehension, follow these suggestions:

1. Do not start out with the most important material. Use your introduction to let the audience adjust to your pronunciation and patterns of emphasis that differ from their own. Usually this will take just a few minutes.

2. Speak more slowly and distinctly than you do in conversation.

3. Be very alert to feedback. If you see confused faces, repeat ideas slowly. Try several synonyms for important words. Unclear vocabulary or mispronunciation of one key word may mystify your listeners. If necessary, check it out directly: "Do you know what I mean by 'plumbum'? No? I think you also call it 'lead'."

pronunciations. The result is quite the opposite of what they wish. Rather than sounding erudite, they, with their grimaces and popping consonants, appear patronizing, melodramatic, and just a little silly. Do not say *thee* in a place where *thuh* is natural. Avoid the false formality of mispronouncing "often" as *off-ten* instead of *offen*. Do not use "would not" where "wouldn't" feels right (Just be sure to say "wouldn't" rather than *wunt*.) Standard usage dictates that some syllables are truncated. Do not reverse this procedure. *Con grat you lations* is an overly precise pronunciation of "congratulations," which most speakers say like *con grad ja lations*.

23c. Reinforce meaning and make your speech more interesting through vocal variety.

The speaker who has a clear speaking voice devoid of vocal tics wastes these good qualities if she or he speaks hypnotically, with no variation in pitch, rate, or volume. Change and movement are intrinsically more interesting than the static or predictable, and, in Sections **15** and **18**, we stress the importance of variety of word choice and variety of examples to maintaining a high level of audience attention. Vocal variety is equally important, and the need for it goes beyond mere desire for novelty. Your voice should not just transmit words; you can use it to underscore and reinforce your message. Suppose your speech on air pollution contained these two sentences:

When the pollution levels are high my hair feels gritty and I have to wash it more often.

AND

Every time pollution reaches the Alert level in our city more people with chronic respiratory problems die.

Delivering these sentences in the same tone of voice could imply that they were of equal importance. Changes in pace and emphasis show your audience what is significant and can signal humor, seriousness, irony, and a range of emotions.

(1) Vary your pitch.

Speaking in a monotone says this to an audience: "I have little interest in the subject or confidence in my ability to interest others in it." A listless vocal performance will negate any dynamism that ordinarily would spring from your word choice and content. Varied inflection implies a high energy level and self-confidence, and generally aids your credibility. The pitch you use for the delivery of a word or phrase can underscore its meaning or imply its opposite. For instance, it is common to indicate disagreement with an assertion or statement merely by speaking it in the inflection used for questions.

If you can sing an octave, on key or not, you can speak an octave. Do not be afraid to use the full range of your voice.

(2) Vary your rate of speaking.

The average pace of your delivery should be geared toward comfortable listening. However, changes in rate at different times during the speech can be effective in establishing moods or in adding emphasis. Speaking slowly can make you seem thoughtful and deliberate, or can impart a sense of drama. Similarly, an extended pause at the end of a sentence will signal to your audience that you consider what you just said important and worth some thought on their part. Rapid delivery shows excitement and activity. A climactic effect is achieved by presenting a series of ideas or examples at a rapid clip, as in the following example:

[slow] Since we adopted this management system, [fast] absenteeism is down, productivity is up, morale is up, sales are up, profits are up.

The preceding example also demonstrates that the shift in rate (in this case, slow-to-fast) is as important to creating a climactic effect as the rate itself. The following passage shows what one can do with a fast-to-slow shift. Were you to read this aloud you would speak faster and faster through the first sentence, but would speak the second sentence very slowly:

In the next hour they looked in her room, checked the tree house, went over to the playground, called several of her friends, drove around the block, asked all the neighbors. No one — had seen — Emily — since — she — got off — the school bus.

The accelerating pace of the first sentence shows mild concern turning to frantic searching, which leads to the sudden moment of grim acceptance contained in the measured delivery of the last sentence.

(3) Vary your volume.

You should speak loud enough that you can drop your voice for effect and still be audible to the people in the far corners. At the same time, you should hold some volume in reserve so that you can raise your voice for emphasis.

Notice how a drop in volume (the sentence below in italics) can pique interest by evoking an air of confidentiality:

I was having an awful week. Few prospects, no sales. It was hard on a young, eager guy just out of school. On the other hand, I never saw old Jones without a customer at his side or a signed contract in his hand. I guess he saw my hangdog look and took pity on me, because he walked over and said, "Smith, you've got the makings of a great salesman, but you're doing one thing wrong."
Now, this is what he said: . . .

Here is an example of raising one's voice for emphasis:

The city council has approved yet another halfway house in the neighborhood. The university is using our streets for its parking lot. The state parole board dumps its parolees downtown. Prostitutes from miles around converge each night on Second Street.
Do you want to know what's coming next?

23d. Use standard, acceptable pronunciation.

(1) Identify words you habitually mispronounce.

Some differences in the ways people pronounce words are inevitable and cause no problem for public speakers. A person from New England will say "I went to a pahty," a Pennsylvanian may have "cot a cold," and a Texan may tell you to come "ovah heah." Unless they have strong biases against some part of the country, listeners rarely make negative inferences about the speaker on the basis of regional pronunciations like these. If, however, a person says "warsh" instead of "wash" or "ax" for "ask," many listeners will consider this substandard and draw conscious or unconscious conclusions about the speaker's educational level, competence, and intelligence. This sort of linguistic snobbery can be unjust and inaccurate, but it will be a lot easier for a speaker to try to change some pronunciations than to change everyone else's attitudes.

Look over this list and see if you make any of these pronunciation errors.

	Proper	*Improper*
GET	get	git
JUST	just	jist
ACROSS	a cross	a crost
NUCLEAR	nu clee ar	nu cyou lar
PERSPIRATION	pers pir a tion	press pir a tion
STRICT	strict	strick
ESCAPE	es cape	ex cape
COMPULSORY	com pul sory	com pul so rary
RECOGNIZE	rec og nize	reck a nize
LIBRARY	li brar y	li berry
MISCHIEVOUS	mis che vous	mis chee vious
THEATER	*thee* a ter	thee *a* ter
PICTURE	pic ture	pit chure
SURPRISE	sur prise	sup prise
COMPARABLE	*com* per able	com *pare* able
LARYNX	lar inks	lar nix
RELEVANT	rel a vant	rev a lant
DROWNED	drown'd	drown ded

If you found on the list one or two words that you mispronounce, you can easily work on correcting them. If you found five or more, you may need more extensive help in the form of coaching or coursework. Due to factors in your background or perhaps a lazy ear for the finer distinctions of speech, you probably are also mispronouncing several other words and impairing your effectiveness in communicating with certain groups of people. Here too, feedback from your practice audience can alert you to errors of which you were unaware.

(2) Check the preferred pronunciation of unfamiliar words.

Your reading vocabulary and your speaking vocabulary are different. There can be words you frequently see and understand yet rarely speak or hear spoken. Without exposure and feedback you might develop your own silent way of saying such a word that involves a mistake like adding a sound or reversing sounds. The incorrect pronunciation will feel right to you because you have said it to yourself so often as you read and did research. If you give a whole speech about the Electorial College (instead of Electoral), your listeners might just wonder how knowledgeable you really are. Or, they may be confused or amused if you constantly refer to the need for a counselor to listen "emphatically" when you think you are saying "empathically," a word that means something entirely different. Check words you encounter in research, but do not use regularly, to be sure you have them right.

As a child you may have been taught to "sound out" unfamiliar words. You also discovered the perils of this technique the first time you pronounced *island* "iz-land," and wrestled with *pneumatic*. You learned then that it was unwise to make assumptions about unfamiliar words; that is still true, especially for the speaker.

Place names are always an area for careful investigation. Looking at the word *Beaulieu* one would expect to say it "Bowl yew." However, the village by that name in Britain is pronounced "Byew lee." Similarly, Leicester is "Lester." The Cairo in Egypt we call "Kie row"; the Cairo in Illinois, "Kay row." Houston Street in New York City is "How ston," but Texans have a "Hyew ston."

There are minor differences in pronunciation that can be troublesome. *Ap*ricot or *ay*pricot? Har *rass* or *Har* rass? Which pronunication of Vietnam, Peking, or Caribbean? A dictionary is not much help when there are several correct pronunciations, or changing ones, or when words become more or less anglicized, or when unusual proper names like Walesa spring upon the scene. It has been said that the arbiters of the most current acceptable pronunciation are the anchorpersons of national news programs. You are usually safe to follow their lead, or other such models as the most articulate and respected leaders of the community.

Refer to these sources for questions of pronunciation:

Colby, Frank O., ed. *The American Pronouncing Dictionary of Troublesome Words*. New York: Thomas Y. Crowell Co., 1950.

Lass, Abraham, and Betty Lass. *Dictionary of Pronunciation*. New York: Quadrangle/The New York Times Book Co., 1976.

24

Physical Delivery

Use your physical delivery to create a visual effect that complements the content of your speech.

Much of how your audience responds to you is a result of what they see rather than what they hear. The words may be confident, but trembling legs and fidgeting fingers tell another story. Slumped posture and a sour expression can give the lie to the statement "I'm so happy to be here!" When practicing and delivering your speech, be aware of the visual image you are creating. As with vocal delivery, the goal is to be natural and to avoid any actions that would distract your audience from your message.

24a. Be conscious of your appearance.

What kinds of first impressions do people have of you? Are they initially intimidated by you because you are football-player big and burly? Do people dismiss you because you look ten years younger than you are? Obviously, you cannot trade in your body; but if such impressions get in the way of your speech goal, you can try to compensate. Correct false impressions, especially in the opening minutes of your presentation, by using speech content and all those physical characteristics you have control over.

As you get ready for a particular speech, consider what your hairstyle, grooming, and clothing might say to your audience. You do not need, or necessarily want, to mimic the dress of your audience. Regardless of differences in sense of style, you should show that you took *care* in preparing, that you consider the event important enough to expend some energy in trying to look good.

Ideally, your clothes should provide a tasteful and unobtrusive frame for your personality and your remarks. Be aware of regional, cultural, and occupational norms. In some parts of the country and in certain professional or social settings jeans and a sport jacket can be considered formal enough for a presentation. When in doubt, though, lean toward conservative, businesslike clothes. There is no need to be drab, but remember that your audience could be distracted by gaudy colors, busy patterns, eye-catching jewelry, unorthodox combinations of apparel, and any clothing they associate with seduction or courtship.

24b. Eliminate distracting mannerisms.

Distracting mannerisms fall into two categories: those you have all the time (pushing your glasses up your nose, tucking your hair behind your ear, cracking your knuckles), and those you have only when giving a speech (noisily fanning and squaring up your notecards, rocking back and forth on your heels, tapping your pencil on the lectern). These are physical equivalents of saying "y'know ... y'know ... y'know." No act is inherently distracting — it is the repetition of that act that becomes distracting. As with vocal mannerisms, you are unaware of the frequency of the act until someone points it out. Thus, the biggest step toward eliminating the problem is becoming aware of it; sometimes this awareness is sufficient to resolve it. Commit yourself to using the practice techniques laid out in **21c** to get feedback on your delivery.

A distracting mannerism did not spring up overnight, and it would be unrealistic to think that it could be eliminated overnight. The primary goal should be a reduction of the frequency of the mannerism by adapting the behavior modification techniques described in **23a(5)**.

24c. Stand or sit with a relaxed but alert posture.

As a general rule, you should stand when speaking. This focuses the attention on you and gives you a better view of your audience. There are exceptions, of course. In an intimate setting, such as a circle of a dozen people, you might choose to speak seated. As a member of a panel discussion, you may be constrained to follow the sedentary lead of the moderator. If, however, you can learn to be comfortable speaking without a lectern, with your weight evenly distributed, your notes grasped casually in one hand at waist level, supported by no props of any kind, then you can easily adapt to any setting. Appropriate variations might include leaning across the lectern to show deep involvement or sitting on the edge of a desk or table to signal the shift to an informal mood. Draping yourself across the lectern, lounging at the side with one elbow extended, or standing in an off-center posture are never compatible with the energetic and controlled image of a polished public speaker. But avoid also the rigid, petrified stance of a military academy cadet. Specifically, be careful never to lock your knees—you risk becoming light-headed or even toppling over.

24d. If you move about during the speech, make the action purposeful and relevant.

You can give a perfectly good and proper speech standing behind a lectern. However, most speeches can be aided by movement at appropriate times. Taking a few steps to the left or right, or moving closer to your listeners can add variety or emphasis to your speech. You also establish contact with that segment of the audience that you have moved toward. Moreover, physical movement during a speech is a constructive way to release tension.

Make your movements purposeful. Pacing nervously around the room is distracting. So are the tentative dances of the speaker who cannot really decide whether to move or not. This speaker shuffles, rocks to either side, extends a toe as if testing the temperature of the water, and then darts back, chilled. If you are going to move at all, be decisive. Take at least two or three normal paces diagonally or directly forward. When you stop keep your body orientation and eye contact toward the most concentrated part of your audience.

The timing of your movement can reinforce your ideas. Generally, it is not effective to move around when explaining complex material or when delivering your most emotional examples or powerful arguments. Physical movement works best at transitional points, where it signals a change in mood, content, or form.

24e. Keep your hands free so you can gesture if it feels natural.

"I don't know what to do with my hands" is perhaps the most frequently expressed concern about delivery. People who use their hands to gesture quite naturally and comfortably in everyday interaction stare with consternation at the two frying pans below their wrists when it is time to give a speech. What you should do with your hands in a speech is exactly what you do with them in normal conversation. For some people, using their hands in this manner means hardly using them at all. For others, this means gesturing a great deal. Whether we gesture a little or a lot, we do it to describe, to point out, to enumerate, to emphasize, to entreat.

There is no need to plan what gestures go with your speech. If you have ever seen a speaker who had prepared a gesture for nearly every word in the speech, you probably began to feel you were watching a game of charades or a person signing for the deaf. Inevitably with such a scheme, the carefully planned gestures get a little ahead of or behind the words, the unfortunate result resembling a movie with its sound track out of sync.

If you are absorbed with your topic and with communicating it to your listeners, the gestures will emerge spontaneously at the appropriate points. But this will happen only if your hands are free to move. Too many speakers immobilize their hands completely, both out of the panicky need to cling to something and the desire to prevent uncontrolled movement. Do not lock yourself into any of these gesture-inhibiting stances:

THE BEAR HUG	Arms across chest, is one of the most common ways of getting a grip on yourself
TEN-HUT!	Arms stiff, wrists firmly nailed to pelvis
THE FLESH WOUND	One arm hangs useless at the side, the other hand serves as a tourniquet above or below the elbow
THE FIRING SQUAD	Legs slightly spread, hands tied behind back
THE CHOIRBOY/GIRL	Hands clasped at waist level, every finger entwined with several others
THE SUPPLICANT	Same as the Choir, but higher: at chest level
THE FIG LEAF	Demurely crossed hands, strategically placed

Actually, all of these are perfectly acceptable transitory postures. The problem with them lies not in the position of the hands but rather in the temptation to remain in one stance, statuelike, while concentrating on what is coming out of your mouth. As you become more involved in your message and the audience's response to it, your natural gestures will come back to you. When these natural impulses collide with the unnatural posture you have locked yourself into, the results are bizarre:

- The Supplicant, who cannot get her fingers untangled when she wants to forcefully jab a finger in emphasizing a series of points, looks like she is holding a pistol in a two-handed police grip and taking pot shots at the audience.
- Another speaker, trying to describe a complex process while in the Ten-HUT! position, finds himself flapping his hands uselessly at his thighs, like a penguin trying to fly.
- The Choirboy starts a dramatic elevating gesture to emphasize his point on the rise in inflation and discovers that since he cannot unclench his hands they have come to a stop against his chin and his elbows are twitching out in the vicinity of his ears.

So, what *do* you do with your hands? First, nothing distracting like nervously shredding notecards or drumming on the table. Second, nothing contrived, no rehearsed gestures. A hand can be at your side, be holding cards at waist level, resting lightly on the other, *gently* grasping the lectern, or casually in a pocket (no change jingling). What matters most is that your arms, wrists, and fingers are relaxed so that your hands can move if you find a need for that movement arising naturally.

24f. Maintain eye contact.

Be familiar enough with your material that you can look at as many members of your audience as possible, as often as possible. In our culture, looking into another's face connotes openness and interest, while looking away or down is interpreted as a sign of insincerity or shiftiness. People would much rather look at your face than the top of your head. Moreover, it can distract them from what you are saying if you stare fixedly out the window or up at the ceiling. After a while the audience's attention begins to shift in those directions, wondering if cue cards are taped to the rafters, or if a major crime is in progress outside. But more essentially, maintaining eye contact allows you to read your listeners' faces to get feedback on how your message is being received. Advice to fake eye contact by looking between heads or looking just over the heads of the people in the back row misses the whole point.

At the beginning of your speech, when you have not yet gotten into your stride, find a few listeners who are responding supportively with nods and positive facial expressions. Look at them and use their support to help you through this uncomfortable period, but as soon as you start to roll, widen your eye contact to include everyone.

Actually look into the eyes of the individual audience members, and hold that contact for at least three seconds. Do not skim across rows of faces. Move your eye contact randomly throughout the room. Do not fall into a head-bobbing pattern: left, center, right, center, left... Have a friend or colleague observe and tell you if you scan mechanically or if you have a tendency to neglect any one segment of the audience.

In any speech, even a manuscript speech, you should have eye contact 85 percent of the time, looking down only to read technical material or to refer briefly to your notes. Most importantly, be sure you have eye contact throughout your introduction and conclusion and during the most telling points and pivotal arguments.

24g. Use facial expression to reflect or forecast mood and tone.

Do not let the tension of a speaking situation force you into a deadpan face. Your natural facial expressions can add one more channel for effective communication. Generally, changes in facial expression precede and forecast shifts in tone or mood. Replacing your cheerful countenance with a concerned frown can be a better transition than that hoary old cliché, "but seriously, folks."

You should not plan a series of mugs, smiles, and grimaces — all you need do is exaggerate slightly those expressions that arise normally. The subtle nuances that work in face-to-face contact will not show up in the back row.

The *one* expression that has the same meaning in every culture is the smile. Most public speakers underuse or misuse this powerful tool. A constant, fixed, jaw-aching grin is as bad as being deadpan. A smile at a sad or serious moment is inappropriate. However, remind yourself to smile genuinely whenever it can reinforce your message. It is one of the easiest ways to establish rapport, show your good will, and put you and your audience at ease.

25

Adapting to the Speech Situation

Anticipate that the actual speech situation may be different from your visualization of it. Be prepared to take advantage of the good variations and to cope with the bad ones.

What would you do if twenty people show up for your speech when you were told there would be 300? What if you expected a homogeneous audience and find a mixed one waiting, or assumed an audience to be favorable but discover they are hostile instead? How would you handle distractions or hecklers during your speech? To cope with these turns of events you must resist the temptation to go on automatic pilot and spew out the speech exactly as practiced. Do not stop thinking the second you start speaking. Despite all your hours of preparation, the actual creation of the speech occurs *now*, as you talk. Dozens of strategic choices cannot be made until during the speech. But you can avoid some unpleasant shocks if you spend some time thinking about the contingencies you face. When you prepare for and practice a speech, consider not only the probable but the possible.

25a. Be alert for opportunities to weave in references to people and events in the immediate setting.

If you have done a thorough audience analysis, you will already have many references to the audience built into the speech and will have made use of attention factors like proximity and familiarity. But there are always other chances to adapt to your audience once you start your speech. Be willing to throw out what you have if you can replace it with something "close to home." Here are some adaptations you might try:

Use the names of people in the audience.

Replace supporting materal with items drawn from the audience's direct experience. Before giving a speech you will often have a chance to meet a few members of your audience. It is often effective to refer to them. Why say "Suppose a business person wants to obtain a loan" when you could say "Suppose Ms. Silver's [nodding toward a listener] hardware business is expanding so rapidly she decides to take out a loan to enlarge her store"?

Refer to the person who introduced you and to other speakers on the program.

> If no nation in history has progressed as rapidly as ours in two centuries (a mere tick-tock in the history of mankind), it seems to me that on the other hand no nation has deteriorated as rapidly in one eighth of that time. Allow me, if I may, to indulge in a personal recollection which Professor Reid mentioned in his very gracious and generous introduction. On another April 13, twenty-five years ago . . .[1]

In a speech class you might come across something like:

> So now that we have examined the causes of stress, let us look at four ways of reducing it. The first of these is physical exercise. Nearly everyone can find an activity she or he likes. Linda was telling us about the joys of tennis. Similarly, aerobic dance is . . .

Refer to details in the immediate setting or from shared experience.

"And all of that expensive atom-smashing machinery was housed in a room not half the size of this one." "Everyone in this class knows about *situational stress*. The five of us giving speeches today are especially aware of it."

---

[1]William Peden, "Is Thomas Jefferson Relevant?" *Representative American Speeches 45, no. 4* (1972–73): 95.

Do not use a hypothetical example of a point or process if you can draw a more concrete example from something that has just happened to the group.

25b. Adapt to the audience response as you give your speech. Plan alternative strategies for reactions you may receive.

The give and take between speaker and listeners is one thing that makes a good speech more than reading aloud. A speaker can present the same report twelve times and not become boring and flat, because he or she experiences the excitement each time of interacting with a new and different audience. The changes and adaptations sustain the vigor of the speech. Adaptation is not a new skill you must laboriously learn; it is nothing but a more structured version of the mood sensing and editing you do all the time in ordinary conversation.

What follows are some common adjustments you might make.

(1) If your audience seems bored or restless, consider the following:

- Use more humor and novelty.
- Use more concrete examples.
- Use more direct references to the audience.
- Invite direct participation—by asking them for examples or to raise their hands to denote agreement, and so on.
- Cut out or simplify technical descriptions and statistics.
- Make your delivery more animated.
- Make a physical change; for example, walk around the lectern and sit on a desk.
- Cut it short. The program might be running late—cut out subpoints, drive home your thesis sentence, and stop.

(2) If you are not getting the agreement you expected, consider the following:

- Stress common ground.
- Modify your goal; do not try to do so much.
- Spend extra time on establishing your credibility.
- Appeal to your listeners' sense of fair play: "Whether you agree with me or not, I'm sure you will hear me out."

(3) If your audience is less informed than you expected, consider the following:

- Check your perceptions. Ask questions like "How many of you know the difference between fission and fusion?" ... "the secret of Damascus steel?"
- Use more supporting materials that are geared toward clarification: definition, explanation, examples, illustration, restatement, and analogies that compare the unknown to the known.
- Delete the more technical materials.

(4) If your audience is more informed than you expected, consider the following:

- Condense your basic material and call it a review. "As most of you know ..."
- Recall and insert the more technical or abstract materials you encountered in your research.
- Introduce the questions and issues that you see as unresolved aspects of the topic.
- Cut the speech short and invite discussion of your topic.

(5) If your audience is more heterogeneous than you expected, consider the following:

- Gear your supporting material and language to what seems to be the typical audience member. Identify the predominant ethnic group, for example, or estimate the average age.
- Add materials that acknowledge the presence of the full range of listeners, but do not change the main thrust of your speech. Add a reference to a television show that children in the audience can relate to, or spend a few minutes establishing your credibility for the 10 percent of the audience that disagrees with you.

CAVEAT: Do not overreact in categorizing your audience. Give your listeners time to adjust to you and give your speech room to make an impression on them. Keep in touch with the mood of the audience and do not play to the extremes.

☐ **Exercise 1.** What if Cunningham, when delivering the speech in the **Appendix**, encountered the following responses? Name one specific adjustment she might make for each.

1. Audience looks mystified at her reference to Quality Circles.
2. Audience becomes restless and begins to fidget at about paragraph 72.
3. She observes that spouses and families of business leaders are present in the audience.

25c. Take several steps to prevent distractions. If distractions do occur, be familiar with the strategies to deal with them.

Murphy's Law is an especially potent force to reckon with in facing the physical setting and the mechanical apparatus of the speech situation. Here are some suggestions on how to avoid or mitigate its effect.

(1) Check your presentation's setting and equipment to detect possible sources of distraction.

Arrive early and survey the room where you will speak. Make whatever changes necessary to insure that attention will be focused on you and your message. For instance, if the room has windows, you may have to draw the blinds or modify the seating arrangement to prevent sunlight from blinding your listeners. An obtrusive object or chart should be covered or turned around. The chairs should be shifted to suit your type of presentation. Test the acoustics to see if you need to close windows against outside noise or need amplification to counteract an undercurrent of environmental sounds.

If you are using electronic aids, find the outlets in the room and actually test both your aids and the outlets for proper functioning. Have backups for your equipment or, if you are being provided with equipment, insist that it come with spare bulbs, batteries, and so on. Now, and not after being introduced, is the time to check the sound level of your microphone.

Inevitably, there will be some sources of distraction that cannot be controlled. The FAA would doubtless not approve of canceling all commercial flights over the building in which you will be speaking, but you should take every opportunity to change what you can: Katharine Hepburn, during the run of the musical *Coco*, was able to convince the construction workers across from the theater to cease riveting during her big solo each matinee.

(2) Fleeting or low-level distractions during your speech are best dealt with by not acknowledging them.

The first rule of dealing with distractions is, naturally, that you yourself must not become or seem distracted. At the same time, though, you should subtly raise your energy level to keep your listeners' attention. When all heads turn as a latecomer enters through the door behind you, do not legitimize the interruption by turning your head also. Do not appear to be flustered when a fluorescent bulb starts to flicker overhead—just speak a little louder, become just a bit more animated, add some extra attention devices such as humor or storytelling.

(3) Sometimes distractions can be turned to your purpose by incorporating them into your speech.

One frequently told story is of the politician whose campaign speech was interrupted by a crying baby. "I can't blame that youngster," he remarked. "She's just thinking about four more years of a Republican administration." In another instance, a speaker had to pause when a waiter noisily dropped a tray of dishes. He continued with, "That's about how the intercollegiate athletics' department came crashing down when the scholarship scandal hit the press. Guess who got elected to pick up the pieces?"

(4) When it is necessary to actually interrupt the continuity of your speech, do so as quickly as possible and then draw your listeners back in.

Your job is to give the speech, not close doors, answer telephones, adjust the thermostat, and so on. If no one seems to want to take care of a problem, then you must interrupt your speech and deal with it so that everyone can quickly return to the business at hand.

There are two levels of interruption. In the first, you do not stop speaking: "... which would justify that course of action. Would someone please unlock that door? There are people wanting to get in. For my second point, I would like you to consider ..."

In the second case, circumstances require that you stop speaking while certain actions are taken by you or members of the audience. After you are satisfied with the result of that action — as, for example, when a victim of heat prostration has been cared for and led from the room — you may continue, backing up in your organization to summarize the progression of your points prior to the interruption: "Thank you for handling that so competently. Now, as you remember, I was just a moment ago talking about . . ."

25d. Do not hand control of the situation over to the verbal or nonverbal heckler. Respond to such interruptions calmly and firmly.

The worst distraction a speaker can face is the intentional interrupter. The problems can range from the listener who has had a little too much to drink and has delusions of wit, to the person who makes a systematic attempt to undermine your speech goal or even to prevent you from speaking. Generally, respond to them by progressing through the steps from **25c**: Ignore; if you cannot, Incorporate; if you cannot, Confront.

Always keep in mind your credibility with the audience and remember that you do not want to do anything that will interfere with achieving your speech purpose. You never want to lose your composure, dignity, or temper; you do not ever want to go to the heckler's level.

(1) The verbal heckler

If you start justifying yourself to a heckler, you have lost control of the situation and have put it in his or her lap. Do not get into a defensive posture. For example, do not defend yourself against name-calling. "You're a crook!" "You don't care about the environment." Do not waste time with denials. deal with the substance, not with the accusations.

First-level tactics:

ESTABLISH AN IMAGE OR TONE OF REASONABLENESS OR FAIR-NESS. Make it clear that you are not opposed to dialogue, even if the heckler is disregarding the polite convention that gives the floor to you. Give the heckler the benefit of the doubt in terms of his or her sincerity.

APPEAL TO FAIR PLAY. "I base my opinions about China on my three months travel there. Will you hear me out while I describe those experiences? *Then* we'll listen to your objections."

BUILD ON COMMON GROUND. "We both want the best schooling for our children. If we didn't think it was vitally important, neither of us would be here."

Never seem to close down the heckler or his or her point of view completely. Each does represent a point of view, and you want the audience to view you as a reasonable person. Of course, you may subtly imply that the heckler, though sincere, has adopted a vastly oversimplified analysis of a complex issue.

Second-level tactics:

In the course of being polite, you do not want your audience to think that you are glad that you have been interrupted and are enjoying the byplay. There comes a time where you have to shut the person off and get on with the speech.

ENOUGH IS ENOUGH. If the heckler has not been mollified or deflated by your reasonableness, then you can say something like, "I think you've made your point. Now I really must ask you to sit down and let me continue my speech." Even if the heckler does not, this will give the audience permission to tell the person to shut up, or the sergeant-at-arms permission to remove her or him.

THE ZINGER. As a last resort it is sometimes appropriate to flatten a heckler with a pithy and pointed comeback. Effective use of the "zinger" depends on two factors: your ability to think of a wise and witty retort (*not* one of the "your mother wears combat boots" variety), and your correct reading of the audience. If your listeners are irritated and impatient with the heckler, they will welcome your initiative. If you have misjudged their mood, however, you run the risk of seeming nasty.

(2) The nonverbal heckler

These are the hecklers you will run into more frequently. Rolled eyes, fidgeting, sighs, whispering, note passing are their trademarks. They do not have quite the nerve to heckle you out loud, but they want you to know that they disagree or are bored. If you focus on their behavior, your self-confidence may start to erode. These people can absorb all your attention as you start playing to them.

By and large, the usual way to deal with the nonverbal heckler is to ignore him or her. Sometimes you might have to completely cut off eye contact with that section of the audience. Instead, make eye contact with the people who are displaying positive signs, and avoid allowing your eyes to drift back to the heckler.

If you find it difficult to ignore the heckler, you may want to try one of the following:

- If you know the person by name, throw the name, in a complimentary sense, into the speech. This may either get their interest or embarrass them into being polite.
- The Evil Eye. If you are superior in status to this person, or if you are sufficiently self-assured, maintain eye contact with the nonverbal heckler until he or she submits.

If the heckling is an ongoing problem, in a class, say, or in a series of business meetings, it may be advisable for you to talk to this person privately and ask for feedback. He or she may be gratified enough by the attention to modify the annoying behavior.

You should avoid, however, projecting your own interpretations too freely onto the members of the audience. Often, teachers have been surprised when the student who has been sitting in class all year with crossed arms and a sour expression comes up at the end and says, "This was the best class I've ever had." The frown in the audience may be the result of a headache, or poor dinner, or merely concentration. Do not be too eager to leap to conclusions about the nonverbal messages your audience is sending you.

26

Answering Questions

Use the question-and-answer period to ensure that your message was understood by as many people as possible. Prepare fully, answer questions directly, and maintain control of the interaction.

The question-and-answer period is a great opportunity to further the goals of your speech. While you spoke, you attempted to address the needs of your audience, and now you can see how close you came. From your listeners' questions you can learn what points are unclear or what arguments and objections they have. Do not approach the question-and-answer period as if facing a firing squad. Communicate an eagerness to interact with the audience and to hear their ideas on your subject. Express your enthusiasm through such reactions as, "I'm glad you brought that up," "That's a good question," "That's intriguing. I never thought of it quite that way."

Do not lose your delivery skills just because the speech is over. Keep eye contact, avoid fidgeting or mumbling. Actually, some speakers' delivery improves during the question-and-answer period because they became more relaxed.

26a. Come prepared for a question-and-answer period.

Keep in mind the importance of the question-and-answer period throughout the stages of preparing your speech. Anticipate the questions that will arise naturally from each of your various points. One aid to this would be to have the friends who listen to your practice sessions ask you questions afterward. Although you can never predict the exact questions that will come up, there are certain ones that are more probable than others. Rehearse aloud possible answers to the most complicated and difficult ones. This is how public figures prepare for news conferences.

Ideally, your research has been so extensive that you have much more material than you were able to use, considering the time constraints surrounding your speech. You should not shove this extra material into a closet and forget about it. Continue to review it so you will be familiar enough with the content to weave it easily into elaboration and explanation in response to questions.

Think of possible applications of particularly effective evidence. For instance, for your speech on women in the labor force (see **5b**), you do not use a delightful story you found about a Japanese woman worker. The day before the speech, though, you go over the details of the story so you can tell it accurately should any of the audience question you about the cross-cultural nature of the topic. Similarly, it takes a minute to memorize Flo Kennedy's wonderful insight — "I know we're termites. But if all the termites got together, the house would fall down." — which you realize might fit into a discussion of the need for women to use their potential power. The statistics used in your speech relating income differences between men and women in San Jose city government jobs may seem vulnerable to some in the audience, so put together a backup notecard that (1) explains the sampling frame for the survey, (2) breaks the statistics down by occupation group, and (3) lists comparable statistics for eight other major cities.

26b. Invite and answer audience questions in a straightforward manner.

Do not worry if there are not any questions immediately, or if at first there are long pauses between questions. It usually takes your listeners a moment to collect their thoughts. In some cases you can start the ball rolling yourself by asking a question of the audience. "What problems have you encountered setting up affirmative action programs in your companies?" can generate counterquestions.

Call on questioners in the order they sought recognition and maintain eye contact while the question is being asked. If you are not sure you understand the question, paraphrase it according to your own interpretation and ask the questioner if it is accurate. When both of you are satisfied, restate or paraphrase it for the entire audience and direct the answer to them.

Be sure you *answer* the question. To avoid oversimplification, you will want to elaborate, expand, or qualify your answer, but if your discussion becomes too diffuse you will appear to be avoiding the issue. Consequently, always include a one-sentence, direct answer in your response to a question. For emphasis, place this sentence first or last, as in these examples:

FIRST: *"Yes, I do oppose building nuclear power plants,* at least until several safety questions are answered satisfactorily. My reasons include ...

LAST: "... so, because of all these serious problems I see, my answer to your question would be: *Yes, I do oppose building new nuclear power plants* at this time."

What if you are asked a question for which you do not have an answer? Do not bluff. Say that you do not know. If you have some idea where the answer could be found, tell the questioner of the source. Ask other audience members to help you out by volunteering what they know. Or, you might promise to look it up, and that if the listener will get in touch with you later, you will have an answer.

26c. Do not allow self-indulgent questioners to distort the function of the question-and-answer period.

The purpose of a question-and-answer period is to clarify issues for the entire audience. When individual audience members attempt to use this time for detailed consultation on a specialized problem, or to get on their favorite soapbox, you have an obligation as the speaker to bring the interaction back on its true course.

Be prepared to keep control of the situation by dealing in a firm and tactful manner with the following types of distracting questioners:

The person who wants to give a speech

This person may agree or disagree with you, or may have a favorite ax to grind that is only tangentially related to your topic. The distinguishing characteristic is that it becomes obvious that he or she has no real question to ask you, but rather is taking advantage of an assembled audience to hold forth. It is rarely effective to ask, "What is your question?" The person will just say, "Don't you agree that . . ." or "What do you think of the position that . . ." and take off for another five minutes. You must just jump in at the end of a sentence, manufacture a question somewhat related to the person's ramblings, answer it, and recognize another questioner on the opposite side of the room. "So, you're saying that there is so much inefficiency in government that you wonder how this or any other problem can be solved. That is a tough question to answer, but I am hopeful that the recent reorganization of our agency will permit us to be successful in our efforts. Next question over there?"

The person who wants to have an extended dialogue

This person might start out with a genuine question, but will not relinquish the floor when you respond. Rather, he or she counter with follow-up questions, comments on your answer, or new lines of discussion. Sometimes this sort of person wants free professional advice or therapy and does not mind seeking it in public. Other times the person simply finds you and your ideas fascinating and wants to converse at length, as though you were both guests at a cocktail party instead of speaker and audience member in a formalized setting. The best way to deal with this sort of person is to end the exchange firmly but with a compliment and/or invitation. For instance, "Thank you, you've given me quite a number of interesting insights here. Maybe you can come up and talk to me about them some more later."

The person who wants to pick a fight

Intellectual confrontation and probing, penetrating questions are to be expected, even welcomed from audience members who disagree with you. But sometimes questioners become inappropriately argumentative and mount hostile, personal attacks against a speaker. It becomes obvious that they are not really seeking an answer to a question, but are trying to destroy your credibility. Do not let them succeed by becoming angry, or by defending yourself against generalized name-calling. See **25d** on heckling. Pick out the part of such a person's diatribe that contains the kernel of a question, paraphrase it, and answer it calmly and reasonably.

Q: "What about all this poisonous junk that you greed-crazed despoilers dump into our river to kill our children and whole species of animals?"

A: "The questioner has brought up the valid and difficult subject of toxic waste disposal. What is our company doing about it? Well . . ."

In short, respond to these disruptive people diplomatically. Remember that, unlike hecklers, their participation has been invited. Do not take cheap shots or direct humor at them to shut them off. Likewise, when you are taken aback by incomprehensible questions, or questions that demonstrate gross ignorance or misinformation, you should react positively. Avoid language that embarrasses the questioner or points out errors:

NOT: "Well, *as I said* in my speech . . ."

BUT: "Let me go over these statistics more slowly . . ."

NOT: "You've totally confused fission and fusion!"

BUT: "Many of those problems relate to nuclear *fission*. The *fusion* reaction is quite different. It works like this . . ."

Try to find ways to dignify bad questions and turn them into good ones. Your listeners' empathy is with the questioner who may be nervous or confused. Your efforts to put others at ease will win you an audience's goodwill.

27

Guidelines for Special Occasions.

Research the specific demands that special occasions place on speakers. Adapt your speech to the specialized formats and expectations of these settings.

This final section looks at a potpourri of public communication settings that differ in varying degrees from the persuasive, informative, and evocative speeches emphasized throughout the book. Some of these, such as chairing a meeting or being interviewed by a group, may not seem like speech occasions. We want you to see how concepts from the *Handbook*, such as audience analysis, introductions, and conclusions, can enhance your performance in these settings. Other situations described here, debates or television speeches, for example, clearly call on all of the public speaking skills covered in previous sections, but require mastering a number of particular techniques as well.

27a. On ceremonial occasions, follow the traditional patterns but adapt them so they are immediate and personal.

Some speeches, classified in this book as evocative, are designed more to fill a ritualistic function than to transmit information or change behavior. When you are asked to present an award, welcome delegates to a convention, propose a toast, nominate a candidate, and so on, be aware that there are standard forms. And as with all ritual, the familiarity of the form is one source of the emotional satisfaction participants derive. Happy moments like winning an Olympic medal or sad ones like mourning a death take on added meaning when accompanied by traditional, familiar ceremony. Certain words, gestures, acts are expected — the Olympic athlete would undoubtedly be disappointed if the medal, three-tiered platform, and national anthem were replaced by a gift certificate presented at a pizza house get-together. As you might imagine from the preceding, you are by necessity forced to tread near that line separating tradition and triteness when you give a ceremonial speech.

Cover the expected bases no matter how predictable they are. Do not be *too* creative. At the same time, you must strive to find ways to make these ceremonial moments special and fresh. Above all, this means avoiding overused phrases and constructions. Unless you prepare carefully, you will hear yourself ad-libbing clichés you would never use otherwise:

On this auspicious occasion . . .
It is indeed an honor and a privilege . . .
. . . this small token of our esteem.
With no further ado . . .

Information exchange is of secondary importance in these speeches; style becomes crucial. Because the two or three ideas you transmit will be pretty basic, you should expend your energy crafting ways to express them, polishing your language and timing. This is made easier by the fact that ceremonial speeches are usually short. Frequently a memorized or partially memorized mode of delivery is best. See **20d**. Your language should be more elevated than in everyday speech, but not so formal as to seem stiff or unnatural.

In preparing all ceremonial speeches consider the following two questions:

What are the needs of the person to whom or about whom I speak?

Although as company president you give a safety award each year and for you it is old hat, it is a special moment for the recipient. What can you say that he or she will remember with pride? Address the *uniqueness* of that person. While the form of the speech may be stylized, the content should be personalized.

What are the needs of the people for whom I speak?

In most ceremonial or ritualistic addresses you can think of yourself as speaking on behalf of some group or community, not just for yourself. People have come together to share emotions as well as—or instead of—information. Yet, these emotions may be unfocused. When you deliver a thoughtful and moving speech you symbolize the feelings of the audience, thus bonding them. You also help them achieve perspective and find deeper meanings in their experiences. Early in the preparation for this sort of speech, envision yourself as a vehicle for group expression. The following internal monologues are examples of this search for group motivations: "All of us feel such affection for Gary. What is the best way to say what each of us would like to tell him as he retires?" Or: "So many people in our city have worked hard to arrange a successful visit for these exchange students. What words can I choose to portray that warm welcome?"

(1) Follow these guidelines when presenting an award or honor:

Unless a surprise is part of the tradition, announce the person's name early in the speech.

Repeat it again in the last sentence in a way that invites applause. "And so, Tim Curtis, for all that you have given to IPMS, of your time, your energy, your leadership—we thank you."

Explain how the person was selected for the honor, and by whom.

Besides listing achievements or qualities, try through a brief anecdote or description to capture some unique qualities of the person.

This may sometimes be done playfully.

If a tangible object—plaque, certificate, key to the city—is presented, explain what it symbolizes.

What is the group really giving? What should the recipient think of when he or she looks at it in years to come?

(2) Follow these guidelines when delivering a eulogy or memorial address:

Do not accept this assignment unless you feel able to keep your composure.

This does not mean that you will show no feelings, but it does mean that you are ready and able to take attention off your own grief and offer comfort to others.

Acknowledge shared feelings of sadness, loss, and anger, but do not dwell on these.

Highlight and celebrate the value of the one being eulogized.

Some people present may have known the person only professionally or only socially, only long ago, or only recently. Touch on several aspects of the person's life. Do not be reluctant to share light, even humorous, moments.

Use phrases that bond the group together.

"All of us who cared for Eleanor . . ." "I see many people here who . . ." "We all know how persistent she could be when she believed in an idea." This sense of sharing can reduce the lonely, alienated feelings of grief, and communicate to the closest survivors a sense of being supported by a loving community.

Try to place the loss in some larger, optimistic perspective.

Themes of the continuity of life, appreciating each moment, and growing through pain are timeless and universal. Presented with moving quotations, a few lines of poetry, or some carefully chosen words of your own, these philosophical concepts are still a source of comfort.

Do not play on the grief of a captive audience to promote a specific religious belief or social or political cause.

It is in extremely poor taste to say, "I know Dave would have wanted you all to show your respect for his memory by boycotting all goods from Japan until it signs a treaty to protect the whales."

(3) Follow these guidelines for a toast:

If the toast is a formal part of the event, make arrangements ahead of time so that everyone will have a beverage in hand at the proper point.

Be sure nonalcoholic alternatives are available so everyone can participate.

Refine your basic idea into a short message of good will and memorize it.

Choose the words carefully. Humor, wordplay, rhymes, metaphors, proverbs all find their way into toasts. If no witty inspiration comes to you and if the toasts in books all seem corny and contrived, then there is absolutely nothing wrong with taking a sincere thought and stating it gracefully and building to an evocative ending:

> Here's to Hilary and Robert. Those of us who first knew just one of them recognize and celebrate today our connection with them both. May they share many years of companionship, good health, prosperity, and, above all, the happiness we see in their faces today.

If the toast is more than a few sentences — really a short speech — do not make listeners hoist their glasses the full time.

Start out as a speech. Then at the end say something like, "Let's raise our glasses to our new laboratory director. Sheila, we wish you luck, success, and may all your troubles be microscopic!"

(4) Follow these guidelines when presenting a public prayer:

Keep it brief.

An invocation, benediction, or grace all come at moments when listeners have other things on their minds.

Keep it nonsectarian and nondoctrinaire.

Unless the occasion is a religious service to begin with, you cannot assume that those present are Christians, or are necessarily religious. It is intrusive and insensitive to dwell on symbols that are specific to a particular sect of a particular denomination. More polite and more effective are appeals to a universal spirituality: "Eternal Spirit," "We look beyond our human understanding for strength and guidance," "This we pray with a deep sense of reverence," and so on.

Make reference to the specific occasion and the purpose the group has for gathering.

(5) Follow these guidelines when accepting an award or tribute:

Unless asked in advance to prepare a major aceptance speech, limit your remarks to a few sentences.

Accept the honor with pride.

Do not let humility and embarrassment make you seem to reject the gesture, saying "I really don't deserve it." Remember how disappointing it is to have a gift or a compliment brushed away.

Share the honor with those who deserve it.

But do not get into an endless thank-you litany of the sort that always makes the Academy Awards run overtime.

Give a gift back to the audience.

Can you offer them a genuine tribute, an insight, even a funny story related to your relationship with them?

End with a future-oriented statement about what the honor means to you.

"In years to come, when I want to remember what we've had together, when I want to think of exciting challenging times full of camaraderie, I will need only to look at this plaque in the place of honor it will have in my house. Thank you, thank you all!"

27b. When participating in a panel, symposium, forum, or debate, tailor your individual presentation to the group format.

(1) Be sure of the format of the program, and clarify expectations about your responsibilities.

There are many versions of group presentations, and too often their standard labels are used interchangeably and inconsistently. You may be invited to be part of a "panel," prepare accordingly, and discover that the organizer has really set up a debate. Here are the definitions most commonly used by speech communication texts:

SYMPOSIUM   A series of short speeches, usually informative, on various aspects of the same general topic. Audience questions often follow.

PANEL   Is composed of a group of experts publicly discussing a topic among themselves. Individual prepared speeches, if any, are limited to very brief opening statements.

FORUM   Basically a question-and-answer format. One or more experts may be questioned by a panel of other experts, journalists, and/or the audience.

DEBATE   A structured argument where participants speak for or against a preannounced proposition. The proposition is worded so that one side has the burden of proof, and that same side has the benefit of speaking first and last. Speakers assume an advocacy role and attempt to persuade the audience, not each other.

Do not assume that the person arranging the program uses the terms this way. Find out as much as possible about the program, asking such questions as:

What is the purpose of the group presentation?
Who is the audience?
How much time is allotted? How will it be divided among speakers?
Will there be discussion among participants? Will there be questions from the audience?

Who are the other speakers? What will they talk about? In what order? Is there a moderator or discussion leader?

(2) Prepare as carefully for a group presentation as for a speech.

Do not be lulled into thinking a group presentation is just a conversation. Even if you already know your topic very well, brush up on your research, plan a general outline, and bring along notes with key facts and statistics. Prepare visual aids if appropriate. Plan an introduction and conclusion for your formal part of the session.

Be prepared to adapt, however, in your best extemporaneous style. Since you are in a group, do not give your talk in isolation — make frequent references to the other panelists. "Ms. Larsen has pointed out some of the reasons mental health care is so expensive," and "I won't get into the medical details. Dr. Ray is the expert on that." Also, unless the panelists coordinate beforehand, overlap is inevitable on related topics. When you hear your favorite example or best statistic being presented, quickly reorganize and substitute the backup material you wisely brought along. Review the principles in **26** for use in the question-and-answer exchange.

(3) Be aware of your nonverbal communication throughout the entire group presentation.

When you speak in a group you should still follow the guidelines for effective delivery. The fact that you might be seated does not give permission to be offhand and overly casual. On the contrary, you may need to project a little more energy to compensate for lack of visibility and movement.

What far too many speakers seem to overlook is that they are "on stage" during the whole presentation. While other speakers are talking, look attentive and be courteous. Nod and respond facially in ways sufficiently subtle that you do not upstage the speaker. Above all, do not distract the audience by whispering, fidgeting, or grimacing in disbelief. Do not hurt your own credibility by looking bored, or by frantically going over your notes.

The previous suggestions, combined with general speaking skills, should get you through most group situations. The public debate presents some additional challenges.

(4) Follow these guidelines for a public debate:

Formal academic debating and competitive tournament debating require skills beyond the scope of this handbook. Excellent texts and classes are available. Any good public speaker, though, can handle informal debates — such as are held during elections campaigns or at public meetings or club functions — by remembering and applying the following prescriptions.

Prepare by considering the opposing point of view.

Research both sides of the topic to see what evidence you will encounter. Get outside yourself and look at the strongest points of your opponent's case and the weakest points of your own. This helps you anticipate the arguments and prepare for them.

Organize your ideas, arguments, and evidence into three general areas:

1. Your own best case for your position. This will be your opening statement or constructive speech.
2. Attacks on or challenges to the opposing position, which you will use to respond to or refute their case.
3. Defense material which you will probably need to answer challenges to your position.

Prepare your opening speech with particular attention to organizational clarity (see 7 and 8) and sound support of assertions (see 12).

Follow the general suggestions for speaking to a hostile audience. See **19a(3)**.

In the refutation phases of the debate follow the guidelines in 19d(2).

Time is usually limited, so address yourself to major issues. Explain the argumentative impact of your points. Show what damage you have done to the underlying logical structure of your opponent's argument. For instance.

> Ms. Hoffman has argued that legalizing abortion will lead to greater promiscuity. Her whole point rests on the assumption that fear of pregnancy substantially restricts sexual activity. I've

just presented authoritative evidence to show that's not the case. Unless she can reestablish that assumption, in spite of this data I've given you, *her entire second point is invalid*.

When you weaken an opponent's case, drive home the point by issuing a specific challenge.

> If increased spending for driver education causes a reduction in accidents, then states with higher per capita expenditures would be expected to have lower accident rates. Mr. Kelly should be able to prove that that has been the case in most states, so he ought to address himself to the examples I gave you from Kansas and New Hampshire, where just the opposite happened.

Save time for a clear and persuasive summary of the argument.

Debates can be confusing, with points flying back and forth. So, even if you have to skip some additional specifics, take the last few minutes to focus the controversy, interpreting how it has emerged during the discussion. Emphasize what points have been agreed or granted, crystallize the key issues that remain. Sometimes a simple analogy is an effective tool.

> Ms. Linden is trying to get you to throw out our entire advertising campaign and try this expensive, untested direct mail system. Now I ask you: if you had a five-year-old car that had served you well and needed just a few hundred dollars for tune-up and repair, would you trade that in on a flashy, expensive vehicle that still was being tested for safety and reliability?

End with a persuasive closing statement and clincher that capitalizes on your strongest point.

Maintain a calm and professional demeanor throughout the debate.

As with sports, card games, or any competitive activity, emotions can sometimes get out of hand. Do not lose perspective: getting the last word on every single point is less important than maintaining your long-term credibility. Even if the other debater distorts or misleads, you should remain courteous and unflappable. Your tone may be vigorous, but never hostile. Address your arguments to the audience, and refer to the other speaker by name, not as "my opponent." Treat her or his arguments respectfully, grant good points that are made. Always assume the honesty and decent intentions of the other speaker. Never say, "That's a lie," but rather, "I think those figures are inaccurate. Here's what I found."

27c. Prepare carefully when you chair a program or meeting. Clarify the format, coordinate the participants, and anticipate contingencies.

(1) Plan the agenda carefully.

Determine what will occur and in what order. In some cases you will find that a format is already set by bylaws and custom. Regardless, try to establish mechanisms whereby all potential agenda items are submitted to you well in advance. How many business meetings and banquets have been thrown off schedule by the surprise request to make a "brief announcement" — one that turned into a fifteen-minute speech followed by a half-hour debate? It is your responsibility to manage the communication so that the group's goals are met efficiently. Be firm in sticking to the agenda and moving the proceedings along.

Generally, an agenda should follow a climactic order. Take care of routine reports, announcements, or introductions early and lead up to the major speaker, presentation, or discussion.

A SAMPLE AGENDA FOR A BANQUET OR CEREMONY
*indicates optional

1. Greeting: Brief Statement of Purpose by MC
   *Invocation, song, patriotic ritual, group ritual
   *More extended theme-setting remarks by MC
   *Formal Welcome (from Mayor, Governor, etc.)
2. Introduction of Honored Guests
   At platform or head table
   *In audience
   *Telegrams, messages from those not present
3. Ceremonial Events
   *Thanks to committees, planners
   *Announcements of elections, etc.
   *Awards, presentations
4. Introduction of Featured Speaker or Event
   Featured Speaker or Event
5. Closing by MC
   *Quick announcements
   *Benediction, song, ritual

Light entertainment — comedy, skits, musical interludes — may be interposed before 2, 3, or 4. When a ceremony is the very purpose of the event, as in presenting the Heisman Trophy, 3 and 4 are usually reversed.

A SAMPLE AGENDA OF A PARLIAMENTARY SESSION

1. Call to Order
   *Check credentials; call roll; introduce observers, parliamentarian; any ceremonial functions
2. Approval of Agenda
3. Reading (or Distribution) and Approval of Minutes of Previous Meeting
4. Treasurer's Report
5. *Reports of Other Officers
6. Reports of Standing Committees
7. *Reports of Special Committees, Task Forces
8. Old Business
9. New Business
10. Announcements
11. Adjournment

(2) Be sure all participants in the meeting or program understand the agenda and the roles they are expected to play.

Give a *written* copy of the agenda to all participants in a formal business meeting. Confirm how and when they will participate. "I'll call on you for the treasurer's report right away. Save your idea for fund raising, though, and introduce it under new business." For a decision-making session, let every participant know what to expect, so they can come prepared with the right information and some prior thoughts. For an informal program such as a banquet, you might not write out the agenda, but you should still apprise each person of your plan. "Right after the ventriloquist performs, I'll introduce you for the presentation of the Scholarship Award."

(3) Be prepared for all contingencies.

As chair of any event or session, you are a coordinator, facilitator, and host. You are not the "star," but are there to serve the group by helping them meet *their* goals efficiently and pleasantly. To this end, prepare by visualizing the event which you will chair. Anticipate the issues that may arise. Will the group need information for its discussion? Perhaps you should bring minutes, policies, reports, and data for reference. Prepare handouts, slides, or charts to put key information before the group. Consider the comfort and convenience of those assembled. At a business meeting are there writing materials, name tags, refreshments, scheduled breaks? At a banquet or public program, oversee or delegate even such small details as seating arrangement, water at the speaker's table, or audiovisual equipment.

Carefully plan your opening and closing statements. Try to develop coherent, even graceful, transitions to bridge the parts of the program so that you do not fall back on "moving right along" or "last, but not least."

(4) Follow these guidelines when chairing a parliamentary session:

Learn the principles that underlie parliamentary procedure.

A. THE PRINCIPLE OF PRECEDENCE OF MOTIONS. In a parliamentary session there is no discussion unless there is a motion on the floor. This serves to focus and limit the discussion, not unlike the thesis sentence of a speech. *Main motions* and their amendments deal with the substantive issues before the house. There can be only one main motion (and only two levels of amendment) on the floor at any time. Other kinds of motions can be made while a main motion is pending. *Subsidiary motions* are those aimed at resolving what to do about the main motion, such as refer it to a committee or postpone consideration until a certain time. *Incidental and privileged motions* are those unrelated to a specific pending motion and are tied to the general decision-making process, such as raising a point of order or moving for a recess. Motions of higher precedence (see Figure 27-1) than the pending motion are in order; those of lower precedence are out of order. Motions of higher precedence are voted on first. If you understand the need for a main motion, the logic of precedence, and the general definitions of main, subsidiary, and incidental motions, you can chair an informal session with the aid of the table.

B. THE PRINCIPLE OF MAJORITY RULE. Democratic groups are governed by the majority, and most matters *not related to members' rights* can be settled by a simple 51 percent vote. When the vast majority of a group clearly wants to go a certain way on a harmless issue, use your power as chair to help them. Do not get tied in parliamentary knots. Tools exist to protect groups from obstructive individuals or minorities who could otherwise use parliamentary procedure to block a majority will.

Some such tools are the need for a quorum, the motion to object to consideration, and the requirement of a two-thirds vote to pass a motion to rescind. See Figure 27-1.

C. THE PRINCIPLE OF MINORITY RIGHTS. The majority will rule in the end, but minorities have every right to extend debate while they try to persuade others to their point of view. As chair you must insure against premature decisions "railroaded" by a bare majority. A number of parliamentary rules are established to protect minority rights, such as the requirement of a two-thirds vote to end debate or to suspend the rules.

D. THE PRINCIPLE OF INDIVIDUAL RIGHTS. Regardless of one's position on a given issue, every member of a group is guaranteed certain rights.

Each person has a right to be safe, comfortable and able to see and hear the proceedings.

Each member has a right to know what is being considered and what the parliamentary status of a motion is at a given time.

Each member has the right to insist that every person present, including the chair, abide by the rules.

Each member has the right to demand a justification of "judgment calls" (such as the chair's ruling on a voice vote) and to challenge those calls.

The three main vehicles — all of which have very high precedence — for protecting these rights are:

• Point of personal privilege.

I don't have a copy of the budget we're discussing.

OR

Please explain what this motion means. If I vote yes, am I voting to buy a new copy machine, or to study buying a new copy machine?

• Point of order.

I rise to a point of order. There's already a main motion on the floor, so I don't think we can consider this now.

• Appeal the decision of the chair.

I disagree that arguments of finance are irrelevant to the amendment. I want to hear these arguments as part of the debate. [The assembly then votes on the two interpretations of relevance.]

FIGURE 27-1   TABLE OF MOST FREQUENTLY USED PARLIAMENTARY MOTIONS AS ADAPTED BY THE NATIONAL FORENSIC LEAGUE

Type	Motion	Purpose	Second Required?	Debatable?	Amendable?	Required Vote	May Interrupt a Speaker
Privileged	24. Fix Time for Reassembling	To arrange time of next meeting	Yes	Yes-T	Yes-T	Majority	Yes
	23. Adjourn	To dismiss the meeting	Yes	No	Yes-T	Majority	No
	22. To Recess	To dismiss the meeting for a specific length of time	Yes	Yes	Yes-T	Majority	No
	21. Rise to a Question of Privilege	To make a personal request during debate	No	No	No	Decision	Yes
	20. Call for the Orders of the Day	To force consideration of a postponed motion	No	No	No	Decision of Chair	Yes
Incidental	19. Appeal a Decision of the Chair	To reverse the decision of the chair	Yes	No	No	Majority	Yes
	18. Rise to a Point of Order or Parliamentary Procedure	To correct a parliamentary error or ask a question	No	No	No	Decision of Chair	Yes
	17. To Call for a Roll Call Vote	To verify a voice vote	Yes	No	No	1/5	No
	16. Object to the Consideration of a Question	To suppress action	No	No	No	2/3	Yes
	15. To Divide a Motion	To consider its parts separately	Yes	No	Yes	Majority	No
	14. Leave to Modify or Withdraw a Motion	To modify or withdraw a motion	No	No	No	Majority	No
	13. To suspend the Rules	To take action contrary to standing rules	Yes	No	No	2/3	No

FIGURE 27-1 (CONTINUED) TABLE OF MOST FREQUENTLY USED PARLIAMENTARY MOTIONS AS ADAPTED BY THE NATIONAL FORENSIC LEAGUE

Type	Motion	Purpose	Second Required?	Debatable?	Amendable?	Required Vote	May Interrupt a Speaker
Subsidiary	12. To Rescind	To repeal previous action	Yes	Yes	Yes	2/3	No
	11. To Reconsider	To consider a defeated motion again	Yes	Yes	No	Majority	No
	10. To take from the Table	To consider tabled motion	Yes	No	No	Majority	No
	9. To Lay on the Table	To defer action	Yes	No	No	Majority	No
	8. Previous Question	To force an immediate vote	Yes	No	No	2/3	No
	7. To Limit or Extend Debate	To modify freedom of debate	Yes	Yes	Yes-T	2/3	No
	6. To Postpone to a Certain Time	To defer action	Yes	Yes	Yes	Majority	No
	5. To Refer to a Committee*	To study further	Yes	Yes	Yes	Majority	No
	4. To Amend an Amendment*	To modify an amendment	Yes	Yes	No	Majority	No
	3. To Amend*	To modify a motion	Yes	Yes	Yes	Majority	No
	2. To Postpone Indefinitely	To suppress action	Yes	Yes	No	Majority	No
Main	1. Main Motion	To introduce business	Yes	Yes	Yes	Majority	No

T—Time to be specified.

*No. 5 Should Include:
1. How Appointed
2. The Number
3. Report When?
    or
To What Standing Committee

*Nos. 3 and 4 by:
1. Inserting
2. Adding
3. Striking Out
4. Substituting
5. Striking Out and Inserting

When a member is not sophisticated about parliamentary procedure but is apparently trying to assert a basic right, a good chair will help the person find a proper way to proceed.

I'm sorry, your motion to postpone this until next week is out of order because there's a motion of higher precedence before us. Would you like to raise a question of privilege and ask for a recess to read this report? I'd be inclined to grant it.

E. THE PRINCIPLE OF BALANCED DEBATE. Once an issue is before the house, a chair should try to see that all views are represented and all arguments explored, yet try to discourage endless reiteration of points already covered. The person who makes the motion should be recognized first to explain it and present the basic case for its adoption. If there is a known "leader of the opposition," that person should be recognized next. The chair should alternate between speakers pro and con, giving priority within each group to the person who has not spoken yet or who has not spoken recently.

If the debate becomes tedious, the chair may try to move it along by structuring questions and comments such as:

Are any of you who seek recognition attempting to make a subsidiary motion?
Are any of you who seek recognition attempting to present an amendment?
Are any of you who seek recognition attempting to raise an argument not yet presented by either side?
In the interest of time, if you merely want to add your public endorsement to a position already presented, will you please try to do so as concisely as possible.

Ultimately, the group may need to waste time and go through certain public rituals before a vote is taken. It is your job as chair to balance expediency, fairness, and participants' ego needs in a way that best serves the entire group. Above all, remain calm, impartial, and patient.

For a more formal parliamentary session, either master the twenty-four basic parliamentary motions and their precedence, or insist on the services of a parliamentarian.

Figure 27-1 provides a table of basic motions, their purposes and requirements.

Study the constitution, bylaws, and customs of the organization.

Most matters of meetings, membership, elections, officers and their duties, are set forth in response to specific needs of the particular organization. Additionally, to cover situations not spelled out in its own constitution and bylaws, a group will adopt a parliamentary authority, usually *Roberts' Rules of Order* or Sturgis's *Standard Code of Parliamentary Procedure*. At the same time, a group may have quite unparliamentary customs, such as discussing a topic generally and then drafting a motion when they are ready to vote. If these customs serve the group better than more formal procedures, while still protecting everyone's rights, then you as chair should honor them.

(5) Follow these guidelines when moderating a forum, panel, or debate:

Be sure the format and ground rules are clear to all participants well in advance.

Let them know who the other speakers are and what they will cover. It may be a good idea to arrange a planning meeting.

Plan an introduction.

Engage and motivate the audience toward the topic to be discussed. See **9**. In the logical orientation step, explain the format to be followed and introduce the speakers.

Make a *brief*, one- or two-sentence transition between each segment of the presentation.

Strictly enforce time limits.

Emphasize the importance of this to speakers before the program and arrange an unobtrusive signal for when the time is almost up. If a speaker goes way overtime, you should interrupt politely but not apologetically. "Excuse me, Mr. Kirste, but will you wrap this up in about a minute? I'm sure we'll have a chance to get into these topics more deeply in the discussion period."

Moderate discussion aspects of the session by keeping the participation balanced.

If one topic, speaker, or audience member is consuming far too much time, again interrupt politely and move the discussion along. And be prepared to summarize, clarify, focus, or even ask questions of your own during a lull. Do not, however, take over the discussion to develop your own ideas.

Wrap up the parts of the presentation with a conclusion.

See **10**. The logical closure should be an extemporaneous summary of the points that have actually emerged. You may compose the psychological closure and clincher ahead of time.

(6) Follow these guidelines when acting as MC of a ceremony or banquet:

Plan opening remarks that establish an appropriate mood.

Whether the occasion is a solemn one, a celebration, or a regular monthly luncheon, make guests feel welcome and set the tone for the events to follow.

Make gracious and concise introductions. Learn to control and invite applause at appropriate times.

When you introduce people, you will not have applause cards to regulate audience response. Direct it by asking them to "hold their applause" or by signalling for it through your phrasing and inflection.
    Our favorite unprepared banquet introduction was:

> And seated next to her is Robert Temple, who's done yeoman's service as business manager, and of course, not without the help of those secretaries back in his office. Having held his job myself I can assure you that without a good secretary you're a dead duck!

Feeble applause followed. Were we applauding dead ducks, secretaries in general, Temple's secretaries, or Temple? A person who has worked all year in a difficult job deserves more thanks than a phrase about yeoman's service buried in the middle of a sentence. Even if he did not feel cheated, the audience was cheated out of a chance to show their gratitude in the traditional symbolic way. This MC, rather than ad-libbing, could have prepared a sentence or two that made the secretary point early, and ended with, "Our energetic and dedicated business manager, Bob Temple!"

(7) Follow these guidelines when introducing a main speaker:

Get current and accurate information about the speaker and his or her topic.

Stress those aspects of the speaker's background and qualifications that will establish credibility for this audience on this topic.

Avoid the biographical recitation as an organizational pattern.

"Hope Clayton was born on March 14, 1963, in Atlanta and attended grammar school in Nashville." An introduction is itself a short speech and should have an attention-seizing opening, should develop a couple of main ideas, and end with a clincher that clearly signals for applause.

Keep the introduction brief, but do tell the audience something they do not already know.

Sometimes speeches of introduction are almost as long as the speech they introduce. In the majority of cases, one to three minutes is adequate. (In certain instances the main speaker is also the recipient of a major award or honor. If so, a longer introductory speech is appropriate. See **27a(1)**.) At the other extreme is the introducer, common at graduation ceremonies, who simply reads off the paragraph from the printed program while the audience reads along. A featured speaker deserves a more personal send-off.

Avoid long strings of empty and embarrassing adjectives.

"Marie Carr is a brilliant, charming, eloquent, all 'round wonderful human being." Be complimentary, of course, but not fatuous.

Talk about the speaker, not yourself.

You may mention your association with the speaker, or tell a story that really captures something special about the person, but do not carry this to self-indulgent lengths.

27d. Prepare for a group interview as if it were a public speech.

Traditionally, the job interview consists of an applicant and a personnel director, with a desk as a prop. However, more and more interviews are being done in a group, with a number of people from different departments and levels talking to the applicant. Other interviewlike events are the press conference and the sales presentation to a committee. In any of these situations, you may not be successful if you come prepared only to answer questions. When you speak to a group, even a small group, you should apply several public speaking concepts, of which the following are the most important.

(1) Analyze your audience.

Learn all you can about the people who will be interviewing you. If possible, get a list both with their names, so you can learn to pronounce them, and with their positions, so you can think about the various perspectives and interests they represent. When you are introduced, you can quickly associate faces with the names and roles you have studied. Throughout the interview you can adapt your answers to their perspectives: "That brings up the whole question of the cost effectiveness of surveys. I'm sure that you confront that issue all the time, Mr. Keenan, being director of marketing research."

(2) Prepare an opening statement.

It is predictable that the first question will be, "Well, tell us a little bit about your background, how you got to where you are now, and how you describe your orientation to our field." Hearing this, you do not want to seem startled or reluctant. Do not chastise them for the breadth of the question. Seize the opportunity to set the tone. Make a brief statement that serves the purpose a speech introduction does: gets their attention, creates rapport, and establishes a framework for the main content to follow. Do not assume that on the day of the interview your résumé or sales brochure is fresh in the interviewers' minds. They may have read it a week ago and need a little memory jogging. Besides reiterating what you sent earlier, you can also update it, if further developments would be of interest to the group.

You may use your opening statement to develop a general philosophy or position. Sometimes you set a vocabulary and theme in your initial remarks that you can keep referring back to as you answer questions. You may highlight aspects of your experience to show trends or directions that lead you to the present interview. Whether you are selling yourself, a service, a product, or an idea, use this opportunity to establish credibility.

It almost never hurts to compliment their organization. Be as specific as possible to show your knowledge of it and its workings.

(3) Answer questions directly and concisely.

Before any interview, review the guidelines for answering questions in **26**.

Try to tie questions together in a group interview. "This question spotlights another side of the training issue Ms. Herman raised a few minutes ago." You can demonstrate your powers of synthesis by pulling through certain common threads and relating them back to your opening position.

(4) Maintain effective delivery skills throughout an interview.

Just as in the panel discussion, you are "on stage" the entire time, even though you are seated and in an informal setting. Look at **23** and **24** for a review of delivery skills.

When you answer a question from one group member, be sure to include the entire group in your eye contact.

27e. Modify your presentation style to meet the special demands of the broadcast media.

In an electronic age you need not be a celebrity to find yourself communicating through the media of radio and television. The following suggestions will help you make the most of your opportunity to speak to such an extended audience.

(1) Take steps to minimize the distraction of an unfamiliar setting.

A television studio can be overwhelming; a radio studio only a little less so. All illusion of spontaneous interaction disappears when you are surrounded by technicians, flashing lights, and microphones. To blunt the uncomfortable novelty, see about visiting a studio in a tour or as part of a studio audience. There are also excellent handbooks to alert you to the technical demands of a media appearance.

When you are composing and preparing for your presentation, do not be embarrassed to ask your contact person questions about the format and equipment. On the day you speak, arrive early with your speech fully prepared. Do not count on finding a private time and place to finish polishing your introduction. Be ready for a rather self-conscious experience before the program, as people hold light meters to your skin, dab powder on your nose, and ask you to repeat your first sentence a dozen times to get a voice level. Review **22** on overcoming fear of speaking, use relaxation techniques and try, as the show begins, to get your concentration centered on your topic.

(2) Time your presentation exactly. Be concise.

For a television or radio speech, such as a free speech announcement or an opening statement, the timing must be so precise that you will need to use a manuscript or memorized mode of delivery. See **20c** for suggestions on how to keep a natural conversational tone.

When being interviewed, you will speak extemporaneously and it is especially important that you keep your comments concise. If you ramble or answer too thoroughly, your first response, given the restraints of time, may also be your last.

(3) Adapt your energy level and tempo to the medium.

Listen to radio and television speaking to see what pace and degree of animation you find most effective. Generally, the electronic media tend to "flatten" speech somewhat, and so require a little faster rate, and greater vocal and facial expressiveness, than face-to-face conversation. For the accomplished platform speaker with an oratorical style, though, it may be necessary to tone down delivery a notch or two for these more intimate media.

(4) Follow these guidelines for a television appearance:

Choose simple clothes, jewelry, and hairstyle.

Avoid busy weaves or prints, glittering or clanking jewelry. Tailored lines, medium color tones with contrasting accents are best. You may want to ask how your wardrobe will blend with the backdrop or set.

Avoid abrupt movements or exaggerated mannerisms.

Remember that you may be on camera, even in close-up shots, at any time. When others are talking, sit calmly and look interested.

Maintain eye contact with the camera (the one with the red light on) during your speech. Look at other speakers during an interview or discussion.

Do not let your eyes wander around, and resist your natural urge to address yourself to the studio audience and production crew.

Do not use notes or a manuscript.

If your material is not memorized, transfer your speech or notes to cue cards or a teleprompter. Consult in advance about the method for doing this, and practice using these aids at the studio. For an interview show, you might take along one or two posters you have made yourself that contain a few key figures, dates, or specific facts. The studio personnel will arrange to have them off-camera where you can see them as you talk.

APPENDIX

Starting a Family Tree, by *Glenn Huxtable*

Glenn Huxtable's speech was given to an audience of twenty-six lower division students at San Jose State University in March, 1983. The group had been together for about eight weeks and had completed two rounds of speeches. Instructor Gary Ruud had assigned a six- to-eight-minute informative speech stressing organizational clarity, variety of supporting materials, and effective use of visual aids.

Gary, an Irish name meaning "the grandson of Gadhra (a kind of bloodhound)." Ruud, a Norweigian name meaning "one with a ruddy complexion." So when we run our speech teacher's name together we find out that he is the ruddy complexioned grandson of a bloodhound. Gary and Ruud, just a couple of names, one of which was given and the other passed on through a family. **1**

We each have a name that we were given at birth and another that was passed on through time, our surnames. We share this family name with our parents, grandparents and many generations of ancestors. Aside from our parents, grandparents and possibly our great grandparents, we never get to meet and really know our ancestors. It's never too late for us to know something about them, though, through tracing our family trees. **2**

This activity, also known as genealogy, is now the second most popular hobby in the U.S., right behind coin collecting. Especially since the TV show *Roots* a few years ago, more and more people have become curious about the details of their heritage. Today, I'd like to explain to you how to trace your family tree. First I will tell you how to begin researching your **3** family's history through consulting three kinds of sources: relatives, family records and public records. Then I'll show two ways to organize and present your findings.

So, if you decide you'd like to undertake a genealogical research 4 project, where do you start? The first step in tracing your genealogy is to collect familial information. The most obvious and direct way to do this is to correspond with and interview your relatives. When you were a kid, I bet you were bored with Great Aunt Jenny's stories from the Depression or Granddad's tales of the War. But I'm also willing to bet that now you wish you'd paid more attention. Your living relatives are a rich source of oral history. Spend an afternoon interviewing each of them, or if that's not possible, communicate by mail or phone.

In this process the logical sequence is to fill in the facts about one 5 generation at a time, starting with your own and working backwards. Get from them as many names of relatives and as much vital information and family folklore as they can remember. After getting the primary data on births, deaths and marriages, flesh this out with other details of people's lives. Ask about education, occupations, military service, honors, awards and residences. Were there any horse thieves among your ancestors? What are the skeletons in your family closet?

You can count on relatives for a second source of genealogical data: 6 family records and mementos. These can take a number of forms, such as family Bibles, diaries, personal letters, photographs, and medical, military and educational records.

When you exhaust your personal sources of information, turn to the 7 public records. You'll be amazed what you can learn about your family by visiting the library and checking public governmental documents. First, make a trip to the library. Look up your family name in a book of surnames so you will be familiar with its various spellings and recognize it in your research. Consult a Gazetteer to see where your family originated.

Several specialized indices exist that document the flow of population 8 from other countries to the U.S. and across this continent. If you have an approximate notion of your ancestors' travels you can verify how, when and where by referring to the *Index of Passenger Lists*, the *Index of Railway Train Lists*, and the *Index of Wagon Train Lists*.

One of the major genealogical reference works is the *International* 9 *Genealogical Index* developed by the Mormon Church in Salt Lake City and available on microfiche at Mormon Branch Libraries. Anyone is welcome to draw on this comprehensive data base.

Other records about your family are available in governmental offices 10
or archives. If it's possible, visit these offices yourself to do the digging.
When you must do your research by mail, be as specific as you can about
what you want. Civil servants don't have time to deal with a request like,
"Did any people named Place live in or around Margaretville in the
1890's?" They might, however, be able to let you know if Frank and Edith
Place registered a marriage between 1890 and 1895. If you make your
letter specific and concise and enclose a self-addressed stamped envelope, you can count on a reply.

This is a list of the kinds of governmental records that can prove useful: 11

- Naturalization Records
- Probate Records
- Birth Certificates
- Death Certificates
- Marriage Records
- Voters lists
- Land transfers
- Census Reports

I should mention that the English census contains details on each member of a household. The United States census did not begin to include the
place of birth of a head of household until 1850.

So far I have just scratched the surface in suggesting ways to start to 12
reconstruct your family tree. When you begin to talk to family members,
examine family records and investigate public records, you'll come up
with more ideas of your own. And you'll be surprised how many people
are willing to help you — from the local librarian to the county recorder
in a little English town. Once you start to compile data concerning your
genealogical background, you will need to organize it so that it is clear
and presentable. I'll show you two of the most efficient ways to do that.

Begin by completing an Individual Worksheet for each person you 13
want to include. Each sheet should have the name of the individual and
an identification code number. By convention, numbers are assigned this
way. Start with yourself as one. Then your father would be two and your
mother three. Work backwards in this way always keeping the male the
even number. On each worksheet include the vital statistics such as birth
and death dates and any other biographical data such as military service.
This sheet represents my great, great, great, great, great, great grandfather, Mathias Schoch and, as you can see, I have noted that he fought in
the Revolutionary War and was present at the Battle of Brandywine.

When the worksheets are completed, you will want to put all of your **14** findings together. This information can be presented in many forms, such as books or charts. One of the most popular charts is the Pedigree Chart, like this one, which shows a direct recorded line of descent. This chart shows three generations of my family, starting with me and going back to my grandparents. If it went back some more generations you would find my great, to the sixth power, grandfather—Mathias Schoch.

I have now introduced you to several ways of gathering familial history, **15** including word of mouth, family records and public records, and you now also realize that you can get information from governmental agencies either by visiting or through the mail. I have shown you just a couple of different ways to document and display your findings, one for the individuals on a Worksheet and one for a group on a Pedigree Chart.

Now that you have seen part of my family tree and know how simple **16** tracing your roots can be, I hope that each of you will dig into your past, document what you find and someday share your history with future generations of your family.

How to Lose a Sale, by *VerLynn Sprague*

The late VerLynn Sprague, Realtor and former sales executive, gave this speech or versions of it to several business groups. A typical audience might consist of thirty to fifty members of a local real estate board in a southern Florida city. Often the speech would be the featured event following a luncheon or a brief business meeting.

Everybody knows it: if you want to get anywhere these days you've got **1** to have a specialty. And when, at the age of fifty-eight, you become associated with a large and active Board of Realtors like the one at Naples, Florida, and you're making an entirely fresh start in what is for you a new and challenging business, you have a problem.

One man is a specialist on acreage. One knows all about motels and **2** hotels. A woman I know has picked condominium apartments. Waterfront houses are the principal interest of another Realtor. Everywhere I looked someone was there before me. Reluctantly, I accepted the truth: all of the good specialties were taken.

But a mature salesman does not give up easily, and out of the experi- **3** ence of years and the new experiences of the present came the inspiration which led me to my specialty. It is one which no one has claimed. I lay claim in the Naples Board, and possibly in Florida Realtor circles, to being the ranking specialist on this one thing — HOW TO LOSE A SALE.

Unlike other fine specialties, this one needs special defense and explanation. It doesn't sound like much; but it is. It is worthy. It merits study, respect and investigation. **4**

I have, in an active selling experience which covers many years, sold **5** many things. I have sold lawn mowers, home freezers, television sets, photographic equipment, petroleum products, mosquito killers, go-carts, air conditioners, automobile radios, women's hats, travel destinations, political candidates and much more. As a Methodist minister for nine years I have even tried my hand at selling heaven. In all of these selling experiences, however, a simple time study of my activities would show that I have always spent a great deal more time in activities which failed to result in actual sales than I have in making sales.

Since I am always trying to sell, it just comes down to this: I have spent **6** at least ten times as much selling time losing sales as I have in making them. This is based on a not-too-modest estimate that I have sold one out of eleven prospects. Now that I am in real estate selling, my record is much poorer than that. Try as I may with the very many prospects I am able to contact daily, weekly and monthly, by letter, phone and personal meetings in my office or on their grounds, I don't think I sell more than one out of twenty. And may I say that I'm doing very well; I am pleased with my progress and with my income.

But — and it is a big "but" — I am spending about twenty times as much **7** time losing sales as in making them, and so, my friend, unless you are some kind of miracle worker I have not yet encountered in this business, so are you.

Let me start with one axiom: Some ways of losing sales are better than **8** others. Why not turn your attention to this other activity at which you spend so much time? Is it possible to improve your methods and techniques for losing a sale and so make even this unsought part of your selling experience a profitable one?

Every senior salesman or seasoned sales manager has at one time or **9** another experienced that tremendous blow to the ego which comes by failing completely in a sales effort while he is being accompanied by a junior salesman. You go out with the younger man to show him how the job is done. You give it your best try . . . and you fall flat on your face.

Some years ago when I was general sales manager for a manufacturer **10** of lawn and garden equipment I had such an experience. A newly employed field man had finished his "inside" training at the factory and I was taking him on a two-day introductory swing through his new territory.

I had been acting as guest instructor for a class in advanced sales-manship in an adult extension course at Columbia and on our way to Walt's territory we stopped there for a final lecture session. Walt sat in with my class. I had carefully hoarded all my best sales success stories for the illustrative material which would make that climactic period an inspirational one for the class. I was in good form. The class was impressed and so was Walt.

After the class we drove on together for about a hundred miles while I basked in the glow of my new salesman's admiration and remembered even more stories. All of them were the same. I had faced the most difficult situations, the toughest of competition, impossible odds, but I had risen to the challenge and made the sale. As I remember the conversation — allowing for the normal amount of exaggeration by a salesman in a "brag session" — the stories were largely true.

We put up in a motel near our first prospect. The next morning, anxious to set a good example, I saw to it that we were up very early and at five minutes after eight walked into an automobile distributorship to make our initial presentation.

Naturally I had exercised the sales manager's prerogative and selected this psychologically important first prospect with some care. He was a strong distributor, well financed and organized and in a productive territory. He had purchased a sizable order of mowers the previous year, paid for them promptly and, to my knowledge, had never presented any problems. He should have been a "pushover" for our new and improved line.

When I introduced myself and my salesman to the man seated at the desk behind the counter, he identified himself as the new manager of the distributorship. He didn't get up. I reached out my hand. He ignored it, but he talked. He talked fast and forcibly.

"I would just like to inquire what you advise us to do with the big inventory of overpriced and broken-down lawn mowers which we have in our stock? The engine distributor in this area went out of business and we have had no one to go to when our customers had engine trouble, and a lot of them had it. Your controls were bad. You sold a better mower at a lower price directly to a local department store and he beat our ears off with a promotion. I never thought an automobile dealer should sell

11

12

13

14

15

16

lawn mowers in the first place and if I were going to, your's would be the last one I'd want to sell. We're out of the mower business. Or least we will be as soon as the weather breaks and I can get rid of our inventory at the damndest sacrifice prices you ever saw." And then, thank the patron saint of salesmen, his telephone rang and he answered it.

I had never been so completely and expertly taken apart in all my years **17** of selling. I knew this sale was lost. I was ready to leave. There was nothing, nothing to do but beat a retreat.

And then I looked at Walt. On his face was a smile that was a mixture of **18** complete confidence and of pity. The pity was not for me, who deserved it, but for the manager who Walt believed only *thought* he wasn't going to buy any lawn mowers. He was remembering the class and my success stories. The sale was lost, but Walt was too inexperienced to know it. He was simply and confidently waiting to be shown how a self-qualified expert salesman handled this type of situation.

What I did next, what I had to do, was not planned. I had to do **19** something, not because I had any faith in it, but because in the face of this dumb trust I couldn't run. I opened my briefcase as the prospect, if I can use such a description, finished his call and turned back to us.

"I can't blame you for feeling the way you do," I told him. "We did have **20** troubles with those engines and unfortunately the service you expected wasn't available. But I want to do something about it. I want to do what we can. I realize that we are going to have to find a new distributor here and normally we move the inventory of parts to that active selling house. But I know your reputation with your dealers. They will look to you for service parts. I'm going to leave you your inventory of parts and honor your orders for replacements as long as you want us to do so. I'm going to send you a supply of controls and a factory service specialist to train your man to replace or repair any defective ones you have. I suggest you have a pre-season sale at reduced prices on your leftover inventory and I'll authorize some factory advertising money to help it along. Is that fair?

"Yes, it's fair," he admitted. "But it is no more than I have a right to **21** expect, and it doesn't mean that I'm happy with the mower business or that I'm going to be in it next season."

"I agree," I told him. "I have done something for you, all I could under **22** the circumstances. Now I want you to do something for me. It won't take two minutes and it won't cost you a cent. We appointed you as our distributor in this market because we thought it was the best automotive distributor here. We still think so. But we are losing you and this is a big market and we must have representation. We trust your judgment and what I am asking will save me a lot of time. Please tell me, who do you think are the three next-best distributors here?"

He hesitated, so I went on. "I guess I can't blame you hesitating to name them. Feeling as you do about the mower business and our line, you probably wouldn't want to wish it even on a competitor." I went on to tell him about the new line of mowers, the improved engine design, the new price and discount schedule. I plunged into my bag and laid out the specifications and price sheets.   23

Walt was then introduced as the new salesman in the area who knew that his future with us depended upon his selling clean and working with his distributors and their dealers. And then I assured him, "So you needn't hesitate to suggest a new distributor to us. We'll not use your name, but you can be sure if he buys our new line with our new prices and promotions that he'd thank you. He'll make sales *and* money."   24

The manager asked, "How much advertising money are you planning to spend in this market next year?"   25

And Walt didn't even look surprised.   26

There's a good way to lose a sale that I learned because I was forced into it. Admit you have lost, give all you can, and ask for help.   27

I have since used this "please point me to a prospect" technique successfully many times. Sometimes the *lost* sale was made. Sometimes I have found good new customers. Always I have parted company with the original prospect on a basis of mutual respect and friendliness.   28

Once I identified myself as an air conditioning salesman to the owner of eight new motel units in Wisconsin. He told me bluntly and quickly that he was not interested and did not want to waste his time or mine discussing a product he would not possibly want to buy. Then, and it was the first time in my experience that it had ever happened to me, he closed the door in my face.   29

I was furious at what I considered rude treatment, but that night I sent him a letter and my product sheets. I thanked him, writing that, after all, his frankness had prevented me from wasting my time, which is all a salesman has for earning a living. I asked him to get in touch with me if he ever had need for my products.   30

Eighteen months later I received a letter from him. "I'm now building twenty units in southern Indiana where you *do* need air conditioning. If you're still in the business, I'm ready to talk." Our Indiana distributor called on him and a twenty-unit sale was made. The Wisconsin sale was lost . . . the good way.   31

Lesson two: perhaps it isn't your failure after all. It may just be that you   32
have the wrong product in the wrong place for your prospect. Perhaps he
wasn't even a prospect. Hang in there. There'll come a day.

Many times I have *lost* sales and my prospects have indicated that they   33
were going to another source where they could "get a better deal." I have
accepted the decision and then offered, as an expert on the particular
product in question, to advise them on what to look for.

Then I have talked about the importance of the features, particularly   34
those I had exclusively on my product. I have suggested questions which
the cautious shopper might ask and given them my answers by way of
illustration. I have explained guarantees and warranties, credit policies
and hidden charges. I have disclosed operating costs and their relation to
original price. I have emphasized service and the importance of dealing
with a salesman who knew and could take care of his product. I have
strongly urged them to come back for other products in the future.

All the time this second sales effort was made on the assumption that   35
the prospect would not buy from me but that I wanted to be helpful just
the same. Many of them decided to change their minds. A few went on to
check the *better deal* only to return with the statement, "You know, that
other salesman really doesn't know much about what he's selling."

Recently, I spent most of an entire Saturday and most of a Sunday   36
morning with an out-of-town couple shopping for a very special lot.
Nothing I had quite suited. Several times we passed a lot on which a "for
sale by owner" sign was posted. I had tried for the listing and failed. I
knew the price and it was just right, no room there for a commission. He
asked about the lot and I told him what I could. He pointed out that he
had but a limited time before catching a plane for the north that evening.
The couple excused themselves and left. I knew just what they were
going to do. An hour later as I was having lunch I told my wife about my
failure. She reminded me that the owner, an elderly neighbor, would
hardly be prepared to close her transaction that afternoon, and she made
a suggestion upon which I acted at once. I grabbed a bunch of contract
forms and walked over to the neighbor's side door. I told her that I was
almost sure that she could sell her lot that afternoon and asked her if she
had blank contracts. Of course she did not. I supplied some and quickly
told her how to complete them. I told her that I was sure the prospective
buyer would build a fine home and make us both a good neighbor. I
suggested she call me if she needed any technical help.

A week later I had a letter from the prospect. He wrote, "Berla and I   37 were sitting around the corner in the living room when you were at the door talking to Mrs M. last Sunday. I'm sure you understand why we didn't buy from you and did buy her lot. We hope you meant that remark about good neighbors. My architect will send you our house plans in a week or two. We want you to find us a builder and handle the construction supervision."

We lost a sale and traded a commission on a lot for one on a home.   **38**

Above all, as you try to make even *losing* a sale profitable, check on   **39** yourself. As frequently as you can, *know* why you lost the sale.

It is easy to know and to tell others how you made a sale. It is harder to   **40** make an honest evaluation of your failure — but try. Sometimes you will be able to come up with the answer, but sometimes you just can't determine what was wrong. *Ask the prospect*. Say, "Do you know, folks, I try to be the best Realtor I can. I thought that this home was right for you. I still do. But somehow I failed to help you make what I think would have been the right decision — for you. Will you please help me? Where did I go wrong?" Many people are willing to tell you where you are wrong and you may find out. Perhaps you will discover some real but unspoken objection which you couldn't answer because you didn't know about. For example, one woman answered me with, "But you didn't do anything wrong. It was that *doberman*." She was afraid of dogs and just wouldn't buy a home near a neighbor who owned a dog she feared. And she wouldn't have confessed what she recognized as a weakness unless I had asked her to help *me*. And I did have some homes with no doberman neighbors.

Learning is a strange thing. Did you ever think about the way a boy   **41** learns to catch a ball? You toss it to him and he misses it. You do it again and again. Finally he catches one. Still, he misses more than he catches. On the basis of his activity he is practicing missing about ten times as much as he is practicing catching. If practice makes perfect then soon he should be a perfect misser. But no, he is actually practicing catching. Despite the misses it is the catching which brings the experience of success, and so he repeats the things he has done right until finally he develops the skill he seeks. But he is practicing. He does watch himself. He fails again and again, but he learns from his failure.

And that is just what this specialty of losing a sale is all about. You lose a   **42** sale, but gain a prospect. You lose *this* sale, but gain a later one. You lose the sale, but gain an insight into your selling technique. You think. You watch. You practice. And some day, if you try hard, you may become such a skillful loser of sales that you will hardly lose any at all.

Productivity and the Corporate Culture: A Return to Balance, by *Mary E. Cunningham*

Mary Cunningham, Vice President, Joseph E. Seagram & Sons, Inc., delivered this speech to the prestigious San Francisco business group, the Commonwealth Club, on February 27, 1981. Although the majority of the thousand people present were successful male business leaders, the audience also contained women executives from major corporations and several dozen students from the Stanford Business School.

Good afternoon, ladies and gentlemen. When I was invited to come 1
here and speak, I had no idea that the California connection would be anything more than a one-luncheon appearance. But as it turned out, this state — by far, the largest wine-producing area in our nation — is going to be very much a part of my future for some time to come. Having accepted a new position as corporate vice president for strategic planning with a major wine and spirits producer, I am very much looking foward to repeated visits to this remarkable and vigorous part of our country.

It was not, of course, because of this connection that you invited me to 2
speak before the Commonwealth Club. Actually, I speculated a bit on why you *did* invite me. I was pleased by the invitation but frankly puzzled, if not a bit intimidated, by reports of a sellout crowd and an overloaded press table.

Perhaps, I said to myself, you wanted to hear my less-than-conventional 3
views on the haste with which the International Monetary Fund instituted its Special Drawing Rights Policy. Or, perhaps, being here on the edge of the Pacific, you were anxious to hear my detailed analysis of the psychological and economic impact that Japanese import quotas would have on California car buyers.

Come to think of it, it is probably my views on both these highly topical 4
and scintilliating subjects that have provoked 60 Minutes, Phil Donahue and many of the major TV stations and motion picture companies to stay in touch on a very regular basis.

Given all of this speculation, I'd like to be very explicit about what I do 5
and do not intend to discuss with you today.

I am not here to do a post-mortem on the circumstances surrounding 6
my departure from a large industrial company. Nor am I here to offer a scathing indictment of the media for turning an otherwise non-event into one of the most sensational fictions of the year. Nor am I here to regale

you with the latest woes of women in top management. Nor do I intend to provide a sequel to the October soap opera that rivaled only "Who Shot J.R."

What I am here to do is offer a fresh perspective on the way in which 7 we as managers might contribute to the nationwide effort to increase productivity.

Productivity is, of course, the central concern this year. And that word 8 will probably be found in the title of more workshops, retreats, senior seminars and planned doctoral theses then even the words "access" and "interface" from earlier years. I have a friend who claims you can get by at most corporate executive meetings this year by using—judiciously, of course—the words "productivity," "macro," and "hands-on."

But cliches or not, these words are telling us something. They fit very 9 appropriately in a discussion of historical trends, trends that alarm people who take the state of business seriously.

Consider a simple index of productivity growth: the United States as 10 compared with Britain, West Germany and Japan.

Between 1870 and 1950, our annual growth in productivity was approx- 11 imately .7 percent higher than in those other countries. And that relatively small but decisive difference contributed to making us first the eco- nomic, and subsequently, the political leader of the world.

But since 1950 and particularly since the mid 60's, those numbers have 12 been reversed. In 1979 and 1980 we actually had a net decline in productivity and the differential of last year is substantially in favor of West Germany and Japan.

Can anyone imagine—would anyone care to imagine—what this will 13 mean in terms of our standing in the world in 1990 or 2000, and how other nations will perceive us?

Those productivity statistics rest on some ominous facts—facts that tell 14 us other countries have produced better products than we have, and have done so at lower costs, with fewer prople, with fewer levels of manage- ment, with far fewer job classifications, with higher quality—and with a far more stable work force.

We business people will be making a mistake if we think that the 15 election of pro-business people to the Congress and the Senate, and a president committed to balancing the budget and "freeing business from government," will solve these problems. It is, of course, essential to improve the investment climate in a variety of macroeconomic ways— whether through a more equitable tax structure, selective decontrol and deregulation, or the encouragement of savings.

But I suggest that we may have become somewhat mesmerized by all   **16**
those macroeconomic plans.

It is not enough, I believe, for us to become cooperative spectators as   **17**
the Administration institutes a series of broad macroeconomic reforms.
In fact, I believe that even if every tax reform and proposed budget cut
were implemented in full we would still remain at a competitive disadvantage with other industrialized nations.

This is because the battle against declining productivity must be fought   **18**
bilaterally, both at the macro-level of government and at the micro-level
of organizational reform.

The present Administration is doing its job by creating a blueprint that   **19**
emphasizes savings, investment, monetary prudence and fiscal restraint.
Our corporations must also do their part by examining what I call the
corporate culture, and instituting the necessary changes in that culture
that will make them more competitive and more productive than they are
at present.

I invite you to examine three concepts with me: **20**

First. The absence of a shared system of values has a measurable   **21**
impact on the bottom line.

Second. A less-than-humane working environment shows up as a   **22**
concealed cost on the profit and loss statement.

Third. Prejudice is an expensive luxury.   **23**

Let me start by admitting that I'm not very pleased with my phrase "a   **24**
shared system of values." Not that it doesn't say precisely what I mean.
But it sounds so impractical and lofty that it might provoke a few yawns.

I can just hear you say, "Does she expect every member of a corpora-   **25**
tion to be a soul-mate of every other?"

I'm not that naive.   **26**

But I do know, as every observer of the human condition knows, that a   **27**
culture is defined in a very important sense by the ethical system that
binds it. Not that everyone in a society practices right and wrong in
identical fashions. But in a fundamental way there is a shared notion of
ethical behavior.

A sub-society, like a corporation, is equally devoid of cohesion if it has   **28**
no common values.

Today, the members of society at large, and of the institutions within it,   **29**
including corporations, are yearning for that sense of meaning that
comes from a well-developed system of values. We need this value system
as individuals to give purpose to our work and therefore satisfaction to
our lives. And the corporation needs it to create unity out of diversity,

loyalty out of selfish opportunism and cooperation out of internally directed competitiveness.

Unfortunately, when you talk about ethical systems in the corporate realm — and that's another reason I hesitated to broach this subject — the word "ethics" suddenly shrinks to puny proportions. All it seems to mean to most people is improper payments and pilferage. Oddly enough, those infringements of ethics, while important, are likely to do much less financial damage than the violations I have in mind. **30**

When I think of ethics in regard to a corporation, I see something with wider repercussions than the usual feeble Corporate Code. I envisage a common value system that causes the members of the organization to function together as a loyal unit. You need only look at the Japanese to see that where there is unity, there is a tremendous increase in productivity. **31**

You are familiar, I'm sure, with Quality Circles in Japan — those weekly meetings where automobile workers, with absolutely no supervisors present, discuss assembly-line problems, quality control, and any other subjects relevant to their work — and look for solutions to present to management. Attendance is absolutely voluntary. The motivating force is precisely the shared sense of values that I say has bottom-line results. **32**

Indeed, the results are measurable. Japanese management receives six to eight suggestions per employee per month. And a measure of the seriousness accorded this exercise is that over 50 percent of the suggestions are adopted. Is it any wonder that, as the flip side of the coin, management regularly rejects courses of action on the grounds that they might "hurt" the employees. **33**

I'd like now to relate this concept of collective identity to my departure four and a half months ago from the company where I used to work. **34**

I must take a moment first to describe the situation. I was hired when I was 27 years old to be executive assistant to the chairman. After a year I was promoted to vice president for corporate and public affairs, and three months after that, to vice president for strategic planning. The question that aroused so much passionate discussion — put in its most objective form — was: Did I merit those promotions? The argument became so distorted, the noise level so intense, and the environment so counter-productive that I decided to spare the organization any further distraction. **35**

Perhaps having heard my perspective on corporate ethics, you now understand why I could not, in good conscience, do what many of the 4,000 letters I received urged me to do. Many people encouraged me to **36** "hang in there" and fight to the bitter end—a kind of female macho. And it would have been a bitter end—not only for me as an individual but for the corporation to which I had a responsibility. I was encouraged to start a law suit, lead a crusade, argue my case on talk-shows, lecture from coast to coast—in other words, become some kind of politicized composite of Irving Shapiro, Ralph Nader and Abbie Hoffman. In short I was being asked to personalize the entire event and to expose or assign blame regardless of the consequences.

But joining an organization is like being born into a family or taking on   **37**
citizenship. With that joining, you take on new responsibilities, the most serious of which is to work for the good of the organization. This does not absolve you from adherence to principle. Nor does it deny your individual rights. It just amends them. It is simply not reponsible to do what is akin to reneging on a contract—not a written one, to be sure, but one that has the same moral force.

I am convinced that as this notion of common purpose takes hold, we   **38**
will find that we are building a new kind of cooperation. The organization will become more humane, more like a family—and this is the second condition I believe is required in order to reverse the trend toward indifference, and create, instead, a climate for increased productivity.

The analogy to the family is a risky one for a woman to make—it   **39**
evokes sentimental, non-businesslike stereotypes. But families have functioned as economic units throughout the history of our species. And because the members had to pull together to survive, cooperation became a necessity—and skills were not wasted.

This kind of organizational framework will, I believe, bring a new   **40**
humaneness and stability to the corporation. And none too soon, for our corporations have become bureaucratic and overly dependent on systems. It is true that sheer size, new technologies, complex government regulations, social pressures and other factors present extremely difficult challenges. But our reaction—indeed, over-reaction to complexity has been to impose a system, and the result has been an artificially satisfying sensation that order has somehow been restored to our universe.

As a result, we have become the victims of the systems we have created.   **41**
Computers, forecasting models, organization charts, and new methods of quantification have been idealized as solutions. Business has become austere and stifling.

Am I suggesting that we abandon all systems, models and computer   **42**
printouts? Not at all. If I did, I'd be out of a job. Used appropriately, they

can contribute to efficiency. What I *am* calling for is a return to balance — not a swing to the opposite extreme, to seat-of-the-pants decision-making. As our respect for numbers grows, our regard for judgment must not diminish.

I am suggesting that in the future, if the organization chart doesn't fit **43** the person, we may well decide to change the chart, not the person.

I would hope that the business schools would sense the need for **44** change and take a leadership role in bringing it about. What I would hope to see is the same emphasis placed on courses in Business Ethics, Organizational Behavior and Human Resource Development as has been traditionally placed on Marketing, Finance and Production. And in giving these subjects their due they should be presented to students not as electives but as part of the core curriculum.

Once again, if we refer to the Japanese example, we will see that this **45** humanizing of the corporation is a major factor in their high level of productivity. I will draw from an industry I became very familiar with during my two years in Detroit. The evidence was gleaned from a Japanese automotive plant — not in Yokohama, but in one of *this* nation's cities. There, the same figures of productivity, the same differentials in cost, quality, and reliability that I mentioned earlier are beginning to appear as though the plant were in Japan. But this time, there's a Japanese management with *American* workers.

A recent study by a large U.S. corporation tells us that "absenteeism" in **46** Japan runs at only 4–5 percent annually, and those figures *include* sick leave and vacation time. If you take out those elements, the statistic drops to 1 percent. Furthermore, the average Japanese worker, entitled to 15 to 20 vacation days a year, takes only an average of five days, because to take more would "inconvenience" his fellow-employees. We need to understand the far-reaching consequences of this spirit.

We could start by asking why Japanese auto workers have only six job **47** classifications at a plant while one of our major producers, for example, has more than 200. Or explore why Japanese and German industry impose less than one half the number of management layers that we do between the chief executive officer and the workman at the machine.

The answer to our competitive disadvantage is not to copy the Japanese **48** style but to adapt the best from their style and stamp it Made in America.

I come now to the third of my basic themes: Prejudice is an expensive **49** luxury.

Much of what I'll say about prejudice in business represents personal **50** observations — not scientific research. And because it depends on observation, it will focus largely with prejudice against women, the situation with which I am most familiar. I know, as you do, that prejudice is not directed exclusively or even primarily at women. Jews, Italians, Irish — virtually every ethnic or religious group — have been victims in the past, and to some degree still are. Blacks, women, Hispanics and other minorities are more common targets today.

So if I talk largely about women, it will be essentially as examples. I will **51** not repeat each time that I'm including in my thoughts other victims. I have not forgotten them and I hope you will not, either.

Prejudice takes many forms. And it changes with time. Five years ago **52** the problem was getting women onto the corporate ladder. Now the problem is moving them up. If the move is exceptionally rapid or involves a very high level appointment, the bewilderment, skepticism, jealousy and resentment are even greater.

It would seem there are no norms for people's minds to rest on when **53** they see a woman set a record in business — so they turn to the very shopworn explanation that she used her sexual charms to get there.

The inability in some to accept a woman's advancement is only one **54** form of sexist prejudice. The other is the failure to promote her at all. In both cases, the observers simply refuse to see merit where it exists. A variant on this is where they see the merit, but, heeding the signs of resentment around them, fear the consequences that might result if they reward it.

I have heard it said that working women must avoid situations which, **55** no matter how pure, can be interpreted as compromising, that appearances may be even more important than reality. There's an ostensibly practical ring to this. In fact there's no question that appearances have consequences. But such advice carried to extremes, quickly turns to nonsense in the attempt to practice it. It means not going on certain business trips or attending conventions relevant to one's work. It means not closing the door when you have to discuss a confidential business matter with a man. It means not staying late to work — and so on.

In other words, at some point the concern for appearances com- **56** promises performance — and it is exactly at that point I believe that a woman must say, "Stop." Corporations have been saying all along they cannot hire women because women cannot perform as effectively as men. You've heard the phrases:

"The customers won't accept her." **57**

"The people at the trade show won't know the difference between her **58** and the models."

"A steel manufacturer would feel she doesn't know what she's talking   **59**
about."

I must conclude that if we buy the "appearances are paramount"   **60**
argument, we end up by justifying the corporation in not hiring women
into positions of high visibility because the performance will, in fact, be
compromised.

Interpretation is in the mind of the beholder. Without interpretation   **61**
these situations mean nothing. Furthermore, even interpretation
wouldn't do much damage if it were not spread through some means of
communication. Photographers at a public function who train their lens,
as they did in my case, on a man and a woman when a wider angle would
have included other officers from the same company are acting irrespon-
sibly and unprofessionally. In such a case, the responsibility lies with the
photographers and their editors to report the full context.

The power of the press to either further prejudice or to combat it is   **62**
awesome. The temptation to capture ratings and wider readership must
be very tantalizing.

But when the press engages in irresponsible and sexist journalism, it   **63**
cannot offer in its own defense that it has no norms for people have who
broken the age barrier. It has—but they have been men. Faced with a
woman with a similar record, they feel obliged to describe the color of
her hair, her shape, and assign an overall 10-point rating. I am still waiting
to hear a detailed physical description of David Stockman who directs
our Office of Management and Budget and was a Congressman at age 30.

Or Samuel Armacost, the young chief executive officer of Bank of   **64**
America, who first became an officer of his bank at age 30.

By consistently focusing on the biologically female side of a woman's   **65**
success, by sensationalizing events, the media does more than hurt the
individuals involved. They deny their readers the formation of vital new
symbols needed to undo old stereotypes. In short, they perpetuate false
notions and betray a public trust.

I have said, and I believe it is worth emphasizing, that American   **66**
management indulges its prejudice at great economic cost. This statement is not subject to the kind of cost/benefit analysis performed on a
calculator. But every good manager knows that our greatest natural
resource is human creativity. It is only a small step from that knowledge
to the realization that corporate attitudes which systematically place the
filter of preconception between the potential candidates for important
corporate posts and the eyes of the personnel decision-maker must
necessarily cost the organization untold earnings.

Beyond the obvious opportunity cost, there are other direct costs   **67**
associated with a corporate culture that does not include women as a
normal part of organizational activity, particularly at the highest levels of
decision-making. The loss in productivity as a result of resentment or
frustration is not obvious but nonetheless real. If such rejection ultimately causes the woman to leave, the time and money spent on her
training is an obvious waste.

There has been no more consistently sounded theme recently in this   **68**
country than the need to recognize that our resources are limited and
that we must exploit them with maximum efficiency and minimum waste.
Oil, coal, water, timber — yes . . . Why not people.

In my opinion, people are our most underutilized resource in America   **69**
today. And to the extent that we continue to accept barriers which
prevent certain talented individuals from achieving the most responsible
levels of corporate power, to that extent we are wasting our greatest
resource, the intelligence, creativity and judgment of our people. Can this
country really afford to pay such a price for discrimination? Is American
industry really willing to provide the receptacle for such waste?

Prejudice is a moral failing in the souls of the people who harbor it.   **70**
But it is also an error in logic — a particularly expensive one that takes the
form of overgeneralization. It is a flaw that has practical consequences,
for unless we free our minds of the generalities that preconceptions
represent, we cannot make room for the exceptions. Yet, it is the exceptions throughout history — in business, in medicine, in politics — that
have made the breakthroughs and moved us forward — not by inches but
by leaps. Bigotry is not only foolish, but destructive — destructive of the
contribution such people could make to the greater group, whether the
corporation, the university or the hospital.

Human creativity is the resource we can least afford to waste. And   **71**
while the creative talent, working in isolation, will always survive and find
some means for expression, we have not yet tapped the special creativity
that could emerge from bringing together people who have not, in the
past, had the opportunity to exchange ideas or attitudes or values. It is not
enough just to give a woman or a black or a young person a job. They
must be made part of the process at all levels of problem-solving to
which they can meaningfully contribute.

I maintain that the continued underutilization of certain segments of   **72**
our work force in America is morally unjust, politically unsound and
commercially stupid. If we do not overcome this tendency, we will resign
ourselves to creating a group of second-class corporate citizens who are

less informed and therefore less effective in the business world, and we will accept a corporate America that is less dynamic, less creative, and less competitive worldwide.

I have no illusion that this talk will cause a sudden shift in corporate **73** goals and organization structure. This will take time. But oddly enough, I am optimistic about cutting the economic costs of prejudice in the near term.

The arguments against prejudice are becoming more convincing as **74** exposure to new faces and new minds reduces the level of ignorance. And as modest successes with strings attached become dramatic break-throughs with great responsibilities, hard-core prejudice must expose its inherent absurdity.

But well before that day, we can work on certain practical remedies **75** that I will share with you now. Once again, I will state them in terms of women, but they are equally applicable to others.

First, make the decision to stick your neck out. Use the leadership you **76** have shown in other areas. Take the first step in putting unusual talents to work and fight the battle to keep them there. You haven't gotten to where you are today by following the pack; don't start now when your example is so badly needed.

Second, treat a woman with potential the same way you would a man. **77** Here, the direct supervisor is the critical determinant of an individual's success. Channel more women into line responsibilities. Don't always point them — or let them point themselves toward staff jobs.

Don't assume what they will or will not be interested in doing. They **78** may be willing to travel even if they have a family. They may be interested in that promotion that requires a geographical relocation even though they enjoy their current job.

Third, give women the difficult assignments. Don't "protect" them by **79** reserving them for the routine or easy jobs — they can't distinguish themselves in that way.

Fourth, and finally, share the critically important social opportunities **80** with them. Introduce them to senior officers. Take them to the important lunches. Permit them the visibility that is essential to corporate mobility.

It is the last area, of course, that may be the most dangerous. It will be **81** the most easily misunderstood by those who desire to misunderstand. Yet, as we in this room all know, it is a component as critical to corporate success as any other. The absence of social entree assures the stifling of upward movement.

As for my other two themes — the importance of a shared value system **82** and the need to humanize the corporation — I believe there's a lot of educating to do. Nonetheless, in many ways, great and small, you have the power, each of you, to personally take action right now. You can look for opportunities to speak out — and if you do, I hope you will agree that it is not only possible but necessary to infuse a practical note into what are normally considered soft themes. Emphasize that a corporate culture will ultimately be played out either as an asset or a liability.

Even more important, you can apply the principles that would guide a   **83**
new corporate ethic and a more humane organization to your own spheres of influence. This will not only bring direct benefit to those immediately affected but it will also become part of the process that will cause those principles to permeate the entire organization.

That is what I intend to do as I resume my role as a manager. I will do it   **84**
not only because it is right but because it is good business ... And the business of Mary Cunningham is business.

The Technical Thesis: Protection in the Power of Those Traditional Values, by *Neil Postman*

> Many university campuses sponsor lectures by well-known speakers to provide a forum for discussion and to link the university to the surrounding community. Such lectures and lecture series are widely publicized and are expected to be both entertaining and intellectually provocative. Seton Hall is a respected liberal arts college in New Jersey, and Neil Postman, a noted educator and author, delivered this speech there on November 9, 1978.

Just about five weeks ago, I received a telephone call from a man,   **1**
unknown to me, who had seen some notice of tonight's lecture. In particular, he had come across a reference to its theme, Mass Communication: Culture in Crisis, and before he committed himself to attending, he wanted to know exactly what my talk would be about. Of course, I hadn't *asked* him to commit himself to attending, but I got the impression, nonetheless, that if I didn't come up with the right answer, I would have to carry on without him.

As it happened, my talk was not then fully conceived or even half   **2**
conceived, but I mumbled my way through an answer anyway, not wishing to lose a potential customer. Perhaps he is here tonight, perhaps

he isn't. My answer couldn't have been very satisfactory. But I mention the episode because I think he was right to call me. So much has happened in America, and continues to happen, that the word *crisis*, as in *culture in crisis*, has probably lost all its meaning; certainly, all its urgency. Everything seems to be in crisis; and every lecture seems to be about one. I believe my caller merely wanted to know which of the 283 crises now available for discussion I was going to choose, since he had doubtless heard 150 of them discussed already. And even though the phrase *mass COMMUNICATION* limited the field somewhat, it could not have been of much help to him. Most of our crises have something to do with what we call the mass media, especially if we mean by that term all the technological changes that have come in such Toffleresque profusion and have led to such Kafkaesque confusion.

In fact, for many weeks prior to his call, and for a couple afterwards, I   **3** was nearly as unsure as my caller as to which of our present media-induced and media-amplified confusions I might give my attention to. And then, on a flight from New York to San Francisco, I chanced to locate the answer in the American Airlines magazine, which, not insignificantly, is called *American Way*. There, I saw an advertisement that struck me at once as one of those rare artifacts—of the kind archaeologists are always looking for—that reveal in capsule form the nature of a culture's most burdensome idea. It was, as I said, an advertisement, and told of a machine called HAGOTH. Anyone can buy it for $1500, making it one of the best bargains of this decade. HAGOTH has sixteen lights—eight green and eight red. If you connect HAGOTH to your telephone, you are able to tell whether or not someone talking to you is telling the truth!

The way it does this is by analyzing the "stress" content of a human   **4** voice. You ask your telephone-caller some key questions, and HAGOTH will go to work in analyzing his or her replies. Red lights go on when there is much stress in the voice, green where there is little. As the ad said, "Green indicates no stress, hence truthfulness." Red, of course, means you are being deceived. HAGOTH, in other words, works exactly like an IQ test. In an IQ test, you connect a pencil to the fingers of a youth, address some key questions to him, and from his replies you can tell exactly how intelligent he is. There is a margin of error, of course, as there is in HAGOTH. But in the main the machinery of both HAGOTH and an IQ test is trusted by our citizenry: it gives us the sort of information we value in a form we respect.

There are several reasons why this is so. The first is that the machines   **5** themselves define what they measure. HAGOTH defines "stress" and thereby "truthfulness" and "deception" by the extent of the oscillations in a voice. Therefore, since (one assumes) it accurately measures oscillations, HAGOTH can't be wrong. It is a self-confirming system. An IQ test defines intelligence as what it measures. Therefore, your score is by definition a precise reflection of your intelligence. Simply, both HAGOTH and an IQ test define what they measure, then measure their definition. In this way we achieve what is called "clarity."

Second, both HAGOTH and an IQ test use numbers. Six red lights **6** mean more lying that two red lights. A score of 136 means more intelligence than a score of 102. If you can count, it is all quite clear. HAGOTH and an IQ test provide us with what are called "objective answers." Thus, we achieve precision.

Third, both HAGOTH and an IQ test are simple. Philosophers may **7** sweat the question, "What is truth?", in books that are a burden to carry, let alone read. HAGOTH bypasses all of this complexity and doubt. If you have a telephone, you have immediate access to the answer. Similarly, intelligence may be elusive to those who must rely on observing how people cope with their problems: such judgments require time and multivarious situations. The answer comes both fast and easy through an IQ test.

Clarity. Precision. Simplicity. Speed. This is our quest. Of course, what **8** we are dealing with here is one of the more overbearing and dangerous teachings of our information environment. And it is this teaching that I shall take as the subject of my lecture, for there is no doubt that we have here the focal point of a serious cultural crisis. I am referring to the idea that it is only through the use of *technique* and *technicalization* that we may find out what is real, what is true, and what is valuable. In its extreme form, this idea amounts to a religious conception, which I have elsewhere called "Eichmannism": the belief that technique is the Supreme Authority and the measure of all things. Both HAGOTH and an IQ test are products of this belief. They do more than merely give us information. They put forth an argument which I find it useful to call "The Technical Thesis," and tonight I should like to expose this thesis to your view so that you may see it, as I do, as an intellectual snare and a cultural delusion.

Before proceeding, however, I must make it clear that I raise no **9** objections against the rational use of technique to achieve human purposes. We are technical creatures, and it is in our predilection for and our ability to create techniques that we achieve high levels of clarity and efficiency. Language itself is a technique, and through it we achieve more than clarity and efficiency. We achieve humanity. Or inhumanity. For the question with language, as with other techniques, is and always has been, Who is to be the master? Will we control it, or will it control us? Thus, my argument is not against technique, without which we would be less than human; my argument is with the triumph of technique, which means technique that subordinates and even obliterates human purpose, technique that directs us to serve *its* purpose, not our own.

What, then, are technique and its progeny, technicalization? This is a **10** complicated matter, which I will here try to simplify by saying that technique is a standardization method for achieving purpose. It may be embodied in machinery or language or numbers or any sort of material than can be made to repeat itself, including, of course, human behavior. In fact, human behavior is itself the fundamental paradigm of technique, for at every level—from physiological to social—we reproduce our behaviors. We are, in a sense, our own clones: Our talk, our dress, our manners, our movements—these are all repetitions of previous behaviors, executed to insure predictability and control, and governed by a set of rules. The rules may not always be known to us, as is the case with those that direct our physiological processes. But they are there nonetheless. Without them, our blood would not circulate through our bodies, our cells would not regenerate themselves. It is the same with language, for the sentences we produce are not randomly created. They are governed by rules of formation and transformation which we have only recently become aware of and do not yet fully grasp. And it is the same with our social behavior, although here we know quite a bit about the nature of the rules, since we have consciously established them to serve specific purposes. For example, a classroom is an ensemble of techniques for standardizing and controlling behavior. So are a courtroom, a restaurant, and a highway. We can write down the rules that govern these situations, and even teach them in a systematic way.

Our artifacts and, in particular, our machinery are also governed by **11** rules, and are designed not only to standardize *our* behavior but to standardize their own. An airplane that is so contructed that it obeys the laws of physics only occasionally is useless, as is a thermometer that responds to heat only when it is "in the mood." We say of such machines that they are "broken," by which we mean their behavior is random, unstandardized, unreliable.

Thus, as I have said, we are technical creatures, and our standardized **12** behavior and machinery—our techniques—make up most of what we call our culture. In saying this, I am saying nothing that is not obvious to everyone. But it sometimes happens that technique begins to function independently of the system it serves. It becomes autonomous, in the manner of a robot that no longer obeys its master. The "purposes" of technique somehow come to dominate a situation, and thereby become a danger to it. The robot, of course, always attacks its master first. Cancer, for example, is a "normal" physiological technique over which we have lost control. Cells regenerate themselves according to blind genetic instructions, without any coordination with the rest of the organism. The body then exists to serve the "purposes" of the process, not the other way around. In a similar way, neurosis is a linguistic technique that has become more important than our own effectiveness. When we generate sentences that produce unsatisfactory results for us, yet cannot stop doing so, then we are in the service of our sentences, not in the service of ourselves.

There are many names for this aberrant process by which a method for 13 doing something becomes the reason for doing it. One of the names is *reification*. To reify a procedure or technique is to elevate it to the status of a purposeful creature, to invest it with objectives of its own. To reify is more than to put the cart before the horse, which is merely bad technique. It is to make sure that both the cart and horse get where they are going, even if the passenger does not. It is to forget that neither a cart nor a horse has any place to go, that they are the means to a human purpose.

But in order for reification of technique to occur certain conditions 14 must obtain, and the most important of these is what may be called *technicalization*. Technicalization is itself a technique. It is a method of transforming a technique into an abstract, general, and precise system. To build a boat requires technique. To draw plans and a set of instructions for building a boat is technicalization. To assess the truth of another's remarks requires technique. To construct HAGOTH is technicalization. To judge someone's intelligence requires technique. To construct an IQ test is technicalization. In other words, technicalization objectifies technique. It removes technique from a specific context, separates the doer from the doing, and therefore eliminates individuality. Whereas technique is a standardized method for doing something, technicalization standardizes the standard. To technicalize is to reduce all possible techniques to one method, to convert *a* method into *the* method. Technicalization en-shrines technique and renders it invariant. It is technique writ large and inviolate.

All cultures are products of technique. Only some are products of 15 technicalization. Through technicalization, we can achieve prodigious scientific and industrial feats, but there is a price to pay. Paradoxically, by objectifying and sanctifying technique, we hide from ourselves what techniques are for. In a culture burdened by technicalization, we must spend most of our time learning the proper methods: learning how to read the plans, learning how to correlate the numbers, learning how to adjust the dials. There is little time to reflect on their purpose or to consider alternative methods. As a consequence, our commitment is to the integrity of our techniques, to the development of our expertise, and to the preservation of our technical definitions and directions. And therein lies the problem. We come to reify our procedures: to believe that procedure supersedes purpose, that in fact procedure is more real than purpose. For to reject is to challenge the basis on which a technicalized culture rests. Such a culture can survive purposes not achieved. What it cannot survive are procedures that are ignored.

It hardly needs to be said that one of the powerful devices for achieving technicalization is the use of numbers, against which mortals always seem defenseless. Imagine someone shouting to you on the telephone, "Help me, please! There's a fire here, my leg's broken and I can't move. Help! Please!" Your HAGOTH would register considerable stress in the person's voice. All eight red lights would flash. Hence, the caller is deceiving you. By numerical definition. Numbers give precision to definitions, and in a technicalized culture, it is precision we want. If the caller is really in danger, so much the worse for him. The machine works. And so it does, in a sense, for in a technicalized culture, what the machine measures becomes, ultimately, the reality. **16**

Everyone must have a favorite and real example of the tyranny of numbers. I have several, the most recent having occurred a couple of months ago. I and several people of reputed intelligence were together in a hotel room, watching a television program called "The Miss Universe Beauty Pageant." Now, even in a non-technicalized culture, a beauty pageant would be, it seems to me, a degrading cultural event. In this one, pure lunacy was added to the degradation by the utilization of computers to measure the measurements, so to speak, of the women involved. Each of the twelve judges was able to assign a precise number to the charm of a woman's smile, the shapeliness of her bosom, the sensuality of her walk, and even to the extent of what was called her poise. But more than this, as each judge assigned a number, a mother-computer, with legendary speed, calculated the average, which was then flashed on the upper right-hand corner of the TV screen so that the audience could **17** know, immediately, that Miss Holland, for example was a 6.231 on how she looked in a bathing suit, whereas Miss Finland was only a 5.827. Now, as it happened, one of the people with whom I was watching believed, as he put it, that there is no way Miss Finland is a 5.827. He estimated that she is, at a minimum, a 6.3, and maybe as high as a 7.2. Another member of our group took exception to these figures, maintaining strongly that only in a world gone mad is Miss Finland a 5.827, and that she should count herself lucky that she did not get what deserved, which, as he figured it, was no more than a 3.8.

Now, the point is that here were two people whose minds had passed **18** the point of crisis and were already in a state of rigor mortis, although they apparently didn't know it. As I left the room and headed for the hotel bar, a similar scene from my high school days came drifting back to me. Because I had received an 83 in English, I had missed by a fraction being eligible for Arista, the high school equivalent of making the Dean's List. I therefore approached my English teacher, a gentle and sensitive man by the name of Rosenbaum, and requested that he reassess my performance with a view toward elevating my grade two points. He regarded my request as reasonable and studiously examined his record book. Then he turned toward me with genuine sadness in his face and said, "I'm sorry, Neil. You're an 83. An 84 at most, but not an 85. Not this term, anyway."

Now, you understand, I trust, that both Rosenbaum and I were crazy. **19** He because he believed I was an 83 or 84 at most, and I, because I believed his belief. He had been fair. He had reviewed the numbers, which were both precise and objective. To him, my performance *was* the numbers. To me, as well. This is reification of technique, from which, several years later, I began to recover almost completely. I often wonder if Rosenbaum got better, too. The disease is not, however, so easy to overcome, because ultimately technicalization is more than a bias of culture. It is a bias of mind. Its assumptions become an interior voice which excludes alternative modes of expression.

What does it take for a person to believe that Miss Finland's shape is **20** no better than a 3.8? What does it take for a teacher to believe, really believe, that a student *is* an 83 (or 84 at most)? It requires, first of all, a belief that it is possible to reduce persons or their behavior to numbers. It requires a total acceptance of the symbols and definitions of a technical system. It requires a belief that a system which supplies precision is, by that virtue, objective and hence, real. It requires, above all, a belief that the technical system can do your thinking for you—that is to say, it requires that calculation supersede judgment.

I remember another instance in my school career that will help me to   **21**
show the power and range of the technical thesis. This time the scene was
a college classroom, where I was taking a course in health. The professor
was giving a lecture on the incidence of hunger throughout the world.
She concluded with the remark that it can be well documented that at
least six billion children go to sleep hungry each night. Our class did not
know much about these things, but we knew that there were certainly not
more than three billion people on Earth — which would make her statement a logical impossibility. The point was raised. She looked startled for
a moment. Checked her notes. Then said, somewhat relieved, "I know it
doesn't sound right, but that's what I've got here."

Now, at first thought, one might say what *we* have here is just a stupid   **22**
professor, or one who has merely made a mistake and is too embarrassed
to acknowledge it. But there is more to it than this. Even if she were
aware that her remark was preposterous, it is significant that she believed
it was an acceptable excuse to refer us to the fact that the remark was
suitably enshrined in her notes. Her notes were, so to speak, a closed and
self-confirming system. Her defense was the equivalent of saying that
eight green lights have flashed, hence the statement is true.

This sort of thinking, by the way, is quite common in our schools, and   **23**
in fact is so well established that special names have been invented to
cover "mistakes," which, in the nature of things, are not acknowledged as
mistakes. I refer, for example to the words "over-achiever" and "underachiever." What is an "over-achiever"? It is someone whose score on a
standardized IQ test is relatively low — say, a 94 — but whose real-life
intellectual performance is consistently high. In other words, the test
can't be wrong. The student *is* a 94. He merely insists on behaving as if he
were not. Perhaps there is even something perverse in him. Certainly,
there is an element of perversity in the underachiever — someone whose
test score is relatively high but who does not perform well in other
respects. The point is that the test score is taken as the reality. The
student's behavior in various contexts is to be judged against this standard. If life contradicts a test score, so much the worse for life. Life makes
mistakes. Instruments do not.

Schools, however, are not by any means the most dedicated promoters   **24**
of the Technical Thesis. One may find the thesis advanced in almost every
social institution, in a variety of ways and with varying degrees of ardor.
The technical thesis consists of more than the tendency to reduce people
to numerical abstractions. Its essence is to get people to submit themselves to the sovereignty of exclusive definitions and formal procedures.

In this sense, there is no more powerful expression of the technical thesis than in the development of the State itself. For the modern state is almost pure technicalization, consisting of nothing else than definitions, procedures, and the means of commanding obedience to them. One of the astonishing political ironies of our own time is the homage paid to large-scale technicalization by "liberals" and "humanists" who, in wishing to expand human freedom, have turned consistently to the formal structure of government for assistance. The guiding principle here would seem to be: that government is best which governs most completely, and most precisely.

It is not enough, apparently, that government should protect against **25** minority discrimination. Government must also insure minority equality. It is not enough that government should care for people who are ill. Government must insure that they are healthy. It is not even enough that government should protect children against child-abuse. It must also protect parents against "child responsibility" (for it is sometimes inconvenient for parents to tend to their own children, in which case government should be available to provide a remedy.)

I do not wish to argue here that any particular responsibility to **26** government is either good or bad. That must be the subject of another lecture by a different lecturer. Rather, I wish to point to the political danger of the technical thesis, which resides in this invariant rule: When technical organizations (that is, bureaucracies) are given power to do something, they always take more of it than they actually need. Tests, computers, machines, *and* governments share this propensity. They always end up controlling more ground than one imagines had been given to them. In yielding to government the sovereignty to implement a "humane" purpose, we always sacrifice some dimension of freedom we had not intended to give. This is the technical trap to which Jacques Ellul refers in his phrase, "the political illusion," the idea that every conceivable problem of social relations may be solved by submitting it to the domain of technical control — i.e., a political solution. The precise cost is that we immerse ourselves in techniques far beyond our capacity to master them. The fact that we have been so eager to do this is a tribute to the power of the technical thesis and its fundamental presupposition: Only through objective, formal, and precise standardization can we control our lives. In other words, through machinery.

This thesis carries far beyond our political and social life. It ultimately **27** forms the core of a religious conception. Consider, for example, the content of most of our popular television programs, including their commercials. These are, of course, parables, and in considering what are their meanings, we may see how deeply the technical thesis cuts, how it comes to form a modern equivalent of The Sermon on the Mount. TV commercials, especially, show this with astonishing clarity. What is the solution to each problem posed by a TV commercial? Where are we directed to seek, and what are we told we will find? The answer is that we shall find happiness through the ministrations of technology. It may be animal technology, vegetable technology, or mineral technology, but it is always technology. That is what we must commune with; that is what we must strive toward. The commercials tell us that, somewhere, there is a drug, a detergent, or a machine to deliver us from whatever shocks our flesh is heir to. Boredom, anxiety, fear, envy, sloth — there are remedies for each of these, and more. The remedies are called Scope, Comet, Cordova, Whisper Jet, Bufferin, and Pabst. They take the place of good works, piety, awe, humility, and transcendence.

On TV commercials, in other words, there do not really exist moral **28** deficiencies as we customarily think of them. Nor are there intimations of the conventional roads to spiritual redemption. But there *is* Original Sin, and it consists in our having been ignorant of a technique or technology which offers happiness. We may achieve a state of grace by attending to the good news about it, which will appear every six or seven minutes. It follows from this that that person is most devout who knows of the largest array of technologies; the heretic is one who willfully ignores what is there to be used.

It is, of course, also part of this religion that people must think of **29** themselves as little more than machines. Like machines, we must submit ourselves to continuous improvement. In fact, it is alleged that we exhibit a certain measure of moral weakness in resisting the opportunities to become new models. Do you think your hair is nice? It isn't. It can be made brighter and softer. Do you think you are attractive? You aren't. You can make yourself thinner or healthier. Do you think you are efficient? You are not. You can improve your productivity three-fold. What's more, you are under a moral compulsion of sorts to do so. Would the Ford Motor Company sell, in 1980, a 1979 model? How can you do the same with yourself? Like machinery, you must progress, streamline and polish yourself, present yourself as forever new.

All of this — technology as salvation — is what Christine Nystrom calls **30** the "metaphysics" of the content of television, by which she means its principal assumptions about what is at the core of human failings and about how we may overcome them. This is another way of saying that television presents us with the technical thesis as a religious conception, as ultimate concern around which people organize their motivations and actions. And we find it preached not only in commercials but on what are called "programs." On action television, typically, the resolution of the struggle between good guys and bad does not recommend to us the force of a traditional moral imperative. It recommends to us the efficiency of a superior technology, technique, or technical organization. Kojak, Starsky, Hutch, Rockford, Jones, et al., are not in any clear cut terms very much morally superior to their adversaries. Not in a traditional sense, they aren't. However, according to the Technical Religion, they *are* morally superior in that their technical skills prevail. Their cars are better, their guns are better, their aim is better, their procedures are better, their organization is better.

What needs to be noticed is that the masters of the media have quite 31 simply pre-empted the functions of religious leaders in articulating the moral values by which we ought to live. From this point of view, the excessive violence on TV, to which so many object, is not nearly so important an issue as is TV's replacement of the traditional moral code with the technical thesis. Even where action shows have reduced significantly their displays of violence, they still stand as celebrations of technique. "Mission: Impossible," which had relatively few instances of overt violence, was a weekly parable on the virtue, indeed, the glory, of technicalization. Its heroes were not people but techniques. Its bad guys were people whose most glaring weakness was their failure to know about or sufficiently appreciate the efficacy of sophisticated machinery. In this sense, "Mission: Impossible" was the most religious program on the TV schedule. And we can be sure that its teachings were not ignored.

In the more benign TV programs, such as "family shows," we find no 32 violence, but nonetheless the technical thesis is there in full force. Almost without exception, the problems which are the focus of each program are about breakdowns or misundertandings in human relations. There rarely arise moral questions of a traditional sort. There are only questions of how to manage one's human relations. This is surely not an insignificant matter, but the point is that living is construed as a purely technical problem. One may solve the problem through amiability or increased communication or artful concealment. But the message of the parable is clear enough: the central human concern is not one's relationship to moral imperatives, but one's technique in solving the problems of relationship management. To put it simply, God is not dead. He survives as Technique.

It is important to say here that I am not contending that television or other electronic media have created the technical thesis. That they amplify, explicate, and celebrate it is beyond doubt. But its origins are probably to be found elsewhere. Lewis Mumford believes that the age of the "mega-machine," i.e., large-scale technicalization, began with the building of the pyramids, the first instance of the massive and systematic use of people as machines. Harold Innis suggests that technicalization began with the printing press, the first example of mass production of communications. Jacques Ellul implies that the invention of the mechanical clock was the first example of the widespread subjugation of human organization to the sovereignty of a machine, from which, he believes, we have never recovered. Ortega Y Gasset argues that industrialization, which produced the specialist and "mass man," also produced a sort of mindless technical man. And Chaim Perelman links the origin of the technical thesis to an age-old desire to be, like God, perfect, such perfection being attainable through precision and objectivity. **33**

It is not to my purpose to try to settle this question, even if I had the wit to do it. The fact is that, in our own time, the technical thesis is advanced so vigorously and on so many fronts that it has created an ecological problem, and a dangerous one. We have a generation being raised in an information environment that, on one hand, stresses visual imagery, discontinuity, immediacy, and alogicality. It is anti-historical, anti-scientific, anti-conceptual, anti-rational. On the other hand, the context within which this occurs is a kind of religious or philosophic bias toward the supreme authority of technicalization. What this means is that as we lose confidence and competence in our ability to think and judge, we willingly transfer these functions to machines, whether they be HAGOTH, IQ tests, computers, or the State. It is no accident that so much energy is being devoted, in computer technology, to the development of "artificial intelligence," the purpose of which is to eliminate human judgment altogether. Or, if not that, to create a situation in which only a few people who are in control of the techniques have the authority to exercise human judgment. He who controls the definitions and rules of technique becomes the master, especially in a situation where people lack the intellectual ability and motivation to understand the assumptions of the technical thesis. **34**

In saying all of this, I am not preparing an argument for a Luddite response. We gain nothing but chaos by banning or breaking our machines or indiscriminately disassembling our social machinery. Although at some time in the future such measures could be taken, they would be **35** the ultimate acts of hysteria of people who live by techniques and who lack the intellectual resources to dominate them. As Ortega Y Gasset remarks, when the masses, in despair and revolt, go searching for bread, their tendency is to destroy the bakeries. In the end, technique is not our enemy. We are. Where then do we turn to protect ourselves against ourselves?

The answers to this question have been given many times and with great eloquence by such people as Lewis Mumford, Jacques Ellul, Erich Fromm, Norbert Wiener, Arthur Koestler, Joseph Weizenbaum, Karl Popper, Marshall McLuhan, and Jacob Bronowski. They all tell us, first and foremost, that we may find protection in the development of our intellect and judgment, and in our continuing quest for knowledge of ourselves and our artifacts. Some of them tell us that we may find protection in the power of those traditional values which stress personal autonomy, community cohesion, family loyalty, and the primacy of human affection. And some also tell us that without a traditional basis of moral authority, we are totally disarmed. We are warned that expertise is no substitute for piety and awe, that efficiency is no substitute for sensitivity and affection, that the State is no substitute for the family, that bureaucracy is no substitute for civilized social relations, that machinery is no substitute for a sense of transcendence. **36**

You may observe that all of these answers are what one might call cliches. And as I come to the close of my lecture, I must tell you that these cliches are all that stand between us and our complete immersion in the technical thesis. But cliches are more powerful than you might suppose. For a cliche is nothing less than a truth that has passed the test of time. And there is this, finally, to say about a cliche: Just at that moment when it is about to pass into the realm of complete fatuousness, it is in its nature, that the truth it embodies is rediscovered and put to work. Let us hope that our cliches will not fail us now. **37**

INDEX

References to sections of this book are printed in boldface type, and italic page numbers indicate where figures or other illustrative materials appear.

R

Reality. *See* Attention-getting techniques, enlivening factors
Reasoning, 11: 126–47
 by analogy, 11d: 140–41
  to draw conclusions, 140
  literal vs. figurative, 11d(2): 141
  similarities between cases, 11d(1): 141
 avoiding fallacies, 11e: 142–47 *See also* Reasoning fallacies
 causal, 11c: 136–40
  oversimplifying, 11c(2): 138–40
  testing validity of, 11c(1): 136–38
 deductive, 11b: 130–36
 developing your speech through use of, 126
 inductive, 11a: 126–29. *See also* Reasoning, deductive
Reasoning fallacies, 11c: 142–47
 absurdly extending argument (*reductio ad absurdum*), 11e(3): 143
 attacking the person (*ad hominem*), 11e(1): 142
 circular reasoning, 11e(4): 143–44
 false dichotomy, 11e(6): 144–45
 hasty generalization, 11e(8): 146
 if/then reversal (affirming the consequent), 11e(7): 145–46
 semantic fallacy, 11e(5): 144
 sequence as cause (*post hoc, ergo propter hoc*), 11e(9): 146–47
 setting up straw figure, 11e(2): 142
Reductio ad absurdum. *See* Reasoning fallacies
Research. *See* Topic research
Resources. *See also* Topic research human, 4c: 48–51; 12e: 163–66
 your personal, 1a(1): 6–9
Restless audience. *See* Speech situations, audiences

S

Secondary points. *See* Organization, of subordinate points

Selecting points. *See* Organization
Semantic fallacy. *See* Reasoning fallacies
Sequence as cause (*post hoc, ergo propter hoc*). *See* Reasoning fallacies
Setting up straw figure. *See* Reasoning fallacies
Shrill voice. *See* Vocal delivery, distracting characteristics, voice quality problems
Simile, 227
Slang, 18c(2): 223–24
Slogans, 152, *173*
Speaking assignment. *See* Topic, selecting, appropriate to audience and occasion
Special occasions. *See* Special speaking occasions
Special speaking occasions, 27: 318–41
 accepting an award or tribute, 27a(5): 323
 acting as MC of ceremony or banquet, 27c(6): 336
 adapting to, 27a: 318–23
 chairing a parliamentary session, 27c(4): 330–35, *332–33*
 chairing a program or meeting, 27c: 328–37
  being prepared, 27c(3): 329–30
  informing participants, 27c(2): 329
  planning agenda, 27c(1): 328–29, *328*, *329*
 debating, 27b(4): 326–28
 delivering a eulogy or memorial address, 27a(2): 321
 introducing main speaker, 27c(7): 336–37
 meeting demands of broadcast media, 27e: 339–41
  adapting to medium, 27e(3): 340
  following guidelines for television appearance, 27e(4): 340–41
  minimizing distractions, 27e(1): 339–40